NVIDIA GPU Infrastructure Fundamentals

A structured guide to NVIDIA GPU infrastructure, from CUDA to production operations

Vivian Aranha

<packt>

NVIDIA GPU Infrastructure Fundamentals

Portfolio Director: Kartikey Pandey
Relationship Lead: Prachi Rana
Project Manager: Sonam Pandey
Content Engineer: Apramit Bhattacharya
Technical Editor: Aysha Nadeem
Indexer: Pratik Shirodkar
Production Designer: Salma Patel
Growth Lead: Vikramaditya Viswanath

First published: August 2026

Production reference: 1250826

Published by Packt Publishing Ltd.
Grosvenor House
11 St Paul's Square
Birmingham
B3 1RB, UK.

ISBN 978-1-80808-749-3
`www.packtpub.com`

About the author

Vivian Aranha is an AI leader and technical educator who leads School of AI, a global learning platform offering more than 80 courses across generative AI, AI product management, quantum computing, cloud technologies, and related fields. Since April 2025, the platform has recorded over 1.5 million enrollments and reached more than 350,000 students. During more than eight years at Delta Air Lines, he has contributed to enterprise AI strategy and digital transformation initiatives. He also works with HeyGen as an AI Pioneer, focusing on AI-driven video innovation. Through curriculum design, video production, and interactive labs, Vivian is committed to making high-quality technical education accessible and helping the next generation of technology professionals develop practical AI skills.

Table of Contents

Part 3: Production AI Platforms and Exam Readiness 137

Chapter 7: Operating the AI Lifecycle with MLOps and Inference 139

Chapter 8: Delivering and Operating NVIDIA AI Platforms 163

Preface

AI infrastructure is no longer defined by the GPU alone. Modern accelerated platforms combine GPU hardware with system software, high-speed networking, storage, orchestration, monitoring, virtualization, MLOps, and inference technologies. Each layer solves a different part of the problem, but the real challenge for infrastructure professionals is understanding how those layers interact and where the responsibility of one technology ends and another begins.

The NVIDIA ecosystem reflects this breadth. CUDA provides the foundation for GPU-accelerated computing, while technologies such as Tensor Cores, NVLink, and NVSwitch influence how workloads execute and scale. MIG and vGPU provide different approaches to sharing accelerator resources, DCGM supports GPU monitoring and management, and Kubernetes and Slurm provide different scheduling models. Beyond the GPU itself, technologies such as InfiniBand, RDMA, GPUDirect Storage, BlueField DPUs, and DOCA shape how data moves through the platform. At the application and operations layers, tools such as NGC, Airflow, MLflow, Kubeflow, ONNX, TensorRT, and Triton help move AI workloads from development into production.

With so many technologies involved, learning them as a catalogue of individual products is rarely enough. An infrastructure decision usually depends on the workload and the boundary at which a problem occurs. A requirement for hardware-isolated GPU resources is different from a requirement for GPU-enabled virtual machines. A model that is starved for input data needs a different response from one that is compute-bound. A container that cannot access a GPU presents a different problem from a pod that cannot be scheduled or an inference service that has poor throughput. Understanding these distinctions is what turns product knowledge into useful infrastructure judgment.

This book presents NVIDIA GPU infrastructure as one connected system. It begins with the foundations of AI workloads and accelerated computing before introducing CUDA and the NVIDIA software stack. You will then examine the architecture and characteristics of NVIDIA data center GPUs and learn how workload requirements influence platform selection. From there, the book moves into the operational layers surrounding the accelerator, including GPU partitioning, monitoring, scheduling, storage, networking, virtualization, and DPU-based infrastructure offload.

The later chapters connect this infrastructure to the AI lifecycle. You will see how Airflow, MLflow, and Kubeflow support reproducible machine learning workflows; how ONNX,

TensorRT, and Triton serve different roles in production inference; and how NGC, Kubernetes, the NVIDIA Container Toolkit, GPU Operator, and monitoring technologies combine into an operable GPU platform. Troubleshooting scenarios throughout the book reinforce the idea that infrastructure should be investigated as a set of connected layers rather than as isolated components.

The aim is not to make you memorize every NVIDIA product or specification. GPU generations, software versions, and platform capabilities will continue to evolve. Instead, this book focuses on the more durable knowledge: what each technology is designed to do, how it relates to the surrounding stack, what trade-offs distinguish similar technologies, and how to reason from a workload requirement or operational symptom to an appropriate infrastructure response. By the end of the book, you should have a structured mental model that allows you to discuss, evaluate, and work with NVIDIA GPU infrastructure with greater confidence.

Who this book is for

This book is for system administrators, cloud and DevOps professionals, data center and networking teams, solution architects, technical managers, presales professionals, and anyone moving into AI infrastructure roles who needs a structured understanding of the NVIDIA GPU ecosystem. It is also suitable for readers who work alongside AI, MLOps, or platform teams and want to understand how compute, networking, storage, orchestration, and inference fit together.

Basic familiarity with IT, cloud, networking, or data center concepts will be helpful, but no previous experience with NVIDIA GPUs is required. You do not need a programming or data science background to follow the book; the focus is on infrastructure concepts, technology boundaries, operational decisions, and platform trade-offs.

What this book covers

Chapter 1, Understanding AI Workloads and Accelerated Computing, introduces the relationship among AI, machine learning, and deep learning and explains why modern AI workloads benefit from GPU acceleration. The chapter then connects common workload families to their compute, memory, storage, networking, latency, and throughput requirements, giving you the foundation for infrastructure decisions throughout the book.

Chapter 2, CUDA and the NVIDIA AI Software Stack, explains how CUDA turns GPU hardware into a general-purpose accelerated computing platform and follows workloads from frameworks through libraries and the CUDA execution model to the GPU. The chapter also introduces cuDNN, cuBLAS, Tensor Cores, Nsight, CUDA Graphs, NGC, TensorRT, Triton, and other layers that make up NVIDIA's end-to-end AI software stack.

Chapter 3, NVIDIA GPU Architecture and Platform Selection, explores the streaming multiprocessors, Tensor Cores, memory systems, and interconnects that determine how NVIDIA GPUs execute AI workloads. The chapter compares the A100, H100, L40S, and B200 and shows you how to match GPU capabilities to training, inference, memory, communication, graphics, and resource-sharing requirements.

Chapter 4, Sharing, Monitoring, and Scheduling GPU Resources, shows how MIG, DCGM, Prometheus, Grafana, Kubernetes, and Slurm turn physical GPU capacity into a shared and observable infrastructure service. You will learn how to partition accelerators, interpret utilization and health signals, and place cloud-native or HPC workloads on the appropriate GPU resources.

Chapter 5, Managing Building High-Throughput Storage and Network Paths, examines how storage performance, network fabrics, and unnecessary data copies can limit even the fastest GPU infrastructure. You will compare Ethernet and InfiniBand and learn how RDMA, GPUDirect Storage, NVMe, and related technologies create faster paths between data, networks, and GPU memory.

Chapter 6, Virtualized GPU Infrastructure and DPU Offload, explores how NVIDIA vGPU and MIG provide different approaches to sharing GPU resources and helps you choose the appropriate model for virtual machines, containers, and multi-tenant services. The chapter then introduces BlueField DPUs and DOCA, showing how networking, storage, security, telemetry, and other infrastructure tasks can be offloaded from the host CPU.

Chapter 7, Operating the AI Lifecycle with MLOps and Inference, follows an AI project from development and training through deployment, monitoring, and the feedback that begins the next lifecycle iteration. You will learn how Airflow, MLflow, and Kubeflow make workflows reproducible before using ONNX, TensorRT, and Triton to turn trained models into optimized production inference services.

Chapter 8, Delivering and Operating NVIDIA AI Platforms, brings together NGC assets, containers, Helm, Kubernetes, the NVIDIA Container Toolkit, device plugin, GPU Operator, and DCGM Exporter to build a repeatable GPU platform. The chapter then moves from deployment to cluster-scale operation, showing how high-speed GPU fabrics and a layered troubleshooting process help keep production AI infrastructure reliable.

Chapter 9, Preparing for the NCA-AIIO Exam and the Next Step, converts the technical knowledge from the preceding chapters into a repeatable method for solving definition, scenario, diagram, and operational-output questions. You will learn how to identify the relevant technology layer, eliminate distractors, strengthen recall, manage exam time, and carry your certification knowledge into further hands-on AI infrastructure work.

To get the most out of this book

You will get the most value from this book if you are comfortable with basic infrastructure concepts such as servers, networking, storage, virtualization, containers, and cloud platforms. Previous experience with GPUs, CUDA, machine learning, or NVIDIA software is not required, as the relevant concepts are introduced as they become necessary.

The chapters are designed to build on one another, so first-time readers will benefit from following them in sequence. Pay particular attention to the comparison tables, architecture diagrams, scenario discussions, and chapter review questions, as these are intended to help you distinguish technologies that solve similar-looking problems at different layers of the platform. When you encounter a new component, focus first on the problem it solves and how it connects to the technologies around it rather than trying to memorize every implementation detail.

No dedicated NVIDIA hardware or programming environment is required to follow the conceptual material in the book. Where product capabilities, software versions, or platform support can change over time, treat the principles in the book as your foundation and verify implementation-specific details against the documentation for the environment you are working with.

Download the example code files

We have code bundles from our rich catalog of books and videos available at `https://github.com/PacktPublishing`. Check them out!

Download the color images

Your purchase includes a color, DRM-free PDF copy of this book, ideal for viewing color images, screenshots, and diagrams. Refer to *Free benefits with your book section* at the end of the *Preface* to unlock your PDF copy.

Conventions used

There are a number of text conventions used throughout this book.

`CodeInText`: Indicates code words in text, database table names, folder names, filenames, file extensions, pathnames, dummy URLs, user input, and Twitter handles. For example: "The `discovery` command lists GPUs visible to DCGM. "

Any command-line input or output is written as follows:

```
dcgmi discovery -l
dcgmi health --help
dcgmi stats --help
```

Bold: Indicates a new term, an important word, or words that you see on the screen. For instance, words in menus or dialog boxes appear in the text like this. For example: "**Compute Unified Device Architecture** (**CUDA**) is the software foundation that opened NVIDIA GPUs to general-purpose computation."

> **Note**
>
> Warnings or important notes appear like this.

> **Tip**
>
> Tips and tricks appear like this.

Get in touch

Feedback from our readers is always welcome.

General feedback: If you have questions about any aspect of this book or have any general feedback, please email us at `customercare@packt.com` and mention the book's title in the subject of your message.

Errata: Although we have taken every care to ensure the accuracy of our content, mistakes do happen. If you have found a mistake in this book, we would be grateful if you reported this to us. Please visit `http://www.packt.com/submit-errata`, click **Submit Errata**, and fill in the form.

Piracy: If you come across any illegal copies of our works in any form on the internet, we would be grateful if you would provide us with the location address or website name. Please contact us at `copyright@packt.com` with a link to the material.

If you are interested in becoming an author: If there is a topic that you have expertise in and you are interested in either writing or contributing to a book, please visit `http://authors.packt.com/`.

Share your thoughts

Once you've read *NVIDIA-Certified Associate AI Infrastructure and Operations (NCA-AIIO) Certification Guide*, we'd love to hear your thoughts! Scan the QR code below to go straight to the Amazon review page for this book and share your feedback.

`https://packt.link/r/1808087496`

Your review is important to us and the tech community and will help us make sure we're delivering excellent quality content.

Free benefits with your book

This book comes with free benefits to support your learning. Activate them now for instant access (see the "*How to Unlock*" section for instructions).

Here's a quick overview of what you can instantly unlock with your purchase:

How to Unlock

Scan the QR code (or go to `packtpub.com/unlock`). Search for this book by name, confirm the edition, and then follow the steps on the page.

UNLOCK NOW

Note: Keep your invoice handy. Purchases made directly from Packt don't require one

Stay Sharp in Cloud and DevOps – Join 44,000+ Subscribers of CloudPro

CloudPro is a weekly newsletter for cloud professionals who want to stay current on the fast-evolving world of cloud computing, DevOps, and infrastructure engineering.

Every issue delivers focused, high-signal content on topics like:

- AWS, GCP & multi-cloud architecture
- Containers, Kubernetes & orchestration
- **Infrastructure as Code** (**IaC**) with Terraform, Pulumi, etc.
- Platform engineering & automation workflows
- Observability, performance tuning, and reliability best practices

Whether you're a cloud engineer, SRE, DevOps practitioner, or platform lead, CloudPro helps you stay on top of what matters, without the noise.

Scan the QR code to join for free and get weekly insights straight to your inbox:

`https://packt.link/cloudpro`

Part 1

Foundations of Accelerated AI Infrastructure

The first part of this book establishes the foundations required to understand AI infrastructure before moving into day-to-day operations. You will begin by identifying how different AI workloads place different demands on compute, memory, storage, and networking. From there, you will examine how CUDA and the NVIDIA software stack expose GPU acceleration to applications before moving inside the GPU itself to understand the architectural capabilities that influence platform selection.

By the end of this part, you will be able to reason from an AI workload to the software and hardware capabilities required to support it. Rather than treating GPUs and NVIDIA technologies as isolated product names, you will understand how workload characteristics, CUDA execution, memory, Tensor Cores, interconnects, and GPU platform choices fit together.

This part contains the following chapters:

- *Chapter 1, Understanding AI Workloads and Accelerated Computing*
- *Chapter 2, CUDA and the NVIDIA AI Software Stack*
- *Chapter 3, NVIDIA GPU Architecture and Platform Selection*

1

Understanding AI Workloads and Accelerated Computing

> **Note**
>
> AI infrastructure begins with the workload: what it must compute, how quickly it must respond, and how much data it must process.

Artificial intelligence has become a broad label for systems that perform tasks associated with human intelligence, but the infrastructure behind those systems varies widely. A rule-based application, a traditional machine learning model, and a deep neural network may all be described as AI, yet they do not place the same demands on compute, memory, storage, or networking. Accelerated computing begins by recognizing those differences and selecting hardware that matches the work.

This chapter first separates artificial intelligence, machine learning, and deep learning so that their relationship is clear. It then explains why graphics processing units are so effective for modern AI workloads and how CPUs, GPUs, and DPUs divide responsibilities in a data center. Finally, it examines four common workload families - **computer vision**, **natural language processing**, **predictive analytics**, and **recommendation systems** - and connects each one to its operational requirements.

By the end of the chapter, you will be able to look at an AI use case and identify the characteristics that matter to infrastructure planning. The goal is not to become a model developer. It is to understand why different models consume resources differently and why GPU acceleration has become central to training and inference at scale.

We will be covering the following main topics in this chapter:

- AI, machine learning, and deep learning
- Why GPUs power modern AI
- AI workloads in the data center

With the chapter route established, the first task is to separate the three terms that are often treated as if they mean the same thing.

> Note
>
> **Download the PDF version of this book**
>
> Your purchase includes a DRM-free PDF copy of this book, the code bundle, and a range of exclusive benefits. To unlock everything, follow the *Free benefits with your book* section in the *Preface*.

AI, machine learning, and deep learning

Artificial intelligence, machine learning, and deep learning form a hierarchy. Each term describes a narrower set of techniques than the one before it. Understanding that hierarchy prevents a common infrastructure mistake: assuming that every system described as AI needs the same hardware profile.

Artificial intelligence is the broadest category

Artificial intelligence, or **AI**, is the broadest of the three terms. It describes machines or software systems that carry out tasks associated with human intelligence. Those tasks can include reasoning through a set of rules, understanding language, recognizing patterns, selecting an action, or making a decision based on available information. *Figure 1.1* makes this hierarchy visible by placing AI as the broadest category and showing machine learning and deep learning as progressively narrower subsets within it.

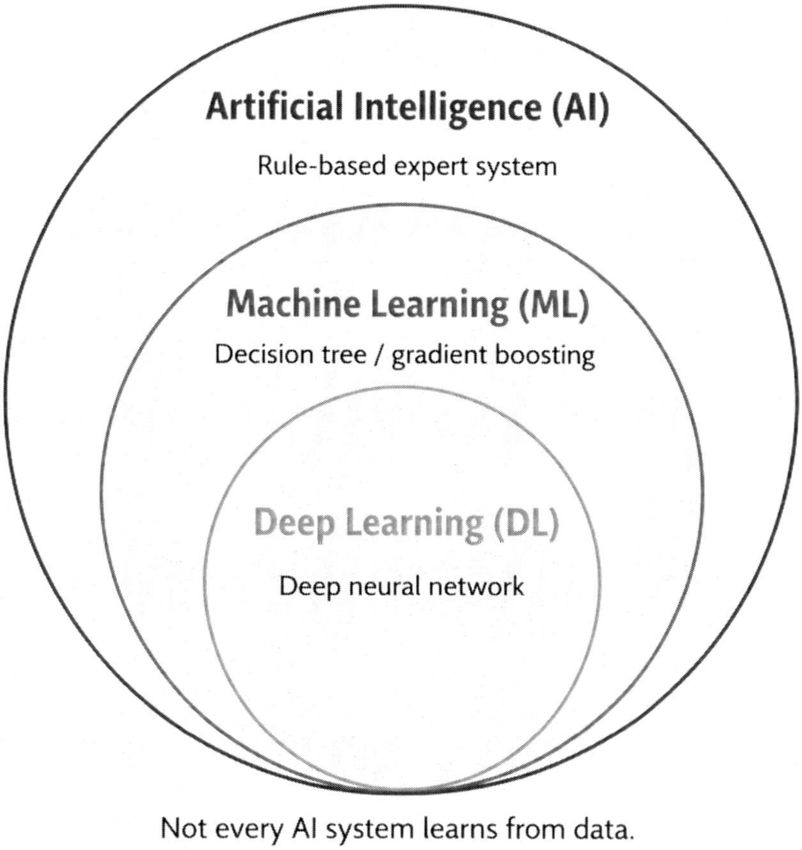

Figure 1.1: The relationship among AI, ML, and DL

Many familiar applications fit under this umbrella. A smart assistant interprets a request and chooses a response. A recommendation service predicts which product, song, or video may interest a user. A vehicle assistance system evaluates conditions and makes driving-related decisions. Each application can be called AI because it performs behavior that appears intelligent from the user's perspective.

AI does not always learn from data. Earlier systems and many current business applications rely on explicit rules, decision logic, and expert knowledge written by people. A rules engine that evaluates a transaction against a fixed set of conditions may be an AI system even though it does not retrain itself. This distinction is important because a rule-based system often has very different compute requirements from a neural network.

The breadth of AI creates the need for a more precise term when a system improves by learning from examples. That narrower category is machine learning.

Machine learning as data-driven pattern discovery

Machine learning, or **ML**, is a subset of artificial intelligence, as shown in *Figure 1.1*. Instead of specifying every rule for every situation, a team supplies examples and allows an algorithm to identify patterns in those examples. The trained model then applies what it has learned to new data.

Consider a spam detector. A conventional rule-based approach might block messages that contain a particular phrase or come from a known sender. A machine learning approach begins with many labeled examples of spam and non-spam messages. During training, the model learns which combinations of words, links, senders, and other features tend to correlate with each label. When a new message arrives, the model estimates which category it resembles.

Machine learning includes techniques such as decision trees, support vector machines, and ensemble methods. These techniques support recommendation, fraud detection, forecasting, classification, and many other business workloads. Some machine learning models can run efficiently on CPUs, particularly when the datasets and models are moderate in size. Others benefit from GPU acceleration when they are trained or applied at high volume. The difference between these approaches becomes clearer when the manually defined rule path is placed beside the data-driven learning path, as shown in *Figure 1.2*:

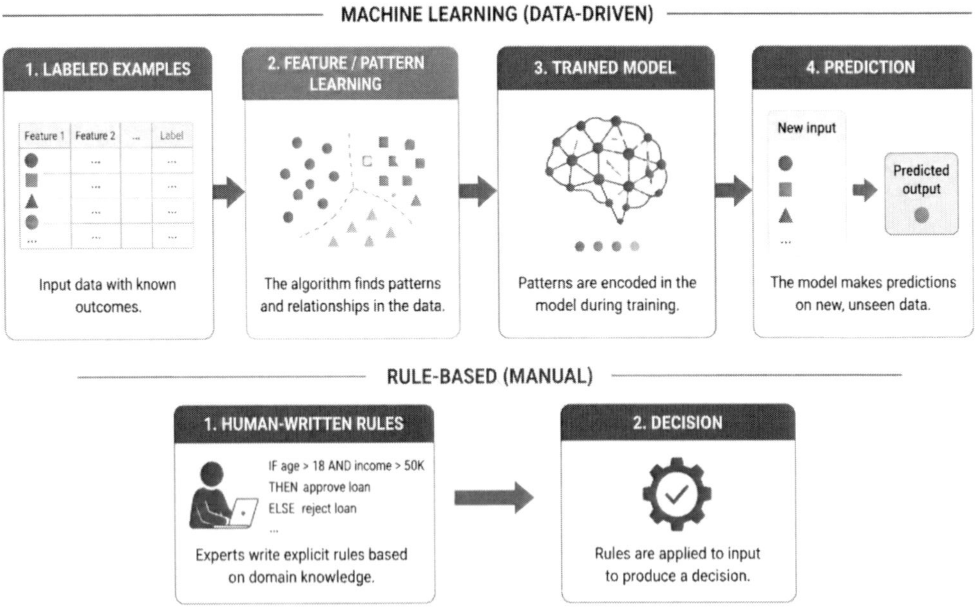

Figure 1.2: Machine learning replaces explicit rule writing with a data-driven learning loop

Machine learning narrows the AI category to systems that learn patterns from data. Deep learning narrows it further by using layered neural networks to learn increasingly complex representations.

Deep learning and layered neural networks

Deep learning is a specialized form of machine learning. It uses artificial neural networks with multiple hidden layers, which is the source of the word "deep". Each layer transforms the data it receives and passes a representation to the next layer. Across many layers, a network can learn patterns that are difficult to express as hand-written rules or manually selected features.

Image processing provides a useful mental model. Early layers may respond to simple edges and changes in brightness. Later layers can combine those signals into shapes, textures, or parts of objects. Deeper layers can then identify larger structures such as faces, vehicles, or other objects. The exact internal representation is learned from the training data rather than specified feature by feature by a programmer. *Figure 1.3* illustrates this progression with an image-recognition example, showing how successive layers move from raw pixels to increasingly abstract representations:

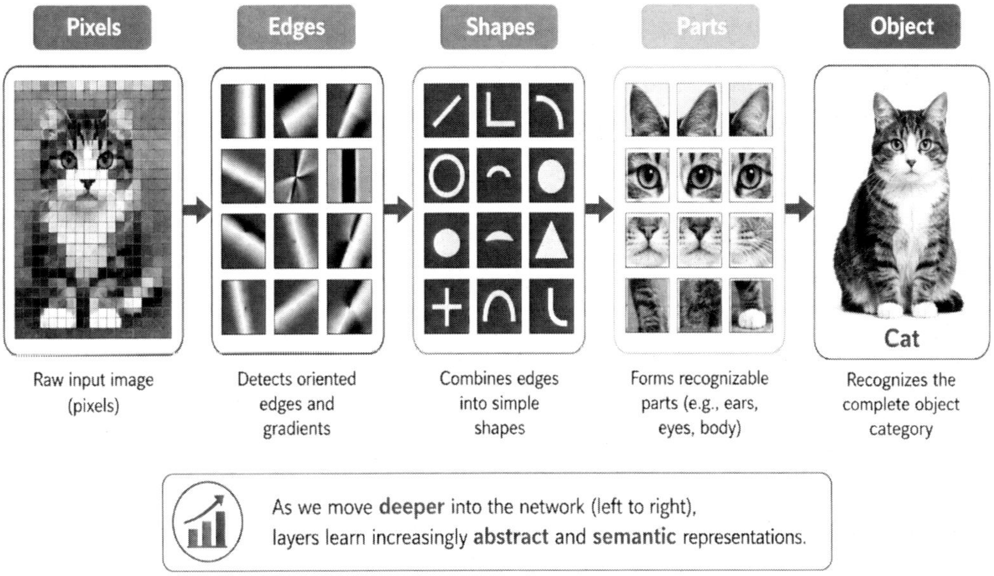

Figure 1.3: Hierarchical feature learning in deep learning

In this figure, the input begins as raw pixels and becomes progressively more abstract as it moves through the network. Early layers identify simple visual features such as edges, later layers combine those features into shapes and recognizable parts, and deeper layers use those representations to identify the complete object. The important infrastructure point is that these transformations require large numbers of repeated numerical operations, which is one reason deep learning benefits so strongly from parallel computation.

The same principle supports natural language processing, speech recognition, medical image analysis, autonomous systems, and large language models. These networks may contain millions or billions of adjustable parameters. Training repeatedly performs matrix and tensor operations to calculate outputs, measure error, and update those parameters. Inference uses the trained parameters to produce predictions or responses for new inputs.

Training and inference use the same model in different ways and therefore place different pressures on the infrastructure. During training, the system repeatedly calculates results, measures error, and updates model parameters. This process typically emphasizes compute throughput and accelerator memory because the system must hold model data together with intermediate information required for learning. Larger training jobs may also spread work across several GPUs, making communication between accelerators important.

During inference, the learned parameters remain fixed, and the system applies them to new inputs. The priorities, therefore, shift toward serving requests efficiently. Depending on the application, this may mean minimizing the latency of an individual request, maximizing the number of requests processed per second, or balancing both goals under concurrent load. A model that was trained on several GPUs may consequently be deployed using a very different serving configuration.

The scale and mathematical structure of deep learning create the strongest demand for massively parallel compute. This is the point at which the hierarchy of AI techniques becomes an infrastructure concern rather than a vocabulary exercise.

Reading the hierarchy as an infrastructure professional

The relationship can be summarized as a set of nested categories: deep learning is part of machine learning, and machine learning is part of artificial intelligence. The following table connects that hierarchy to the way an infrastructure team should interpret the terms:

Category	Core idea	Example approaches	Typical infrastructure implication
Artificial intelligence	Systems perform tasks associated with intelligence	Rules, expert systems, search, planning, and learned models	Requirements vary widely; the AI label alone does not prove that a GPU is necessary

Category	Core idea	Example approaches	Typical infrastructure implication
Machine learning	Models learn patterns from examples rather than relying only on fixed rules	Decision trees, support vector machines, ensembles, and neural networks	Training data volume and model type determine whether CPU or GPU acceleration is appropriate
Deep learning	Multilayer neural networks learn hierarchical representations	Convolutional networks, transformers, and other deep neural networks	Large tensor operations create strong demand for GPU compute, memory bandwidth, and scalable data movement

Table 1.1: AI, machine learning, and deep learning from an infrastructure perspective

When a stakeholder says that an application uses AI, an infrastructure professional should ask a second set of questions. Is the workload rule-based or learned? Is it being trained or only used for inference? How large is the model? What is the input data type? What latency and throughput targets apply? Those questions reveal the resource profile that the general AI label hides.

> **Tip**
>
> This distinction also supports exam reasoning. A scenario involving a small rules engine may not justify a GPU. A scenario involving transformer training, image classification across a large dataset, or real-time neural inference is much more likely to require GPU acceleration. The technology choice follows the computation, not the marketing label.

Why AI has advanced so rapidly

Modern AI capability has advanced through several developments occurring together rather than through a single change. Larger and more accessible datasets have provided more material from which models can learn, while advances in neural-network architectures and training techniques have made it possible to solve increasingly complex problems. At the same time, GPU-accelerated computing has made the large volumes of parallel computation required by these models practical.

Improvements in the surrounding software ecosystem have also lowered the barrier to using acceleration. Frameworks, optimized libraries, packaged models, and deployment tools allow teams to use GPU capabilities without implementing every operation from scratch. Access to scalable data centers and cloud infrastructure has further allowed organizations to experiment with larger workloads and deploy AI services to more users.

These factors reinforce one another: better algorithms create greater demand for computation, accelerated hardware makes larger models practical, and mature software and infrastructure make those capabilities easier to deploy. Understanding this combination helps explain why AI adoption has expanded so quickly across industries.

The hierarchy now explains why some AI systems remain modest while deep learning places extraordinary demands on infrastructure. The next section examines the processor architecture designed to meet those demands.

Why GPUs power modern AI

The central advantage of a **graphics processing unit** (**GPU**) is not that it replaces every function of a **central processing unit** (**CPU**). It is that the GPU is designed to execute large numbers of similar operations at the same time. Modern AI workloads contain exactly this kind of work, especially the matrix and tensor calculations used in neural networks.

Sequential control and parallel computation

A **central processing unit**, or CPU, contains a relatively small number of powerful cores. Those cores are well-suited to general-purpose logic, operating system services, control flow, and workloads in which one step depends heavily on the result of the previous step. CPUs also handle frequent task switching and a wide variety of instructions efficiently.

A **graphics processing unit**, or **GPU**, takes a different approach. It contains many smaller execution resources designed to apply the same or similar operations to many pieces of data in parallel. This architecture was originally developed for graphics, where many pixels and vertices must be processed concurrently. **Compute Unified Device Architecture** (**CUDA**) later made the same parallel resources available for general-purpose computation. *Figure 1.4* contrasts these processor designs, showing how a CPU concentrates on a smaller number of control-oriented tasks while a GPU applies similar operations across many data elements in parallel:

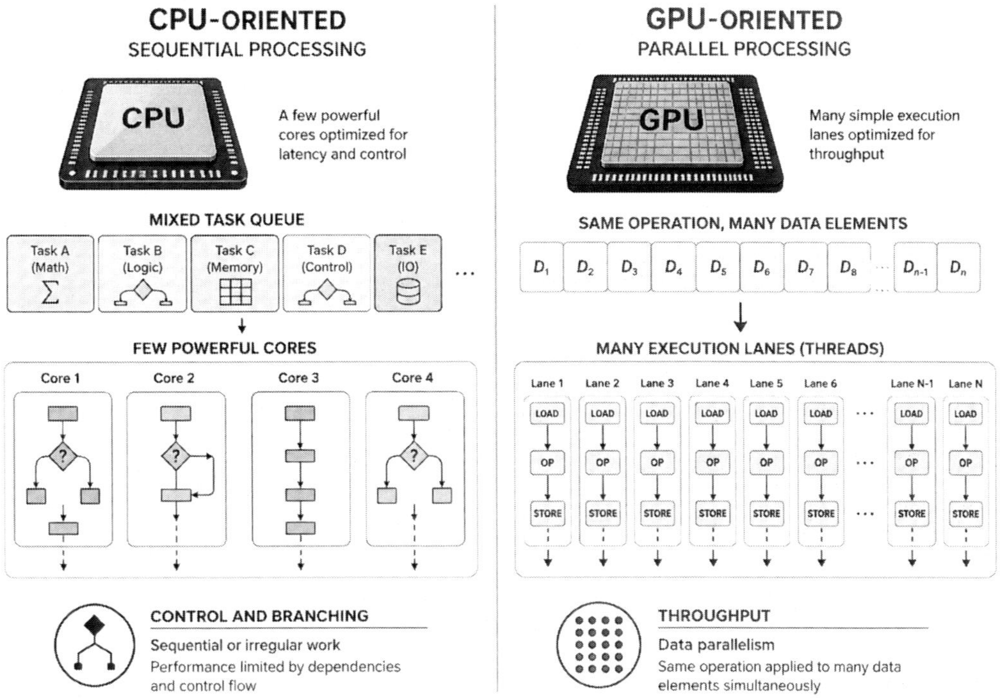

Figure 1.4: CPU-oriented sequential processing compared with GPU-oriented parallel processing

The left side of *Figure 1.4* emphasizes the CPU's strength in control flow, branching, and varied sequential tasks, while the right side shows the GPU applying similar operations across many execution lanes at the same time. The figure therefore illustrates why the appropriate processor depends on the structure of the workload: work dominated by control and dependencies suits a CPU, whereas highly repetitive data-parallel work can make much better use of a GPU.

The contrast is not simply fast versus slow. A CPU may be the better choice for a highly sequential task, while a GPU may deliver a dramatic advantage for a task that can be divided into thousands of similar calculations. Understanding the shape of the work is therefore more useful than treating either processor as universally superior.

Neural networks provide a clear example of highly parallel work, so the next step is to connect their mathematical operations to the GPU architecture.

Why tensors and matrix operations map well to GPUs

Deep learning operates on tensors, which are multidimensional arrays of data. Images, text embeddings, model weights, activations, and gradients can all be represented as tensors.

Training and inference repeatedly perform operations across these arrays, including matrix multiplication, convolution, normalization, and nonlinear transformations.

Two memory characteristics are useful to keep separate. **Memory capacity** describes how much model data and runtime state can reside on the GPU at one time, while **memory bandwidth** describes how quickly data can move between GPU memory and the processing resources that use it. A workload can therefore have enough capacity to fit on a GPU but still be limited by the rate at which its data can be supplied to computation.

During a forward pass, the model transforms input data through its layers to produce an output. During training, a backward pass calculates how the model parameters contributed to an error, and an optimization step updates those parameters. Many elements of these calculations can be performed independently or in parallel.

A GPU can distribute this work across many execution units. Instead of calculating one matrix element at a time, the device processes many elements concurrently. This parallelism shortens the time required for compute-heavy stages and increases the amount of work completed per unit of time. For large training jobs, the difference can determine whether an experiment completes in a practical window. The following figure maps this principle onto matrix multiplication by showing how independent regions of an output matrix can be distributed across parallel GPU execution groups:

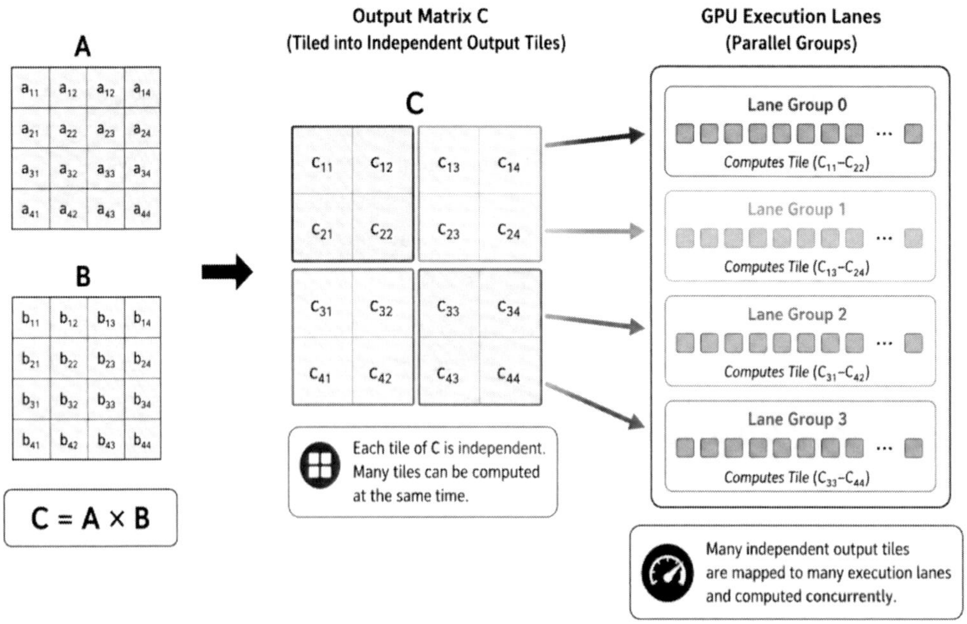

Figure 1.5 Mapping tensor operations to GPU parallelism

The above image makes the parallelism more concrete by dividing the output matrix into separate tiles and mapping those tiles to different GPU execution groups. Although each output value still depends on the required input data, many output elements or tiles can be calculated concurrently. The benefit comes from exposing enough independent work for the GPU to keep many execution resources busy at once.

Inference benefits for a related reason. A production service may need to process many requests, images, or data records at once. Batching those inputs allows the GPU to apply the same model operations across multiple items in parallel. The result can be high throughput, while carefully optimized deployments can also meet demanding latency targets.

Parallelism explains the fundamental fit, but NVIDIA GPUs add specialized technologies that strengthen it further.

Specialized acceleration in the NVIDIA platform

CUDA provides the programming platform that allows software to send general-purpose work to NVIDIA GPUs. Tensor Cores provide specialized hardware for matrix operations used heavily in deep learning. **NVLink** provides a high-bandwidth connection between supported GPUs so that multi-GPU workloads can move data more efficiently than they could through a conventional peripheral connection alone.

It is also useful to distinguish accelerator interconnects from the broader data center network. NVLink provides high-bandwidth communication between GPUs within supported NVIDIA system or GPU configurations. Communication between separate servers typically relies on a data center network such as InfiniBand or high-performance Ethernet. A distributed AI workload may therefore depend on both forms of connectivity: fast communication among local GPUs and an efficient network between nodes.

Data center GPUs such as the A100 and H100 add features intended for training, inference, and shared infrastructure. **Multi-Instance GPU**, or **MIG**, can divide a supported physical GPU into isolated instances. Mixed-precision support allows selected calculations to use lower-precision formats that improve performance and reduce memory use while retaining the accuracy required by the workload.

Hardware is only one part of the advantage. The NVIDIA software stack includes optimized libraries, inference tooling, model servers, and packaged assets. CUDA-aware frameworks can use these components without requiring every model developer to write low-level GPU code. This full-stack integration is one reason GPU acceleration can be adopted across the model lifecycle rather than only in specialized research code.

Even with this specialization, the GPU does not operate alone. Production systems assign different kinds of work to different processors.

The CPU, GPU, and DPU as complementary processors

In a typical AI system, the CPU remains responsible for control-oriented work. It runs the operating system, coordinates processes, prepares data, manages scheduling, and handles parts of the application that do not benefit from massive parallelism. The GPU performs the dense model computation. A **data processing unit**, or **DPU**, can offload networking, storage, security, and data-movement functions that would otherwise consume CPU resources.

In this context, offload means moving infrastructure processing away from the host CPU and assigning it to hardware designed for that work. Networking, storage movement, encryption, packet processing, and related functions are often part of the server's data path. A DPU can perform selected functions close to that path so that the CPU can spend more of its resources on application and control-oriented work.

The following table summarizes the division of labor among the three processor classes:

Processor	**Primary strength**	**Representative responsibilities in AI infrastructure**
CPU	General-purpose control and sequential logic	Operating system tasks, orchestration, scheduling, data preparation, and application control flow
GPU	Massively parallel and matrix-oriented computation	Model training, tensor operations, high-throughput inference, and other compute-heavy AI stages
DPU	Infrastructure data processing and offload	Networking, storage I/O, encryption, packet processing, telemetry, and isolation services

Table 1.2: Complementary roles of CPUs, GPUs, and DPUs in AI infrastructure

This division is best understood as a cooperative design. The CPU does not become unnecessary when GPUs are installed, and the DPU does not replace either CPU or GPU. Each processor handles the work that matches its architecture. When the allocation is effective, the CPU spends less time on data-plane tasks, the GPU receives data consistently, and the application can use the available compute more efficiently. *Figure 1.6* brings these responsibilities together within one server, showing how the CPU, GPU, and DPU cooperate while accessing the memory, network, and storage resources required by the workload:

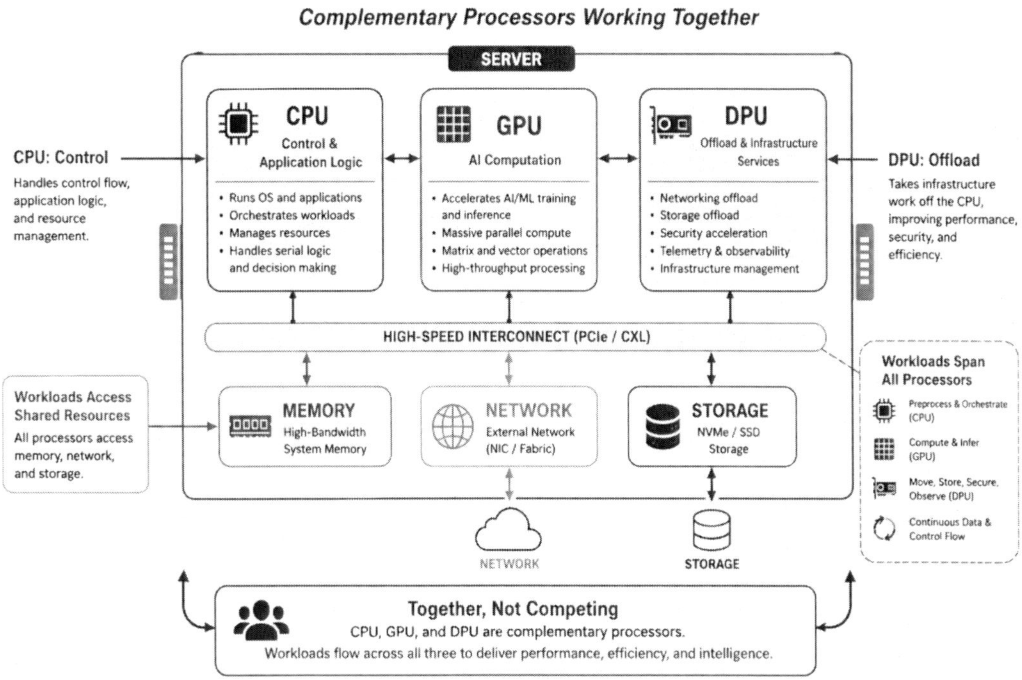

Figure 1.6: CPU, GPU, and DPU work as a coordinated system

Figure 1.6 shows that an accelerated server operates as a coordinated system rather than as a collection of competing processors. The CPU remains responsible for application and control logic, the GPU performs the dense AI computation, and the DPU can take on infrastructure-oriented networking, storage, security, and telemetry work. All three ultimately depend on the surrounding memory, network, and storage paths, so accelerator performance is influenced by the complete system.

For infrastructure planning, this means that buying a powerful GPU is not enough. The host CPU, system memory, storage path, network, and software environment must be able to feed and coordinate the accelerator. Later chapters will examine those supporting systems in detail.

You have now connected neural-network mathematics to GPU parallelism and placed the GPU within a cooperative CPU-GPU-DPU system. The final section of this chapter applies that foundation to common data center workloads.

AI workloads in the data center

AI is not a single workload profile. Computer vision, language processing, predictive analytics, and recommendation systems differ in model structure, input data, latency sensitivity, and scale. Infrastructure teams, therefore, need to recognize the operational signals associated with each family. *Figure 1.7* provides a first-pass view of these four workload families by connecting each one to a representative input, processing pattern, and infrastructure pressure.

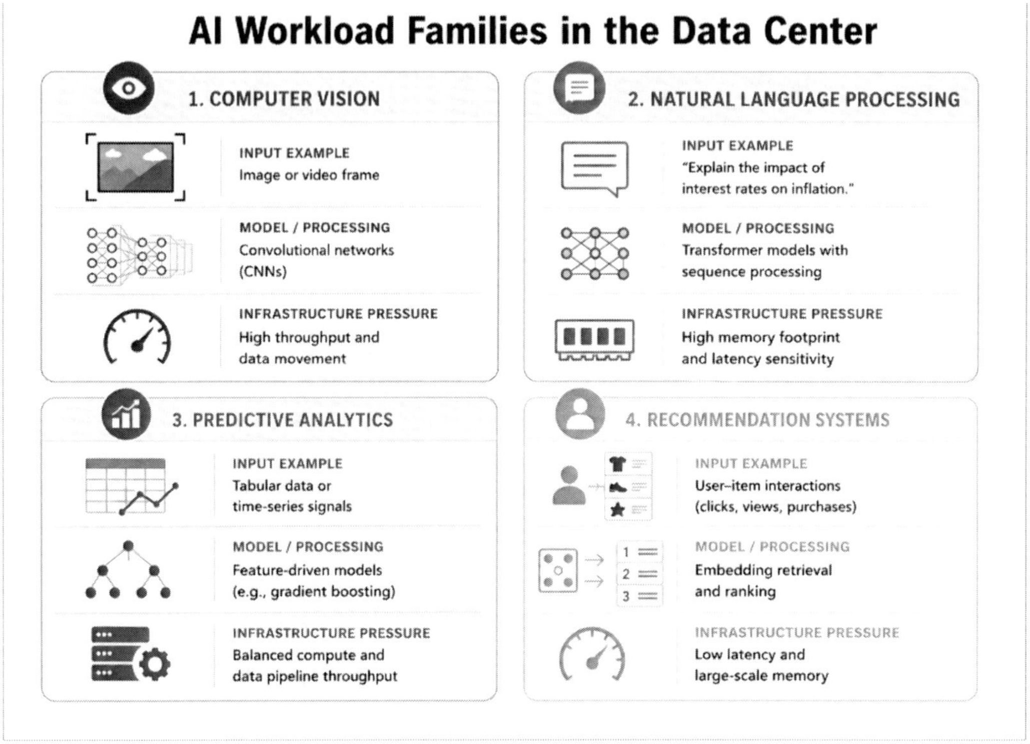

Figure 1.7: AI workloads in the data center

The four quadrants in *Figure 1.7* show why the phrase AI workload is not specific enough for infrastructure planning. Computer vision places strong pressure on data movement and throughput, NLP commonly introduces substantial model-memory and latency requirements, predictive analytics can range from CPU-friendly models to accelerated workloads, and recommendation systems often combine high request volume with strict response-time targets. These differences explain why the workload must be understood before the infrastructure is selected.

Computer vision

Computer vision systems analyze images or video. Common tasks include image classification, object detection, and semantic segmentation. These tasks support self-driving and driver-assistance systems, industrial inspection, smart retail cameras, and medical image analysis.

Vision models often use deep convolutional networks such as ResNet, YOLO, or U-Net. Training may require large collections of high-resolution images and many repeated convolution operations. GPUs accelerate those operations through CUDA, Tensor Cores, and optimized deep learning libraries. When the system processes live video or safety-related input, inference latency can be as important as training speed.

The data path is also significant. Images and video are large, and a GPU can become underutilized if storage or preprocessing cannot supply frames quickly enough. A vision workload may therefore require not only compute capacity but also high-throughput storage, efficient data loading, and a network capable of carrying streams or distributed training traffic.

Computer vision demonstrates that workload planning must consider the input pipeline as well as the model. Natural language processing creates a different pattern, with particularly strong pressure on memory and matrix computation.

Natural language processing

Natural language processing, or **NLP**, includes text classification, sentiment analysis, question answering, document analysis, and conversational AI. Transformer-based models such as BERT, GPT-style models, and Llama-family models have made these workloads central to enterprise AI.

Transformers rely heavily on attention mechanisms and matrix operations. Large models also contain many parameters, which increases memory requirements. Training can require several GPUs when the model, optimizer state, and intermediate data do not fit on one device. Inference may need to serve many requests while maintaining an acceptable response time.

NVIDIA GPUs support these workloads with large memory configurations, Tensor Cores, lower-precision formats, and high-speed interconnects. In production, an NLP model may be optimized for inference with TensorRT and served to applications through Triton Inference Server. The operational challenge is to balance memory use, throughput, batching, and latency rather than focusing on raw compute alone.

Language workloads show why model size and memory capacity often become selection criteria. Predictive analytics can be less uniform because it may use either conventional machine learning or deep learning techniques.

Predictive analytics

Predictive analytics uses historical or streaming data to estimate future events or identify likely outcomes. Examples include demand forecasting, inventory planning, supply chain modeling, and fraud detection. Inputs may be tabular records, time-series data, or a combination of structured and unstructured information.

Some predictive workloads use decision trees or gradient-boosted models, which may run effectively on CPUs at a modest scale. Others use recurrent neural networks, long short-term memory networks, or transformer-based approaches that benefit from GPU acceleration. The correct resource choice, therefore, depends on the model, the data volume, and the required response time.

Batch inference can tolerate a longer processing window and may prioritize throughput. Streaming fraud detection or operational forecasting may need low latency and predictable processing. At a large scale, even a model that is not individually demanding can justify acceleration because the organization must process many records or many models concurrently.

Predictive analytics is a useful reminder that GPUs should not be assigned automatically. The infrastructure team should evaluate whether the workload can use the accelerator effectively. Recommendation systems bring this decision into a highly latency-sensitive, high-volume environment.

Recommendation systems

Recommendation systems predict what a user is likely to engage with next. They appear in e-commerce, video and music services, social feeds, and other digital platforms. A production recommendation pipeline may combine collaborative filtering, feature processing, and deep neural networks to generate personalized results.

The operational challenge is often latency at scale. Recommendations may need to be produced in milliseconds while many users browse simultaneously. The system must retrieve features, run model inference, rank candidates, and return results without noticeable delay. GPUs can provide the parallelism and throughput needed for this process, especially when many inference requests are batched or when deep models are used.

Recommendation workloads also highlight the importance of efficient serving. The model may be only one stage in a larger pipeline, so optimization must include data access, preprocessing, and request routing. A fast GPU cannot compensate for a slow feature store—the system supplying model-ready input features—or an overloaded network.

Across these four workload families, the recurring task is to translate application behavior into infrastructure requirements.

Matching workload characteristics to resources

A practical assessment begins with a small set of questions. What data type enters the system? Is the workload training or inference? How large is the model? How much accelerator memory is required? Is the priority low latency, high throughput, or both? Does the job run on one GPU, several GPUs in one server, or many GPUs across nodes? Must several teams or workloads share accelerator resources while maintaining predictable isolation?

Two performance terms appear repeatedly in AI infrastructure scenarios. **Latency** is the time required to complete an individual request or unit of work, whereas **throughput** describes how much work the system completes over a period of time. The two goals can interact. For example, combining several inference requests into a batch can improve GPU utilization and throughput because the requests are processed together, but waiting to form a larger batch can also add latency. Production configuration, therefore, depends on which performance target the application values most.

Table 1.3 summarizes the workload signals introduced in this chapter. It does not replace measurement, but it provides a useful first-pass model for scenario analysis:

Workload family	Common pressure points	Infrastructure emphasis
Computer vision	Large image or video input, convolution-heavy models, and real-time frame processing	GPU compute, efficient data loading, high-throughput storage, and predictable inference latency
Natural language processing	Large parameter counts, attention operations, model memory, and concurrent requests	Large GPU memory, Tensor Core acceleration, multi-GPU interconnects, and optimized model serving
Predictive analytics	Mixed model types, tabular or time-series data, and batch or streaming execution	Choose CPU or GPU according to model and scale; emphasize throughput and pipeline integration
Recommendation systems	High request volume, strict response times, and multi-stage ranking pipelines	Low-latency inference, batching, scalable serving, and fast access to features and candidate data

Table 1.3: Common AI workload families, pressure points, and infrastructure priorities

> **Tip**
>
> Exam scenarios often provide one or more of these signals and ask for a suitable technology. The strongest answers identify the bottleneck before selecting the component. A memory-bound transformer problem points toward a GPU with sufficient memory. A multi-node synchronization problem points toward a low-latency

interconnect. An underutilized vision GPU may point toward the storage or preprocessing pipeline rather than toward a larger accelerator.

Workload Characteristics	Large-memory GPU	TensorRT/Triton	Accelerated storage	InfiniBand/ NVLink	MIG
Large model	✓ fits large parameter sets	✓ optimizes inference latency	✓ moves data faster	✓ fast multi-node communication	—
Real-time latency	✓ keeps more data on device	✓ optimizes inference latency	✓ reduces I/O bottlenecks	✓ low-latency transport	✓ predictable latency
High-volume media	✓ handles larger batches	✓ high-throughput inference	✓ moves data faster	✓ fast multi-node communication	—
Distributed training	✓ stores larger models	—	✓ fast checkpoint I/O	✓ fast multi-node communication	—
Many small tenants	✓ supports higher consolidation	✓ efficient per-tenant inference	✓ handles many small I/O streams	—	✓ isolates shared tenants

Figure 1.8: Workload symptoms to infrastructure choices

Figure 1.8 should be read as a set of possible relationships rather than as a prescriptive sizing table. For example, a large model may make additional GPU memory the first concern, while distributed training can make high-speed communication critical, and a multi-tenant environment may make MIG attractive. Storage acceleration, optimized inference software, interconnects, and GPU partitioning become relevant only when the corresponding workload bottleneck or operational requirement is present. The correct choice, therefore, comes from identifying the limiting factor first and validating the proposed technology against the actual workload.

This workload-first approach will remain useful throughout the book. Every later technology - CUDA, Tensor Cores, MIG, DCGM, InfiniBand, GPUDirect, vGPU, and BlueField - can be understood as a response to a specific compute or operational need.

Summary

This chapter established the workload foundation for AI infrastructure. Artificial intelligence is the broad category, machine learning is the data-driven subset, and deep learning is the neural-network subset that creates the strongest demand for parallel compute. The distinction is important because the word AI alone does not identify a hardware requirement.

You then saw why GPUs fit modern deep learning. CPUs excel at control flow and general-purpose work, GPUs execute large numbers of parallel tensor operations, and DPUs can offload networking, storage, and security functions. These processors form a cooperative architecture rather than a sequence of replacements.

Finally, the chapter connected computer vision, NLP, predictive analytics, and recommendation systems to practical concerns such as memory, throughput, latency, data movement, and scale. The goal was to help you interpret an AI use case as an infrastructure profile. You can now begin that analysis by identifying the model type, data path, execution mode, and performance target.

The chapter has moved from the meaning of AI to the resource profile of real workloads. With that foundation in place, the next step is to examine CUDA and the software stack that turns NVIDIA GPU hardware into an accessible AI platform. *Chapter 2* moves from workload requirements to the CUDA programming model and the NVIDIA software stack that exposes GPU acceleration to frameworks, libraries, and production services.

Chapter review questions

1. Which statement correctly describes the relationship among artificial intelligence, machine learning, and deep learning?
    a. AI contains machine learning, and machine learning contains deep learning.
    b. Deep learning contains AI, and AI contains machine learning.
    c. The three terms describe unrelated computing approaches.
    d. Machine learning contains AI, and deep learning contains machine learning.
2. A system uses a fixed set of human-written rules to approve or reject transactions. Which description is most accurate?
    a. It is deep learning because it makes a decision.
    b. It is machine learning because it processes business data.
    c. It is AI, but it is not necessarily machine learning.
    d. It cannot be considered AI because it does not use a GPU.

3. Why are GPUs generally better suited than CPUs to the matrix operations used in deep learning?
    a. GPUs use only one highly optimized core.
    b. GPUs eliminate the need for system memory.
    c. GPUs provide many parallel execution resources for repeated operations across large data arrays.
    d. GPUs run operating-system control logic faster than CPUs.
4. A training team doubles a model's size and the number of examples in each batch. Which infrastructure pressure is most likely to increase first?
    a. The need for a hypervisor
    b. The number of firewall rules
    c. Device-memory demand and compute demand
    d. The need for a graphics display connector
5. A real-time computer-vision service has a powerful GPU, but utilization remains low while frames arrive slowly from storage. What is the most likely limiting layer?
    a. Model registry
    b. GPU instruction precision
    c. Input and data-movement pipeline
    d. Credential-badge service
6. Which workload characteristic most strongly suggests a need for a large-memory GPU?
    a. A large language model whose parameters and runtime state require substantial GPU memory
    b. A low-volume cron job that copies text files
    c. A rule-based script with a small lookup table
    d. A network firewall applying a fixed access list
7. An inference service must respond to individual requests within a strict latency target. Which operational priority is most important?
    a. Consistent low response time under expected load
    b. Storing all experiment notes in one notebook
    c. Keeping every GPU idle between requests
    d. Maximizing only total training epochs

8. Which processor-role mapping is correct in an accelerated server?
    a. CPU: storage encryption only; GPU: user authentication; DPU: model training only
    b. CPU: AI matrix computation; GPU: firewalling; DPU: operating-system control
    c. CPU: control and general-purpose logic; GPU: parallel AI computation; DPU: infrastructure offload
    d. CPU, GPU, and DPU perform identical tasks and differ only in price.
9. A recommendation service must score a very large number of candidates for many users. Why can GPU acceleration be valuable even if each individual prediction is small?
    a. A GPU removes the need for input data.
    b. Recommendation services can run only on GPUs.
    c. The aggregate workload exposes substantial parallelism and throughput demand.
    d. A GPU converts all recommendation models into rule-based systems.
10. Which first question best supports an infrastructure decision for an unfamiliar AI workload?
    a. Can the team avoid monitoring after deployment?
    b. Which product name is most familiar to the operator?
    c. Which GPU has the newest architecture name?
    d. What are the workload's compute, memory, latency, throughput, data, and isolation requirements?

Answer key and explanations

Use the explanations to verify both the correct choice and the layer of the stack being tested.

1. A. AI is the broad category. Machine learning is a data-driven subset of AI, and deep learning is a neural-network-based subset of machine learning.
2. C. Rule-based systems can perform behavior associated with AI without learning patterns from examples. GPU use is not part of the definition.
3. C. Neural-network work contains large amounts of data-parallel arithmetic. A GPU can execute many similar operations concurrently, while a CPU is optimized for broader control and sequential work.
4. C. Larger models and batches occupy more device memory and require more arithmetic. The other choices are not direct consequences of the change.

5. C. The GPU is waiting for input. Storage throughput, preprocessing, and the transfer path must be examined before adding more compute.
6. A. Large model weights, activations, and runtime state place direct pressure on GPU memory capacity and bandwidth.
7. A. Real-time inference is judged by response latency and consistency as well as throughput. Training-epoch count is not the serving objective.
8. C. The processors are complementary: the CPU coordinates general logic, the GPU accelerates parallel computation, and the DPU can offload networking, storage, security, and telemetry.
9. C. Large request volumes and candidate sets create many independent calculations that can be batched and executed in parallel.
10. D. Infrastructure selection should begin with workload constraints. Product choice follows only after the requirements are understood.

2

CUDA and the NVIDIA AI Software Stack

> **Note**
>
> GPU hardware becomes useful to AI teams when a software platform can express parallel work, optimize common operations, and carry models into production.

Compute Unified Device Architecture (**CUDA**) is the software foundation that opened NVIDIA GPUs to general-purpose computation. Before CUDA, GPUs were associated mainly with graphics rendering. CUDA provided a programming model, runtime, and ecosystem that allowed developers and frameworks to send scientific, analytical, and AI calculations to the GPU. This connection between software and hardware is central to accelerated computing.

This chapter begins with the CUDA execution model, including threads, blocks, grids, and streaming multiprocessors. It then introduces the optimized libraries and development tools that support deep learning, such as cuDNN, cuBLAS, Nsight, CUDA Graphs, and Tensor Cores. The final section widens the view to the full NVIDIA AI stack, showing how hardware, system software, libraries, frameworks, NGC assets, and production services fit together.

By the end of the chapter, you will be able to explain how an AI framework reaches the GPU and why NVIDIA describes its platform as a full stack rather than a collection of independent products. The objective is to follow a workload from high-level model code down to parallel execution and then forward into deployment.

We will be covering the following main topics in this chapter:

- The CUDA programming model

- CUDA libraries and development tools
- The NVIDIA AI stack from hardware to deployment

The chapter starts at the software-hardware boundary, where CUDA turns a computational problem into work that can be distributed across the GPU.

The CUDA programming model

CUDA is NVIDIA's parallel computing platform and programming model for running non-graphics workloads on NVIDIA GPUs. CUDA allows software written through languages and frameworks such as C, C++, Python, PyTorch, TensorFlow, and JAX to use GPU resources for computation.

From graphics processor to general-purpose accelerator

A GPU was originally designed to repeat similar mathematical operations across many pixels and geometric elements. The same architecture is valuable for scientific simulation, weather modeling, analytics, high-performance computing, and AI because these fields also contain calculations that can be divided into many parallel pieces.

CUDA made this capability accessible without requiring every application to be written as a graphics program. In CUDA terminology, the **host** is the CPU-side system that coordinates the application, while the **device** is the GPU that executes accelerated work. A function launched to run in parallel on the GPU is called a **kernel**. When an application launches a kernel, CUDA creates many threads that execute that kernel over different portions of the workload. Developers could define computational functions, move data to GPU memory, launch work on the device, and collect the results. Over time, frameworks and libraries added higher-level interfaces so that many users could benefit from CUDA without managing each low-level operation directly.

For infrastructure professionals, CUDA is important even when they do not write kernels. Driver compatibility, CUDA runtime versions, container images, library versions, and GPU support all affect whether an application can use the accelerator. CUDA is therefore both a development platform and an operational dependency.

To understand why CUDA scales, the next step is to examine how it organizes parallel work.

Threads, blocks, and grids

The CUDA programming model divides a problem into threads. A thread performs a sequence of instructions on a portion of the data. Threads are grouped into blocks, and blocks are grouped into a grid. This hierarchy allows the same program to describe work that can scale across GPUs with different numbers of execution resources. *Figure 2.1* makes this execution hierarchy concrete by showing how individual threads are grouped into blocks and how multiple blocks together form the grid associated with a kernel launch.

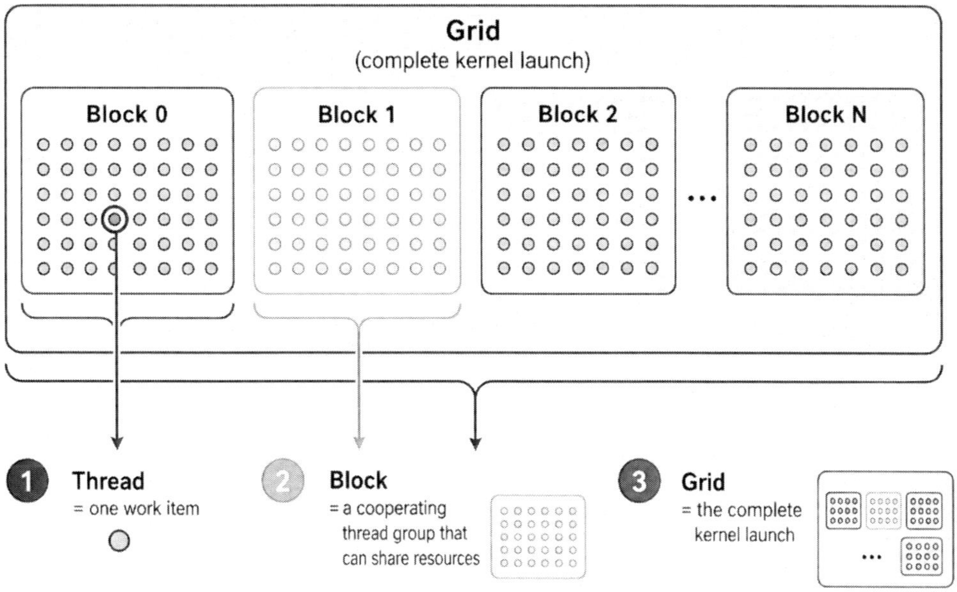

Figure 2.1: The CUDA programming model

The above figure shows the hierarchy from the smallest unit of CUDA work to the complete kernel launch. A thread performs work on a portion of the data, threads cooperate within a block, and multiple blocks form a grid. This structure allows an application to expose large amounts of parallel work without specifying exactly which physical GPU execution resource must process each individual thread.

A **block** is scheduled on a **streaming multiprocessor**, or **SM**, which is a primary compute unit inside the GPU. An SM manages many threads and executes them in groups called warps. Because a data center GPU contains many SMs, it can keep large numbers of threads active at the same time. The software hierarchy becomes more meaningful when it is mapped to the GPU hardware that executes it, as shown in *Figure 2.2*:

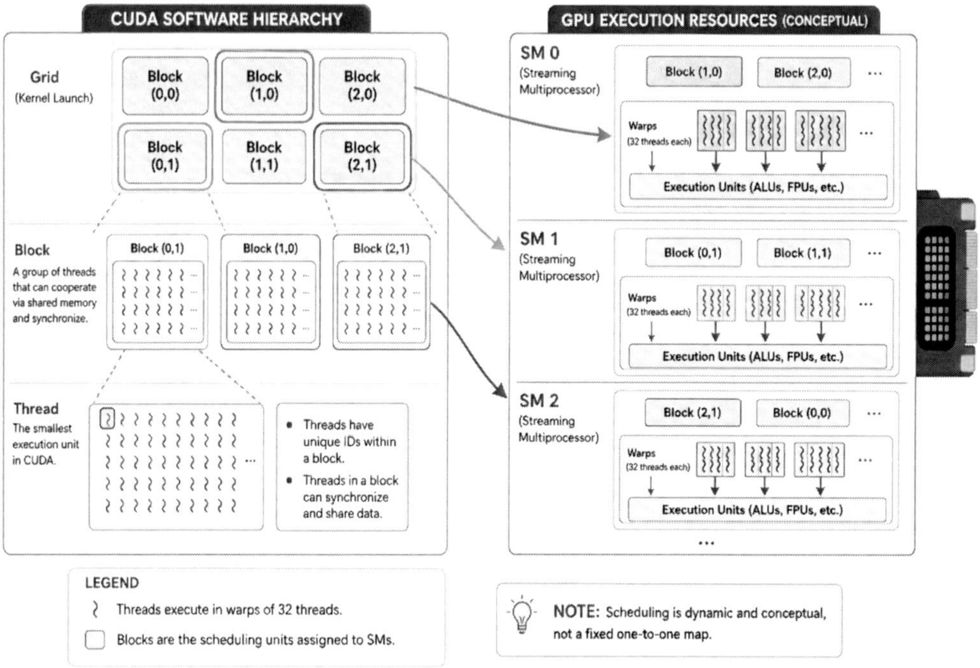

Figure 2.2: From CUDA hierarchy to GPU execution resources

Figure 2.2 connects the CUDA software hierarchy on the left with GPU execution resources on the right. Blocks from the grid are assigned to available streaming multiprocessors, where their threads are organized into warps for execution. The assignment is dynamic rather than a permanent one-to-one mapping: an SM can execute more than one resident block when resources permit, and new blocks can be scheduled as earlier work completes. This separation allows the same CUDA workload to scale across GPUs with different numbers of SMs.

A block remains associated with one SM while it executes, but an SM is not limited to a single block. Several blocks and many warps may be resident on the same SM when registers, shared memory, and other resources allow it. The SM's warp schedulers then select warps that are ready to execute. This ability to keep multiple warps available helps the GPU continue doing useful work while other warps are waiting on data or dependencies.

The grid-block-thread structure gives developers a way to express parallelism without manually assigning work to every physical core. The GPU scheduler maps blocks and warps to available execution resources. When a problem contains enough independent work, the hardware can remain busy even while some threads wait for data or other operations.

The model is especially suitable for array and matrix processing. A program can assign different elements, rows, tiles, or samples to different threads and blocks. The same conceptual structure appears underneath higher-level deep learning operations, even when the framework hides the kernel launch details.

The execution hierarchy explains how work is distributed. The next question is why deep learning provides so much parallel work to distribute.

CUDA in training and inference

Deep learning repeatedly applies mathematical operations to tensors. A forward pass calculates model outputs. A backward pass calculates gradients. An optimization step updates weights. Convolutional networks, transformer attention, normalization, activation functions, and linear layers all contain operations that can be parallelized.

CUDA enables those operations to be offloaded to the GPU. The accelerator can process many tensor elements and training examples at once, reducing the time required for each step. Larger batch sizes can also increase the amount of parallel work, although batch size must be balanced against memory capacity and model behavior.

Inference uses the same underlying model operations but has different operational goals. Training often prioritizes total time to completion and scaling efficiency. Inference may prioritize latency for one request, throughput across many requests, or a balance of both. CUDA remains the execution foundation, while tools such as TensorRT and Triton address production-specific optimization and serving. *Figure 2.3* places training and inference side by side to show which CUDA-accelerated operations they share and which additional computations are required during training.

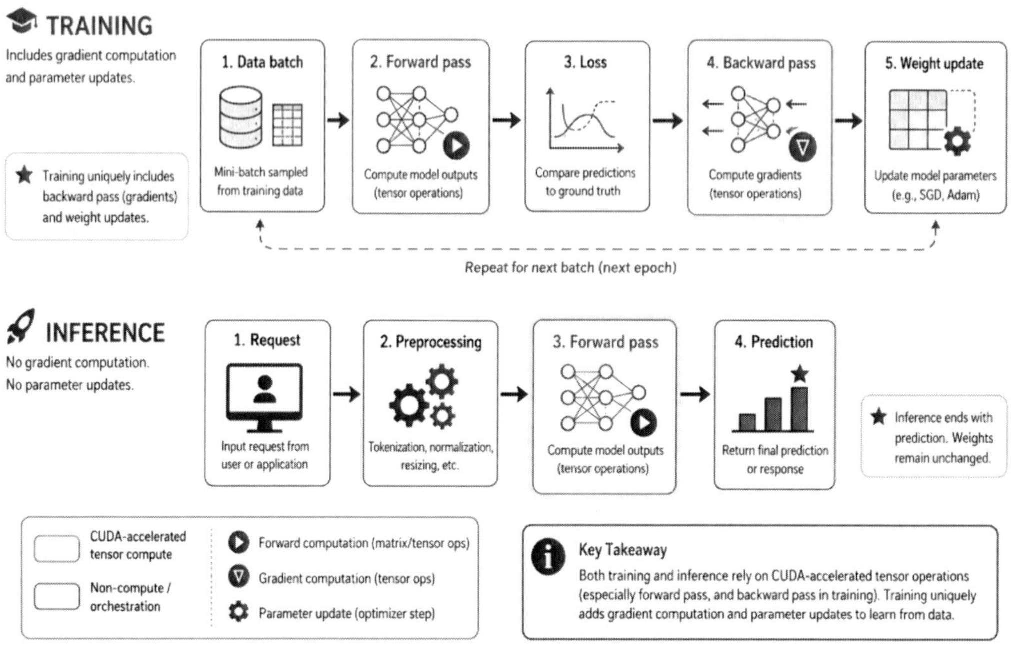

Figure 2.3: CUDA in training and inference

The figure above highlights the shared and different stages of training and inference. Both paths use a forward pass to execute tensor operations on input data, so both can benefit from CUDA acceleration. Training adds loss calculation, gradient computation during the backward pass, and parameter updates before repeating the process with further training data. Inference uses the learned parameters without updating them and ends by returning a prediction or response. These differences explain why training generally emphasizes sustained computation and scaling, while inference places greater emphasis on serving latency and throughput.

The role of CUDA is therefore consistent across the lifecycle: it provides the route from software operations to GPU execution. Frameworks make that route easier to use.

How AI frameworks use CUDA

Popular AI frameworks are CUDA-aware. When a supported NVIDIA GPU and software environment are available, frameworks such as PyTorch, TensorFlow, and JAX can place tensors and operations on the device. The framework selects or generates GPU kernels, calls optimized libraries, manages memory, and coordinates execution. *Figure 2.4* shows how these framework abstractions sit above the CUDA software layers and ultimately translate high-level model operations into work executed by the GPU.

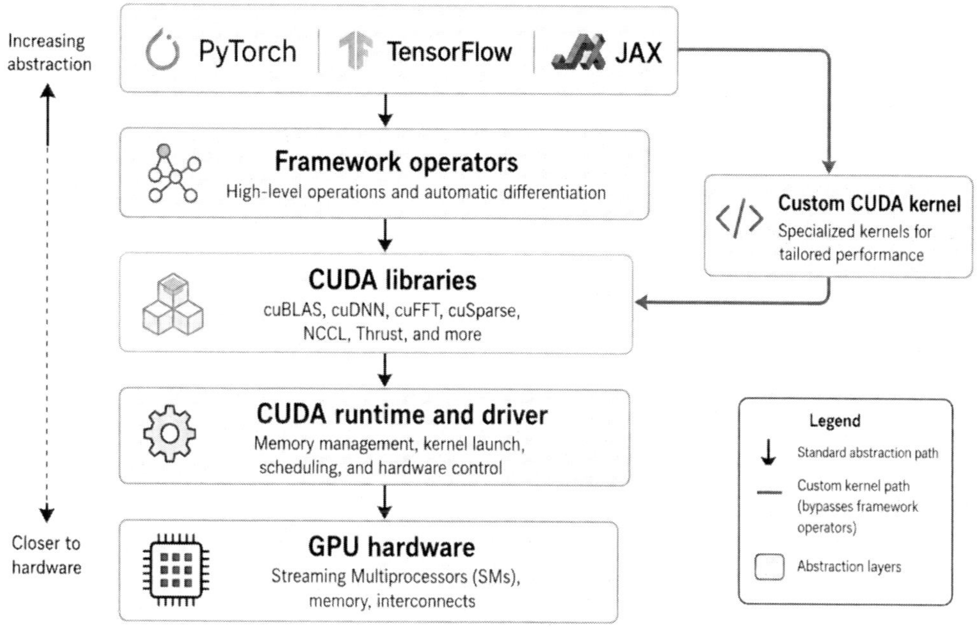

Figure 2.4: How AI frameworks reach the GPU

The main path in *Figure 2.4* shows the abstraction that most AI developers use. PyTorch, TensorFlow, or JAX expresses high-level operations, the framework relies on optimized CUDA capabilities beneath those operations, and the CUDA runtime and driver ultimately coordinate execution on the GPU. The side path represents specialized code in which a developer uses a custom CUDA kernel when greater control or workload-specific optimization is required. For an infrastructure operator, both paths still depend on a functioning and compatible CUDA software environment and GPU.

It is useful to distinguish the CUDA runtime from the NVIDIA driver. The runtime provides application-facing CUDA services such as memory management and kernel launching, while the installed NVIDIA driver provides the lower-level interface that communicates with the GPU. Framework containers can include CUDA runtime libraries and other dependencies, but the host still requires a compatible NVIDIA driver. This is why containerizing an AI workload does not completely remove host-side GPU compatibility requirements.

This abstraction is important. A data scientist can define a model using framework APIs while the underlying stack uses CUDA, cuDNN, cuBLAS, and other libraries. The infrastructure team supports that process by supplying compatible drivers, runtimes, containers, and GPU resources.

The abstraction does not eliminate operational issues. A model can fail if the container expects an unsupported runtime, if the driver is incompatible, if GPU memory is exhausted, or if the device is not exposed to the process. Understanding that the framework depends on CUDA helps an operator investigate these failures at the correct layer.

CUDA also supports workloads beyond model computation. Data processing, simulation, analytics, and custom preprocessing can use the same parallel platform, allowing more of an AI pipeline to remain accelerated.

You have now followed CUDA from general-purpose GPU computing through the thread hierarchy and into framework-based training and inference. The next section examines the optimized libraries and tools that turn this programming model into a practical developer ecosystem.

CUDA libraries and development tools

Writing every mathematical operation as a custom CUDA kernel would be inefficient and difficult to maintain. NVIDIA therefore provides optimized libraries for common operations and tools for profiling, debugging, and reducing execution overhead. These components allow frameworks and applications to reuse tuned implementations.

cuDNN for deep neural network primitives

The **CUDA Deep Neural Network library**, or **cuDNN**, supplies GPU-optimized implementations of operations used repeatedly in deep learning. These include convolution, pooling, activation functions, normalization, and related building blocks.

Frameworks can call cuDNN automatically when they detect a supported operation and environment. This means a model developer may receive GPU acceleration without invoking cuDNN directly. The library selects and executes implementations designed for NVIDIA hardware, reducing the need for each framework to create and tune every primitive independently.

From an operations perspective, cuDNN is part of the compatibility chain. A container or framework release is typically built and tested with particular CUDA and cuDNN versions. Using validated combinations reduces the risk of runtime errors and inconsistent behavior.

Deep learning primitives are one class of reusable work. Linear algebra is another, and it forms the mathematical backbone of many model layers.

cuBLAS and matrix computation

cuBLAS is NVIDIA's GPU-accelerated **Basic Linear Algebra Subprograms library**. It provides optimized routines for vector and matrix operations, including the matrix multiplication used extensively in neural networks.

Matrix multiplication appears in dense layers, transformer projections, attention calculations, and many other components. Efficient implementation requires careful use of memory, parallel execution, and specialized hardware. cuBLAS provides tuned routines so that frameworks can call a reliable building block instead of reimplementing the operation for each GPU generation.

Together, cuDNN and cuBLAS show how the CUDA ecosystem separates concerns. CUDA provides the execution platform, while domain-focused libraries provide optimized operations. This layering increases portability across supported devices and allows NVIDIA to improve implementations without changing the high-level model definition. *Figure 2.5* summarizes this division of responsibility by contrasting the deep learning primitives commonly handled by cuDNN with the linear algebra operations accelerated by cuBLAS.

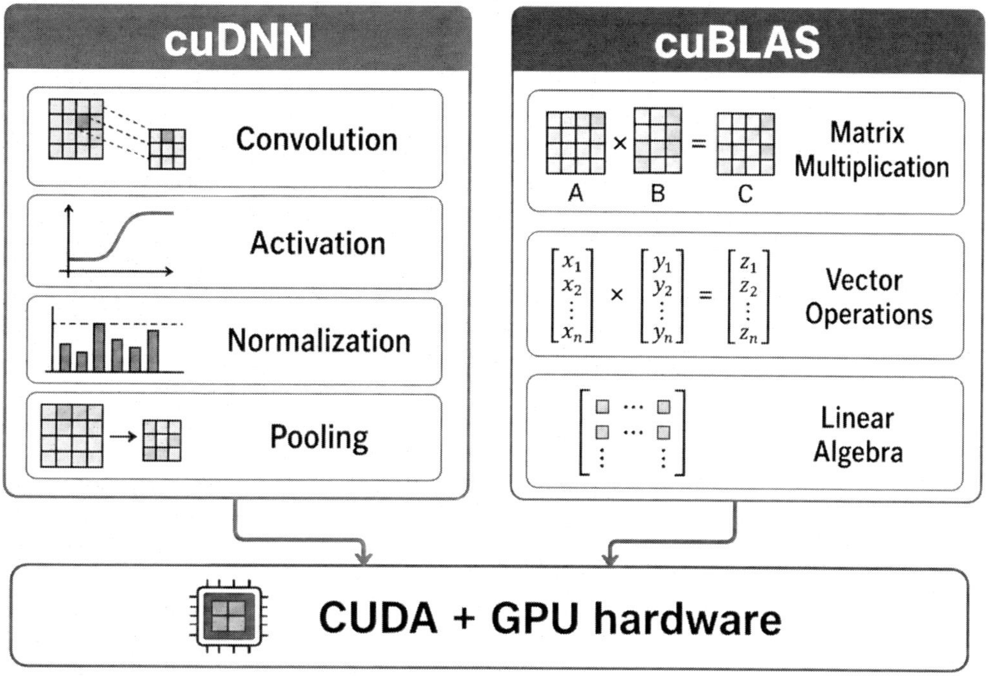

Figure 2.5: Major CUDA libraries by operation type

Figure 2.5 illustrates that cuDNN and cuBLAS solve different classes of reusable computation. cuDNN provides operations associated directly with deep neural networks, including convolution, activation, normalization, and pooling, while cuBLAS provides optimized matrix, vector, and other linear algebra operations. Both sit above CUDA and use the GPU underneath, allowing frameworks to reuse optimized implementations rather than creating every operation from scratch.

cuDNN and cuBLAS are software libraries, whereas Tensor Cores are hardware execution units inside supported NVIDIA GPUs. A library or framework can select operations that make effective use of Tensor Cores when the operation, data format, GPU generation, and software configuration support them. The layers, therefore, complement one another: software selects and organizes the work, while specialized GPU hardware executes it. Specialized Tensor Cores add another level of acceleration for selected matrix operations and precision formats.

Tensor Cores and mixed precision

Tensor Cores are specialized hardware units designed to accelerate matrix-multiply-and-accumulate operations. These operations are central to deep learning, so moving them to dedicated hardware can increase training and inference performance.

Tensor Cores support several numerical formats, including formats such as **FP16**, **BF16**, **TF32**, **INT8**, and **FP8** on appropriate GPU generations. Numerical formats differ in both the number of values they can represent accurately and the range of magnitudes they can express. Reducing precision can improve performance for supported operations and, when the representation itself uses fewer bits, can reduce storage and memory-bandwidth requirements. However, reduced precision can introduce rounding, overflow, or other numerical effects. Mixed-precision workflows, therefore, use different formats for different parts of the computation rather than assuming that the lowest available precision is always appropriate. Lower-precision formats can process more values with less memory and higher throughput than full FP32 calculation. The trade-off is that the application must preserve sufficient numerical accuracy for the model and task.

Automatic mixed precision allows a framework to use lower precision where it is appropriate while retaining higher precision for operations that need it. This approach can improve performance and reduce memory consumption without requiring the entire model to use one numerical format.

The trade-off among numerical formats becomes easier to understand when precision, computational efficiency, memory use, and numerical sensitivity are considered together, as shown conceptually in *Figure 2.6*:

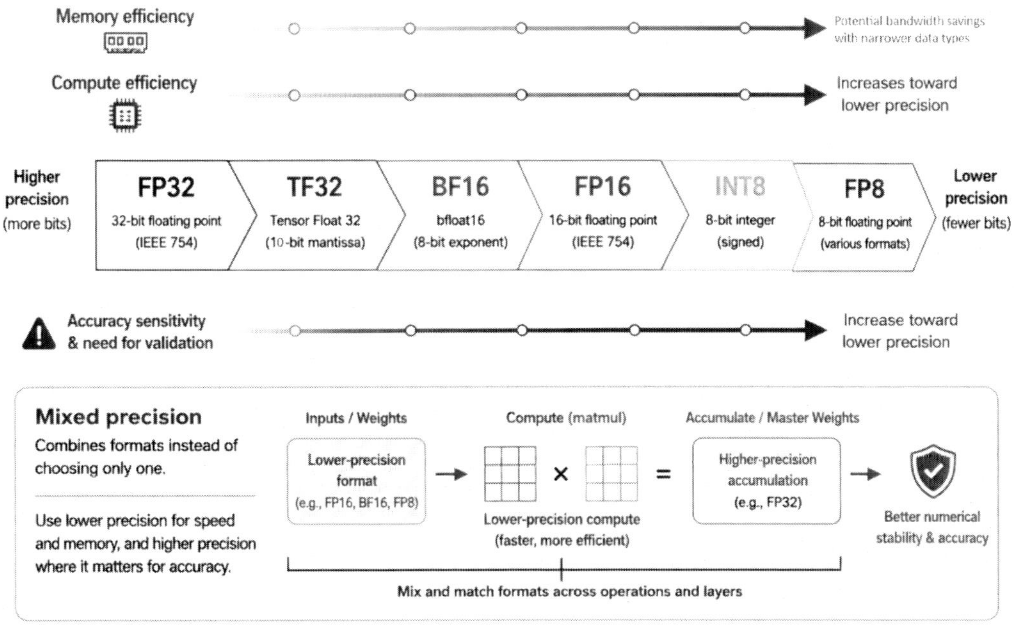

Figure 2.6: Precision formats and mixed precision

Figure 2.6 presents numerical precision as a performance and accuracy trade-off rather than as a simple progression in which lower precision is always better. Reduced-precision formats can allow supported GPU operations to perform more work efficiently, and formats that use fewer storage bits can also reduce memory consumption and data movement. The lower panel shows the principle of mixed precision: use lower precision where it provides a performance advantage while retaining higher precision where additional numerical range or accuracy is required. The appropriate combination must always be supported by the hardware and validated against the model's accuracy requirements.

Note that in the above image, the exact support for formats varies by hardware and software. Infrastructure teams do not usually choose a precision format in isolation, but they should understand why a newer GPU or optimized model may deliver more work within the same memory and power envelope. Precision support is one of the capabilities that links GPU architecture to software optimization.

Performance depends not only on the mathematical operation but also on how kernels, memory transfers, and CPU coordination interact. Profiling tools make that interaction visible.

Nsight tools for profiling and debugging

NVIDIA Nsight tools help developers and performance engineers understand GPU application behavior. Nsight Systems provides a system-wide timeline that can show CPU activity, GPU kernels, memory transfers, synchronization, and gaps between stages. This view is useful for identifying whether a GPU is waiting on the host, data movement, or another dependency.

Nsight Compute focuses on individual GPU kernels. It can expose metrics related to occupancy, instruction execution, memory use, and stalls. These details help engineers determine whether a kernel is limited by compute resources, memory access, or launch configuration. *Figure 2.7* shows how the two Nsight tools operate at different levels of detail, moving from an application-wide performance view to analysis of an individual GPU kernel.

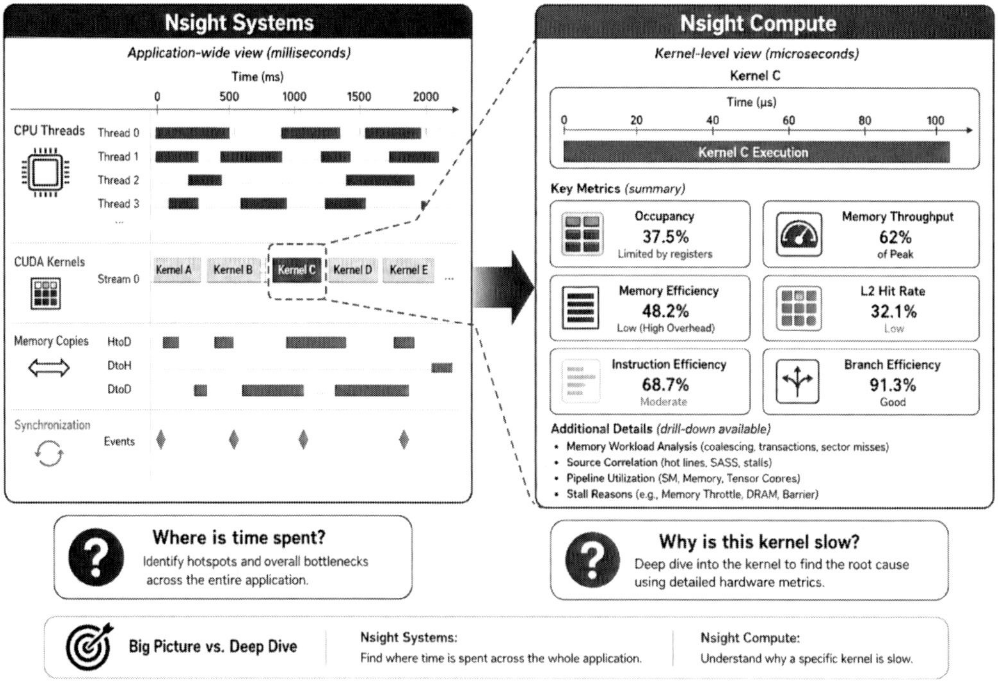

Figure 2.7: Nsight Systems vs Nsight Compute

This figure illustrates a useful profiling workflow. Nsight Systems provides the broad view, allowing an engineer to see CPU activity, CUDA kernels, data transfers, and synchronization across the application timeline and answer the question, "Where is time being spent?" Once a problematic kernel has been identified, Nsight Compute provides the deeper view needed to investigate occupancy, memory behavior, instruction execution, stalls, and other kernel-level characteristics. The tools are therefore complementary rather than competing alternatives.

Tip

A practical rule is to **start broad and then narrow the investigation**. Use Nsight Systems when the question is where application time is being lost across CPU activity, GPU work, transfers, or synchronization. Use Nsight Compute after a particular kernel has been identified, and the question becomes why that kernel is performing poorly.

For an infrastructure professional, the important point is that low GPU utilization does not always mean the GPU is too small or too slow. The cause may be a data loader, synchronization point, memory transfer, or application pattern. Nsight tools complement fleet-level monitoring by explaining what the workload is doing inside a node.

Some production workloads also suffer from overhead when many small operations are launched repeatedly. CUDA Graphs addresses this pattern.

CUDA Graphs and launch overhead

Launching GPU kernels requires coordination between the host and device. When a workload repeats the same sequence of many small operations, the launch overhead can become significant relative to the useful computation. A CUDA Graph represents operations and their dependencies as a reusable execution graph. Instead of paying the full host-side setup cost each time the same sequence is submitted, the application can instantiate the graph and launch the prepared workflow repeatedly. The greatest benefit, therefore, appears when repeated GPU work contains enough small launches for host launch overhead to become significant.

CUDA Graphs allows an application to capture a sequence of operations and replay it with less repeated launch work. This can improve efficiency and predictability, particularly in inference paths where the execution pattern is stable and low latency matters.

CUDA Graphs does not change the model itself. It optimizes the way an existing sequence is submitted to the GPU. The feature illustrates a recurring theme in AI infrastructure: overall performance depends on coordination overhead and data movement as well as arithmetic speed.

The library and tooling ecosystem can now be placed within the broader NVIDIA platform, from physical accelerators to production services.

This section established the reusable components that sit on CUDA: cuDNN for neural network primitives, cuBLAS for linear algebra, Tensor Cores for specialized matrix operations, Nsight for profiling, and CUDA Graphs for reducing repeated launch overhead. The final section assembles these components into the complete NVIDIA AI stack.

The NVIDIA AI stack from hardware to deployment

NVIDIA presents AI infrastructure as an end-to-end stack. Each layer depends on the one below it and provides services to the one above it. The value of this approach is integration: hardware capabilities are exposed through system software, optimized through libraries, consumed by frameworks, and carried into deployment by production tools. *Figure 2.8* brings these components together as a layered stack, showing how hardware and system software support optimized libraries, frameworks, packaged assets, production services, and orchestration.

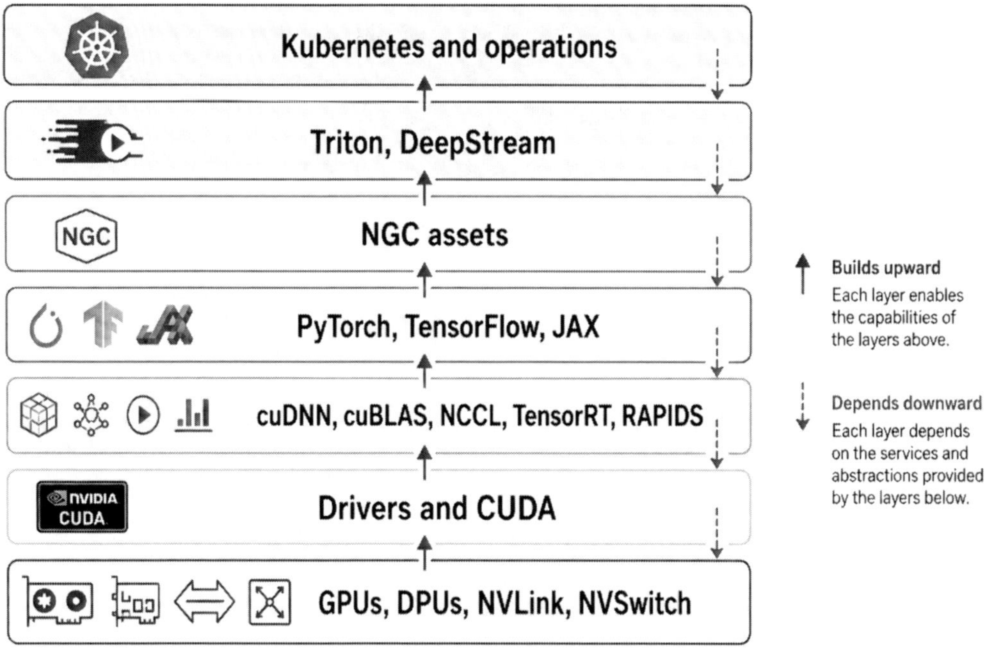

Figure 2.8: The NVIDIA AI Stack from hardware to deployment

Figure 2.8 shows the NVIDIA AI environment as a dependency stack. The stack is a conceptual dependency model rather than a requirement that every workload use every layer or component shown. GPUs, DPUs, and high-speed interconnects form the physical foundation. Drivers and CUDA expose those resources to software, optimized libraries provide reusable acceleration, and frameworks give model developers higher-level abstractions. NGC assets help package and distribute software and models, while tools such as Triton and DeepStream support production workloads. Kubernetes and operational tooling sit above these layers to deploy, scale, and manage services. Reading downward reveals what each layer depends on; reading upward shows how lower-level capabilities are assembled into an AI application.

Hardware and interconnect foundations

The base of the stack contains GPUs and, in some systems, DPUs. GPUs provide parallel compute and specialized Tensor Cores. DPUs can offload networking, storage, and security processing. High-bandwidth interconnects such as NVLink and NVSwitch connect GPUs so that multi-device workloads can exchange data efficiently.

This hardware layer determines fundamental limits such as device memory, memory bandwidth, supported precision formats, inter-GPU communication, and partitioning capabilities. Software can optimize within those limits, but it cannot remove them. Platform selection, therefore, begins with the workload requirements established in *Chapter 1*.

Hardware must then be exposed safely and consistently to the operating system and applications. That is the role of the system software layer.

Drivers, CUDA, and system software

NVIDIA drivers allow the operating system to communicate with the GPU. CUDA provides the runtime and programming model used by applications. cuDNN, cuBLAS, and related libraries supply optimized implementations. These components form the software foundation on which higher-level AI environments depend.

Version alignment is operationally important. A framework container may include a CUDA runtime and libraries, but it still depends on a compatible host driver. A cluster that contains inconsistent driver versions can produce workloads that succeed on one node and fail on another. Validated images and controlled upgrade processes reduce this risk.

System software also includes monitoring and management interfaces. Tools such as NVIDIA-SMI and DCGM expose device state, utilization, health, power, temperature, and error information. These tools connect the execution stack to day-to-day operations.

Above the system layer, specialized libraries and SDKs provide capabilities for training, inference, data analytics, and communication.

Optimized libraries, SDKs, and frameworks

The stack includes TensorRT for optimizing inference execution, NCCL for collective communication among GPUs during distributed workloads, and RAPIDS for accelerating data-processing and analytics workloads on GPUs. Each component addresses a different part of the AI workflow while using CUDA and the underlying GPU resources.

Frameworks such as PyTorch, TensorFlow, and JAX sit above these libraries. They provide model-building abstractions and can call optimized NVIDIA components underneath. A model defined in a framework can use cuDNN during training, NCCL during distributed execution, and TensorRT when it is prepared for production inference.

This layered design avoids forcing one tool to perform every function. The framework expresses the model. CUDA and libraries execute the operations. Communication libraries coordinate devices. Inference optimizers transform the trained model for serving. The infrastructure team ensures that the layers are compatible and observable.

Once a model and its dependencies are ready, packaged assets and model-serving tools shorten the path to deployment.

NGC as a source of optimized assets

NVIDIA NGC is a catalog and registry of GPU-optimized software assets. It includes containers for frameworks and services, pretrained models, SDKs, Helm charts, and sample notebooks. These assets are designed to reduce the work required to assemble and validate an environment from individual packages.

A framework container can provide a tested combination of the operating system libraries, CUDA runtime, cuDNN, framework version, and supporting tools. A pretrained model can provide a starting point for fine-tuning or inference. A Helm chart can package the configuration needed to deploy a service to Kubernetes.

NGC does not remove the need for operational control. Teams still need to select versions, scan and approve images, manage credentials, test workloads, and plan upgrades. Its value is that the starting assets are organized around NVIDIA hardware and common AI workflows.

The production layer uses these assets to serve models and process data at scale.

Triton, TensorRT, and DeepStream in production

TensorRT optimizes trained models for inference. It can improve execution by selecting efficient kernels, applying supported precision changes, and reducing unnecessary operations. The goal is to lower latency, increase throughput, and reduce memory use on supported NVIDIA hardware.

TensorRT and Triton address different parts of inference. TensorRT optimizes how a model executes, while Triton manages how one or more models are exposed and served to client applications. A deployment can therefore use a TensorRT-optimized model inside Triton rather than choosing one tool instead of the other.

Triton Inference Server provides a production model-serving layer. It supports models from multiple frameworks and formats, can serve several models, and can use features such as dynamic batching and model ensembles. Triton can be deployed in containers and integrated with Kubernetes, monitoring systems, and load-balancing infrastructure.

DeepStream is focused on real-time video analytics. It connects video ingestion, decoding, inference, tracking, and output stages into accelerated pipelines. Unlike a general model-serving layer, DeepStream focuses on end-to-end streaming-media pipelines in which video ingestion, decoding, inference, tracking, and downstream processing must operate together. This makes it relevant to smart cities, retail analytics, industrial automation, and other computer vision environments.

These tools demonstrate the top of the stack: models are no longer only files produced by a training job. They become managed services with request handling, batching, scaling, monitoring, and lifecycle requirements.

Reading the stack as one operational system

The following table summarizes the major layers introduced in this chapter. It is useful to read it from bottom to top when deploying a workload and from top to bottom when troubleshooting a failure.

Layer	Representative components	Operational question
Hardware and fabric	GPUs, DPUs, NVLink, and NVSwitch	Does the platform provide the memory, compute, partitioning, and communication required by the workload?
System software	NVIDIA drivers, CUDA runtime, and management interfaces	Are the host, runtime, and device versions compatible and healthy?
Optimized libraries	cuDNN, cuBLAS, NCCL, RAPIDS, and TensorRT	Is the workload using tuned implementations for its compute, communication, analytics, or inference path?
AI frameworks	PyTorch, TensorFlow, and JAX	Can the model definition access the accelerator and required libraries?
Packaged assets	NGC containers, models, SDKs, notebooks, and Helm charts	Is the environment reproducible, approved, and suitable for the target platform?

Layer	Representative components	Operational question
Production services	Triton Inference Server and DeepStream	How will the model be served, scaled, monitored, and integrated with applications?

Table 2.1: Layers of the NVIDIA AI stack and their operational responsibilities

A failure at one layer can appear as a symptom at another. A model server may fail because the model repository is missing, the container may fail because the host driver is incompatible, or a distributed training job may run slowly because the interconnect is saturated. The stack model helps an operator locate the boundary where expected behavior stops.

The same model also explains NVIDIA's full-stack advantage. The hardware, programming platform, libraries, frameworks, packaged assets, and deployment tools are designed to work together. For the certification exam, this relationship is more important than memorizing a disconnected list of product names.

You can now trace an AI workload from a framework through CUDA and optimized libraries to the GPU, and then forward through NGC, TensorRT, Triton, or DeepStream into production. The next chapter moves inside the hardware to examine SMs, Tensor Cores, NVLink, and the major data center GPU families.

Summary

This chapter explained how CUDA turns NVIDIA GPUs into general-purpose accelerators. CUDA organizes work into threads, blocks, and grids, which the GPU schedules across streaming multiprocessors. Deep learning supplies large amounts of parallel tensor computation, while frameworks such as PyTorch, TensorFlow, and JAX provide higher-level access to the CUDA platform.

You also examined the libraries and tools that make the ecosystem practical. cuDNN accelerates deep neural network operations, cuBLAS provides optimized linear algebra, Tensor Cores speed supported matrix calculations, Nsight tools reveal performance behavior, and CUDA Graphs can reduce repeated launch overhead.

The final section assembled the full NVIDIA AI stack, from GPUs and interconnects through drivers, CUDA, libraries, frameworks, NGC assets, TensorRT, Triton, and DeepStream. The chapter objective was to follow a workload from model code to hardware and then into production. You can now identify the role of each layer and understand why compatibility and integration matter operationally.

The next chapter focuses on the physical GPU architecture and compares the A100, H100, L40S, and B200 as platforms for different classes of AI workload.

Chapter review questions

Choose the single best answer for each question. The answer key and explanations follow the complete set for this chapter.

1. What is CUDA's primary role in the NVIDIA platform?
    a. It is a physical GPU interconnect.
    b. It is a model registry used only after training.
    c. It is a parallel-computing platform and programming model for using NVIDIA GPUs.
    d. It is a hypervisor for creating virtual machines.
2. Which sequence correctly orders the CUDA execution hierarchy from smallest to largest?
    a. Block, thread, grid
    b. Thread, grid, block
    c. Thread, block, grid
    d. Grid, block, thread
3. How are CUDA blocks related to streaming multiprocessors?
    a. Blocks are scheduled onto available SMs, where their threads execute.
    b. An SM can execute only one thread for the lifetime of a program.
    c. Blocks run only on the CPU and copy completed results to the GPU.
    d. Every block is permanently tied to one physical core before compilation.
4. Which library is the best match for optimized convolution, activation, pooling, and normalization operations?
    a. MLflow
    b. Helm
    c. DCGM
    d. cuDNN
5. Which library is primarily associated with dense linear algebra and matrix operations?
    a. cuBLAS
    b. Kubeflow

   c. DeepStream
   d. DOCA

6. Why is mixed precision used in many AI workloads?
   a. It combines precision formats to improve throughput and memory efficiency while preserving acceptable accuracy.
   b. It disables Tensor Cores to reduce power use.
   c. It guarantees identical numerical results for every model.
   d. It moves all computations back to the CPU.
7. An engineer needs to identify long CPU gaps before GPU kernels begin. Which tool is the better first choice?
   a. MLflow Model Registry
   b. Nsight Systems
   c. NVIDIA vGPU Manager
   d. Nsight Compute
8. What problem does an NGC container primarily solve?
   a. It replaces the physical GPU.
   b. It partitions a GPU at the hardware level.
   c. It creates NVLink connections between servers.
   d. It packages a tested combination of framework, CUDA libraries, and supporting dependencies.
9. Which component is designed to optimize a trained model for efficient NVIDIA GPU inference?
   a. Airflow
   b. TensorRT
   c. Slurm
   d. Prometheus
10. A framework call reaches the GPU through several layers. Which ordering is most accurate?
    a. GPU hardware -> application framework -> driver -> CUDA library
    b. NVIDIA driver -> model registry -> hypervisor -> GPU hardware

c. Application framework -> DPU -> Helm -> GPU hardware

d. Application framework -> optimized CUDA library/runtime -> NVIDIA driver -> GPU hardware

Answer key and explanations

Use the explanations to verify both the correct choice and the layer of the stack being tested.

1. C. CUDA exposes GPU compute for general-purpose workloads and provides the programming and runtime foundation used by higher-level libraries and frameworks.
2. C. Individual threads are grouped into blocks, and blocks are grouped into a grid for a kernel launch.
3. A. The GPU scheduler assigns blocks to SMs as resources become available. An SM may have multiple blocks resident at the same time when resources permit. This supports scalable execution without the developer managing each core.
4. D. cuDNN provides GPU-optimized primitives commonly used by deep neural networks.
5. A. cuBLAS is the CUDA Basic Linear Algebra Subprograms library and accelerates matrix and vector operations.
6. A. Mixed precision uses lower precision where safe and higher precision where needed. The model must still be validated for accuracy.
7. B. Nsight Systems provides an application-wide CPU/GPU timeline. Nsight Compute is used later for detailed analysis of a specific kernel.
8. D. NGC containers reduce dependency and version-alignment work by providing curated GPU-optimized software environments.
9. B. TensorRT performs graph and kernel optimizations and can use lower-precision execution to improve inference latency and throughput.
10. D. Framework operators can use optimized CUDA libraries and the CUDA runtime, which rely on the NVIDIA driver to execute work on the GPU. This is a conceptual stack ordering; the exact software call path varies by operation and framework.

3

NVIDIA GPU Architecture and Platform Selection

> **Note**
>
> A data center GPU combines general parallel execution, specialized matrix hardware, high-bandwidth memory, and interconnects designed for workloads that extend beyond one device.

A GPU is more than a collection of arithmetic cores. Its performance depends on how work is scheduled across streaming multiprocessors, how specialized Tensor Cores execute matrix operations, how data moves through memory, and how multiple devices communicate. These architectural features determine which workloads a GPU can support efficiently.

This chapter first examines the internal components that matter most to AI infrastructure: Streaming multiprocessors, warps, Tensor Cores, precision formats, and NVLink. It then compares four NVIDIA data center GPUs: the A100, H100, L40S, and B200. The final section turns those specifications into a selection process based on training scale, inference latency, memory needs, graphics requirements, and multi-GPU communication.

By the end of the chapter, you will be able to describe what happens inside a GPU at a practical level and match major platform capabilities to workload requirements. The objective is not to memorize every product specification. It is to understand why architectural differences influence performance, density, and operational fit.

We will be covering the following main topics in this chapter:

- Inside a data center GPU
- Comparing the A100, H100, L40S, and B200
- Matching GPU capabilities to workloads

The comparison begins inside the device, where streaming multiprocessors and Tensor Cores turn CUDA work into parallel execution.

> Note
>
> **Download the PDF version of this book**
>
> Your purchase includes a DRM-free PDF copy of this book, the code bundle, and a range of exclusive benefits. To unlock everything, follow the *Free benefits with your book* section in the *Preface*.

Inside a data center GPU

Three architectural elements are especially important for AI infrastructure:

- **Streaming multiprocessors**: Execute and schedule parallel work inside one GPU
- **Tensor Cores**: Accelerate matrix operations
- **NVLink**: extends the system by connecting supported GPUs with higher bandwidth and lower latency than a conventional PCIe-only path

Figure 3.1 places these capabilities inside a conceptual data center GPU, showing how SMs, Tensor Cores, device memory, and NVLink interfaces form a connected compute and data-movement system:

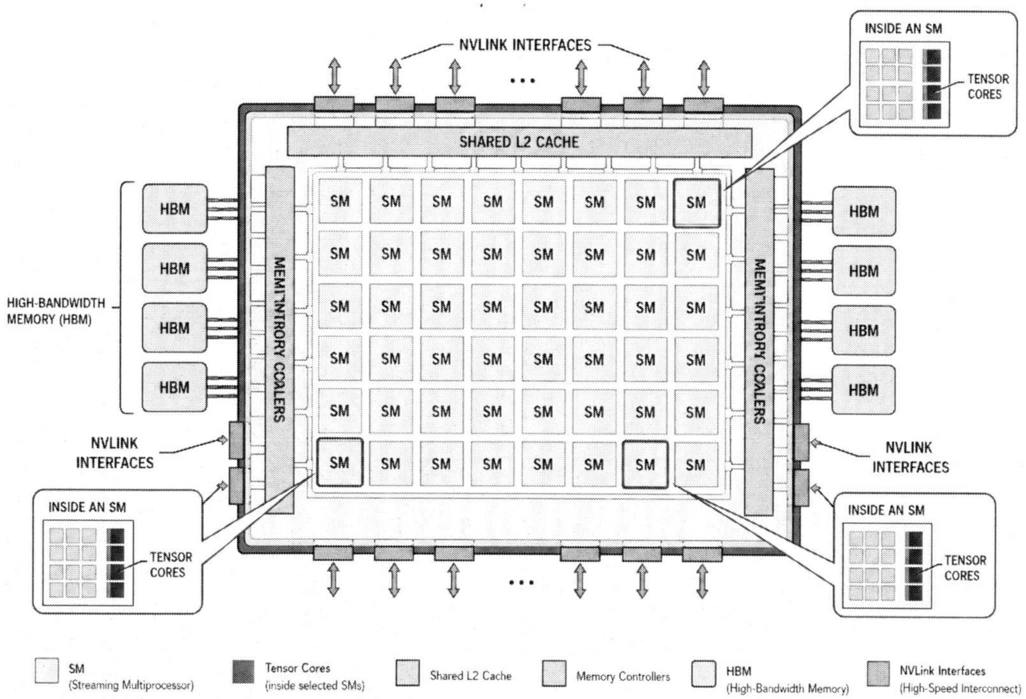

Figure 3.1: Inside a data center GPU

From the above figure, it can be seen that GPU performance depends on more than the number of compute units. The central array of SMs provides parallel execution, while Tensor Cores within the SMs accelerate supported matrix operations. Around those execution resources, memory controllers and the shared L2 cache help move and reuse data from device memory, while NVLink interfaces provide high-speed connectivity to other supported components. The diagram therefore presents the GPU as an integrated compute-and-data-movement architecture rather than as a collection of independent cores.

GPU compute performance depends on supplying the execution units with data quickly enough. Device memory provides the large-capacity storage used for model weights, activations, inputs, and other working data. Data center GPUs may use **high-bandwidth memory (HBM)** or technologies such as GDDR6 depending on the product. Memory controllers move data between device memory and the rest of the GPU, while caches reduce the need to fetch the same information repeatedly from the highest-latency levels of the memory hierarchy.

Two characteristics should be kept separate. **Memory capacity** determines how much model and runtime data can reside on the device, whereas **memory bandwidth** describes how quickly data can be moved to and from that memory. A workload can therefore fit within a GPU's memory capacity and still run below its potential if memory bandwidth or the wider data path cannot feed computation quickly enough.

Streaming multiprocessors as execution engines

A **streaming multiprocessor**, or **SM**, is a primary compute engine inside an NVIDIA GPU. It contains execution resources, registers, shared memory, cache, scheduling logic, and other components needed to run groups of CUDA threads.

When a CUDA application launches a grid, blocks from that grid are assigned to SMs. The SM schedules threads in groups called **warps**. Many warps can be active or ready at the same time, which allows the device to switch among available work while other operations wait on memory or dependencies. *Figure 3.2* follows CUDA threads into an SM to show how threads are organized into warps and how the scheduler selects ready work for execution:

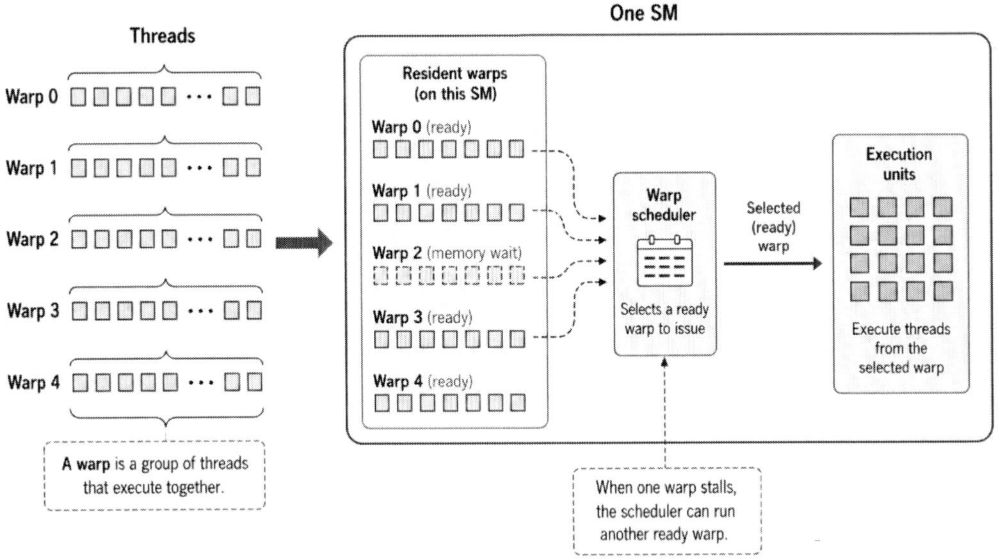

Figure 3.2: Thread, warp, and SM scheduling

Figure 3.2 shows how the SM keeps multiple warps available for execution. CUDA threads are organized into warps, and several warps can be resident on the SM at the same time. The warp scheduler selects a warp that is ready to make progress and issues its instructions to the available execution units. If one warp must wait for data or another dependency, the scheduler can select other ready work instead. This ability to maintain several groups of work is one of the mechanisms that helps a GPU tolerate latency and keep its execution resources productive.

An SM attempts to keep several warps available so that a delay affecting one group of threads does not necessarily stop the whole compute engine. For example, if one warp is waiting for data to arrive from memory, a scheduler may issue instructions from another ready warp. This ability to overlap available work is commonly described as latency hiding. It does not eliminate the cost of slow memory or dependencies, but enough ready parallel work can prevent those delays from leaving all execution resources idle.

The number of SMs and the design of each SM contribute to overall compute capability. I will use the A100 with 108 SMs and the H100 with up to 132 SMs as examples. Exact counts and capabilities can vary by GPU configuration, but the operational principle remains the same: more capable SM resources allow more concurrent parallel work when the workload can supply it.

SMs do not guarantee high utilization on their own. The workload needs enough parallelism, and data must arrive quickly enough to keep the execution resources busy. Poorly sized batches, slow input pipelines, or synchronization gaps can leave an advanced GPU underused.

General CUDA execution handles a broad range of operations. Deep learning adds a large volume of matrix work that can be directed to specialized Tensor Cores.

Tensor Cores for matrix-heavy AI

Tensor Cores are specialized units designed for matrix multiply-and-accumulate operations. Neural networks use these operations repeatedly in dense layers, convolutions, attention mechanisms, and other components. By handling selected matrix work in dedicated hardware, Tensor Cores can deliver substantially higher throughput than general-purpose FP32 execution for supported formats and operations.

I will highlight formats including **FP16**, **BF16**, **TF32**, **INT8**, and **FP8**. Each format represents values with a different number and arrangement of bits. Lower precision can reduce memory use and increase throughput, but the workload must maintain acceptable accuracy. Training commonly uses mixed precision, while inference can use quantized formats when the model has been prepared and validated for them.

Tensor Core performance depends on the full software path. The framework, CUDA libraries, and model must issue operations in a form that can use the hardware. cuDNN, cuBLAS, and TensorRT help select and execute optimized implementations. A GPU with powerful Tensor Cores will not deliver their full benefit if the workload falls back to unsupported operations or uses an inefficient data layout. *Figure 3.3* separates these execution paths, showing where Tensor Cores accelerate matrix-heavy AI operations and where general CUDA-core execution remains appropriate:

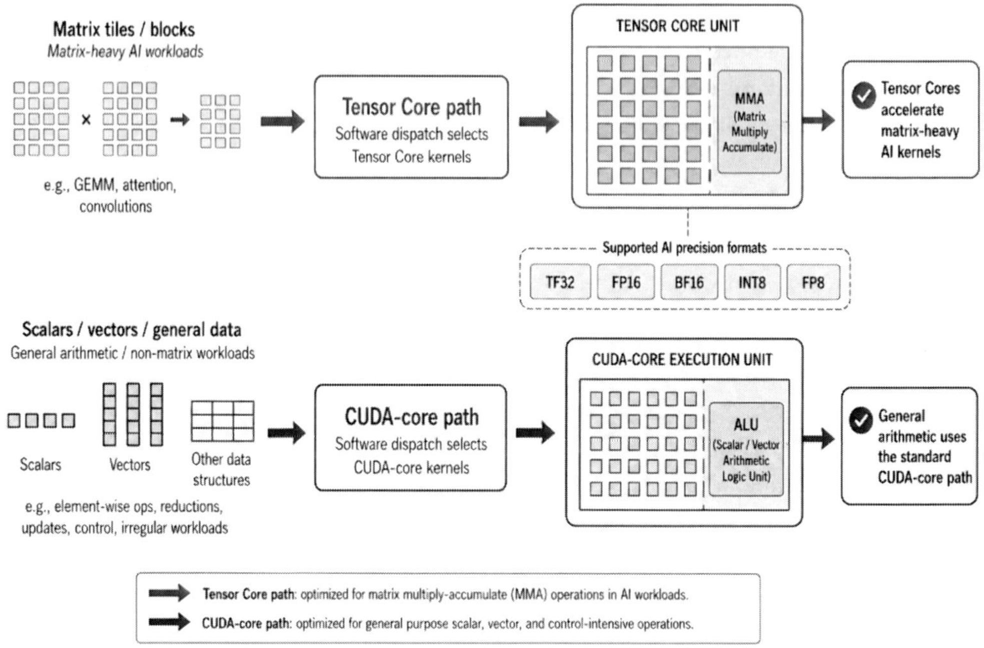

Figure 3.3: Tensor cores and general CUDA-core execution

In the figure above, two complementary execution paths are explored. Matrix-heavy operations such as matrix multiplication, attention, and convolution can use Tensor Cores when the operation and numerical format are supported, while scalar, vector, control-oriented, and other general calculations continue to use the broader CUDA execution resources. Software libraries and frameworks determine which optimized path can be used for a particular operation. Tensor Cores therefore enhance the GPU's general execution capability rather than replacing it.

It is useful to separate general GPU execution resources from specialized Tensor Core acceleration. CUDA cores support a broad range of arithmetic and control-oriented operations, whereas Tensor Cores target supported matrix operations and numerical formats. A neural-network workload can use both during the same execution. The performance benefit of Tensor Cores therefore depends on how much of the workload can be expressed through operations and data types that the software stack can map to that specialized hardware.

The relationship between SMs and Tensor Cores is cooperative. SMs schedule and execute the overall workload, while Tensor Cores accelerate the matrix portions. This combination provides both general parallelism and AI-specific throughput.

As model size grows, the challenge expands beyond one GPU. High-speed interconnects then become part of the effective compute architecture.

NVLink and multi-GPU communication

NVLink is NVIDIA's high-bandwidth interconnect for supported GPUs and systems. It allows GPUs to exchange data more quickly and with lower latency than a PCIe-only connection can typically provide. This is important when a model or training job is distributed across several devices.

Large models may not fit in the memory of one GPU. Training may also be divided across devices to shorten completion time. In both cases, GPUs must exchange activations, gradients, parameters, or other intermediate data. If communication is slow, devices wait for one another and scaling efficiency falls.

NVLink helps reduce this communication penalty within a server or supported platform. **NVSwitch** can extend the concept by providing a switching fabric that connects multiple GPUs with high-bandwidth paths. NVIDIA DGX and HGX platforms use these technologies to create systems in which several GPUs can participate in one workload.

NVLink does not make multiple GPUs identical to one larger GPU in every software context. Applications still need a distributed or multi-device execution strategy. Libraries such as NCCL coordinate collective communication, while the interconnect supplies the physical bandwidth needed for that strategy to perform efficiently.

The architecture can now be summarized as three connected capabilities:

- SMs provide broad parallel execution
- Tensor Cores accelerate matrix operations
- NVLink supports communication when the workload extends across devices

Figure 3.4 focuses on the communication component of this architecture by contrasting a PCIe-based multi-GPU path with direct NVLink connections between supported GPUs.

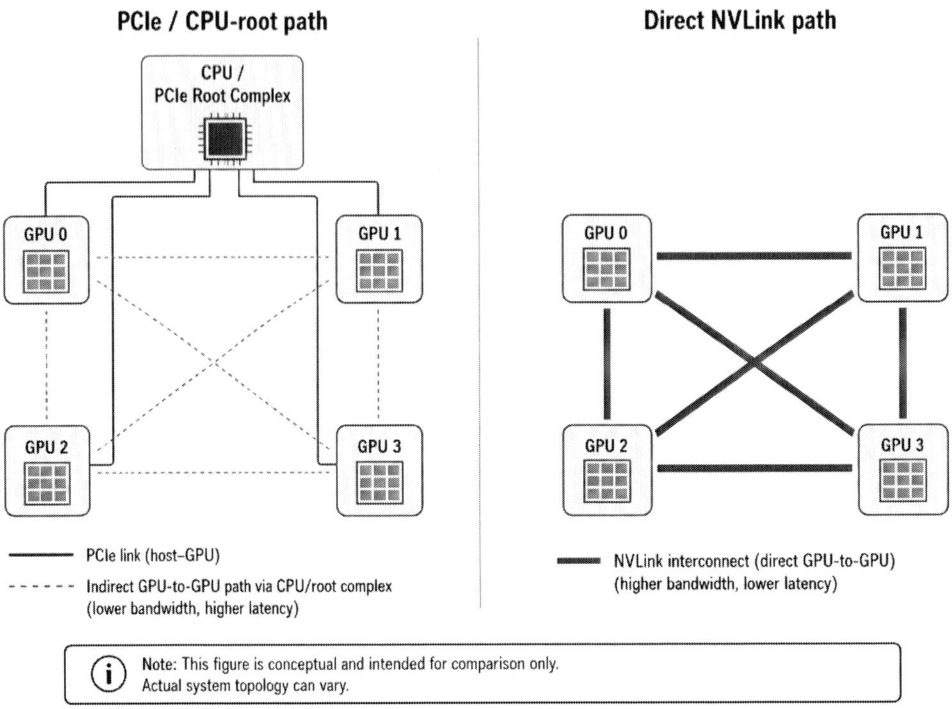

Figure 3.4: PCIe-only versus NVLink-connected multi-GPU communication

The left side of *Figure 3.4* represents GPUs communicating through the system's PCIe topology, while the right side shows supported GPUs connected through direct NVLink paths. The additional GPU-to-GPU bandwidth and lower communication latency of NVLink can reduce the time devices spend waiting for exchanged data during tightly coupled multi-GPU workloads. The figure is conceptual, however; the exact PCIe, NVLink, and NVSwitch topology depends on the server or platform being deployed.

NVLink, NVSwitch, and the data center network solve related communication problems at different scopes. NVLink provides high-speed connections among supported components, and NVSwitch can create a broader NVLink fabric among GPUs within supported systems. When distributed training extends across separate servers, traffic must also traverse a cluster network such as InfiniBand or high-performance Ethernet. Software such as NCCL coordinates collective GPU communication while using the communication paths available to the system.

The internal architecture explains where GPU performance comes from. The next section compares how four NVIDIA GPU families combine memory, precision support, graphics capability, partitioning, and interconnect features for different data center roles.

Comparing the A100, H100, L40S, and B200

The **A100**, **H100**, **L40S**, and **B200** are not interchangeable products with only different performance numbers. They represent different GPU generations and design priorities:

- A100 is a mature, flexible accelerator
- H100 is a higher-performance platform for large AI
- L40S is a balanced inference and graphics GPU
- B200 is a next-generation platform for very large generative AI workloads

Figure 3.5 provides an at-a-glance comparison of the four GPU families across the workload characteristics that most strongly influence platform selection:

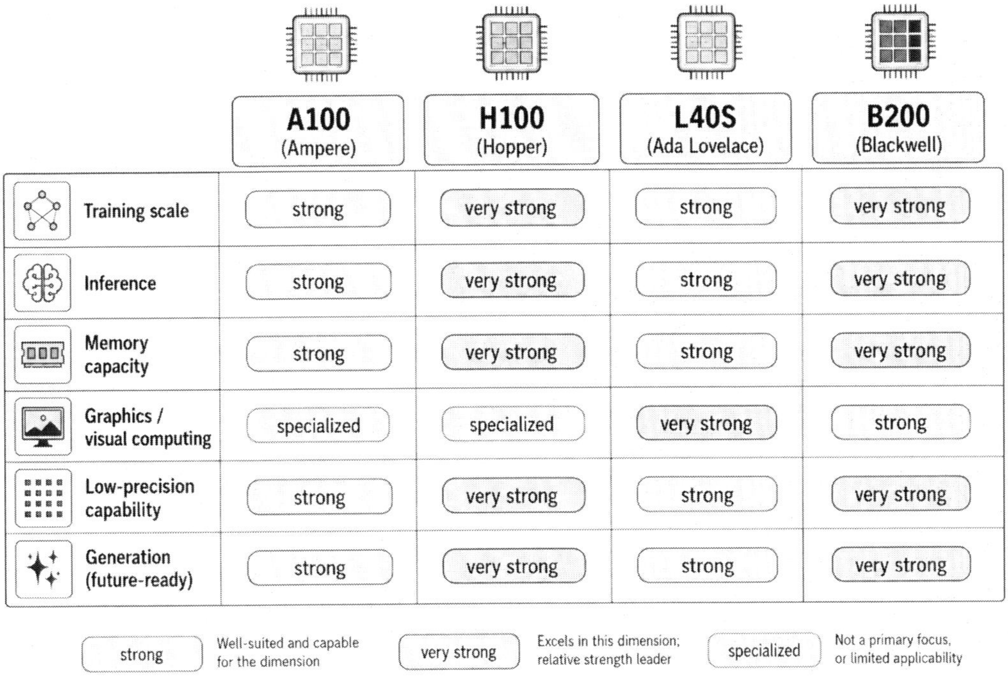

Figure 3.5: At-a-glance positioning of A100, H100, L40S, and B200

Figure 3.5 should be read as a relative workload-positioning guide rather than as a benchmark or absolute ranking. The A100 represents a mature platform that can support a broad mixture of AI workloads, while the H100 emphasizes higher-end AI training and inference. The L40S stands apart because graphics and visual-computing capability are central to its design alongside AI acceleration. The B200 represents the Blackwell generation's emphasis on very large AI workloads, additional memory, and newer low-precision execution. Actual performance and suitability still depend on the exact model, system configuration, and software environment.

> **Note**
>
> A GPU family name does not always identify one fixed set of specifications. Memory capacity, memory bandwidth, form factor, power limits, and interconnect capability can differ among PCIe, SXM, NVL, or system-specific configurations. The product descriptions that follow are therefore representative comparisons. For deployment decisions, specifications should always be checked against the exact GPU and server configuration being considered.

A100: A mature general-purpose AI accelerator

The **A100** is based on the Ampere architecture. It is one of the most widely used data center GPUs for deep learning training, inference, and data analytics. It is available in configurations with 40 GB or 80 GB of HBM2e memory, providing high memory bandwidth for models and datasets.

A major operational feature is **Multi-Instance GPU** (**MIG**) support. MIG can divide a supported A100 into several isolated GPU instances, allowing one device to serve multiple smaller workloads. This makes the A100 useful in environments that need a balance between large-job performance and shared-resource efficiency.

The A100 appears in DGX systems, cloud instances, and enterprise clusters. Its value is not only peak performance but also platform maturity, broad software support, and flexibility across training and inference. For many organizations, those qualities make it a dependable baseline accelerator.

The H100 advances the same data center role with newer memory, precision, and interconnect capabilities targeted at very large models.

H100: Hopper architecture for large-scale AI

The **H100** is based on the Hopper architecture and succeeds the A100 in NVIDIA's data center lineup. It has an 80 GB HBM3 configuration with memory bandwidth up to 3 TB per second. This memory system is designed to feed demanding training and inference operations more effectively.

Fourth-generation Tensor Cores add support for FP8, a lower-precision format intended to accelerate suitable deep learning workloads while maintaining model quality through appropriate scaling and training methods. The H100 also supports a newer NVLink generation and can participate in NVSwitch-based systems for high-bandwidth multi-GPU communication.

H100 is associated with large language models, foundation models, transformers, and distributed AI. These workloads place heavy demands on memory capacity, memory bandwidth, Tensor Core throughput, and communication. The H100 is, therefore, positioned for environments in which model scale and training time justify a high-performance platform.

The L40S serves a different need. It combines enterprise AI inference with graphics and visualization capabilities rather than focusing primarily on the largest training jobs.

L40S: Enterprise inference and visual computing

The **L40S** is based on the Ada Lovelace architecture and includes 48 GB of GDDR6 memory. It is designed for enterprise AI inference, graphics rendering, virtual desktop infrastructure, and mixed AI-graphics workloads.

This profile suits real-time applications such as recommendation services, chatbots, virtual assistants, digital twins, and simulation environments. The L40S can support visual workloads associated with platforms such as NVIDIA Omniverse while also providing AI acceleration.

Its role is therefore not simply lower or higher than the training-oriented GPUs. It is optimized around a different combination of low-latency inference, graphics capability, and enterprise deployment. An organization that needs model serving and visualization on the same platform may value this balance more than maximum large-model training throughput.

The B200 extends the comparison into the Blackwell generation, where emphasis is on memory capacity and low-precision performance for the next wave of generative AI.

B200: Blackwell for next-generation generative AI

The B200 provides very high low-precision Tensor Core performance, including FP4 capability, for large generative AI training and inference workloads. It also introduces support for FP4, an ultra-low-precision format intended to improve inference efficiency when the model and quantization approach can use it successfully.

The B200 is positioned for exascale AI, multimodal foundation models, and real-time generative AI pipelines. These workloads combine very large models, high throughput, and intensive communication. The additional memory can allow larger model portions or batches to remain on each device, while newer precision support can increase the amount of inference work completed per unit of hardware.

Product availability, system configurations, and validated software support evolve over time, so an implementation should always use the specifications for the exact platform being deployed. The important point is the direction of the architecture: larger memory, newer Tensor Core formats, and system-level scaling for increasingly demanding AI.

A compact comparison helps reveal the intended role of each GPU:

GPU	**Architecture and memory characteristics**	**Primary strengths**	**Representative workload fit**
A100	Ampere; 40 GB or 80 GB HBM2e	Mature platform, broad training and inference support, and MIG partitioning	Enterprise AI clusters, mixed training and inference, analytics, and shared GPU services
H100	Hopper; 80 GB HBM3	FP8 support, high memory bandwidth, and advanced multi-GPU connectivity	Large language models, foundation models, transformers, and distributed training
L40S	Ada Lovelace; 48 GB GDDR6	Low-latency inference combined with graphics and visualization	Enterprise inference, VDI, recommendation, digital twins, simulation, and visual computing
B200	Blackwell; up to 192 GB memory in this comparison	Very large memory and newer low-precision AI performance including FP4	Next-generation generative AI, multimodal models, and extremely large-scale AI systems

Table 3.1: Comparison of NVIDIA A100, H100, L40S, and B200 capabilities and representative workload fit

The table should be read as a workload map rather than a ranking. A newer GPU may offer more performance, but the best platform is the one that meets the model, latency, graphics, sharing, and budget requirements of the deployment. *Figure 3.6* reinforces this workload-first view:

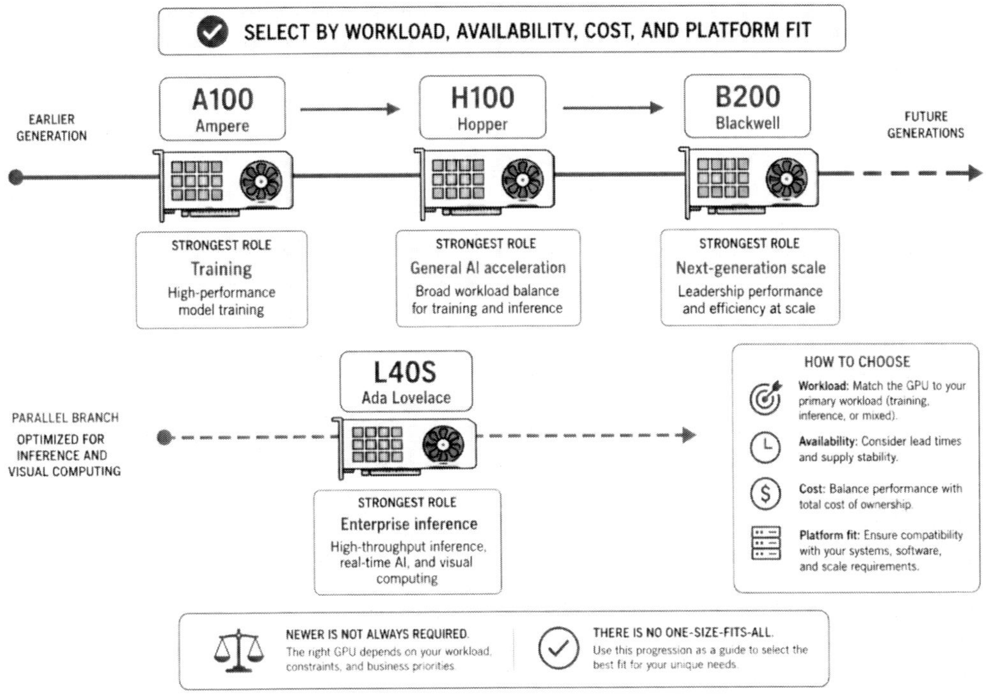

Figure 3.6: Architecture and capability progression

Figure 3.6 makes an important distinction between architectural progression and workload fit. Moving from Ampere through Hopper to Blackwell introduces newer capabilities for increasingly demanding AI workloads, but this does not make every older platform unsuitable. The L40S follows a different design priority by combining AI acceleration with strong graphics and media capabilities. GPU selection should therefore follow the workload, availability, platform compatibility, and cost rather than simply selecting the newest generation.

You have now compared the major capabilities and intended roles of the four GPU families. The final section turns that comparison into a repeatable selection method for scenario-based questions and real infrastructure planning.

Matching GPU capabilities to workloads

GPU selection should begin with workload constraints and only then move to a product. The most useful criteria that we will be considering are **model scale**, **device memory**, **training versus inference**, **precision support**, **graphics requirements**, **multi-GPU communication**, and **resource-sharing needs**.

Start with training or inference

Training updates model parameters and stores intermediate values needed for backpropagation. It can consume substantial memory and compute, especially for large networks and batches. A large training workload may also require multiple GPUs and high-bandwidth communication between them.

Inference applies a trained model to new input. It may need less memory than training because optimizer state and training intermediates are absent, but production inference introduces strict service requirements. Latency, request concurrency, batching behavior, and reliability can become more important than total job completion time.

The A100 supports both training and inference and is presented as a flexible workhorse. The H100 is emphasized for demanding large-model training and inference. The L40S is emphasized for enterprise inference and visual workloads. The B200 is positioned for very large generative AI systems and highly efficient low-precision execution.

Once the execution phase is clear, memory becomes the next major filter.

Evaluate model and memory requirements

A model must fit within the available device memory along with the runtime data required for the operation. Training may need space for model weights, gradients, optimizer state, activations, and batch data. Inference needs the model, runtime buffers, and request-specific state. Large language models may also use significant memory for sequence-related state during serving.

When one GPU is not sufficient, the workload can be distributed across several devices. This introduces communication overhead and makes NVLink, NVSwitch, and collective communication libraries more important. A GPU with more memory may reduce the number of partitions, but the choice must still consider cost, availability, and system design.

MIG creates a different memory decision. A supported physical GPU can be divided into smaller instances with fixed compute and memory allocations. This is useful for smaller workloads, but each instance must still provide enough memory for the assigned model. *Figure 3.7* makes the memory constraint more concrete by breaking GPU memory consumption into model data, runtime allocations, working data, and operational headroom.

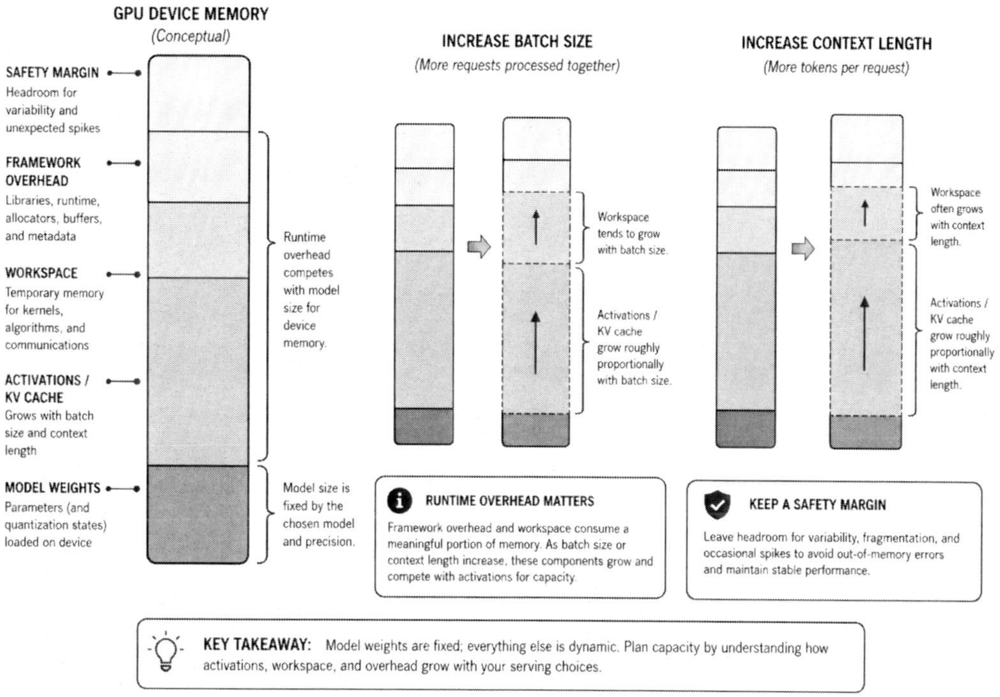

Figure 3.7: How device memory is consumed

Figure 3.7 illustrates why usable GPU memory must be larger than the model weights alone. In a serving workload, memory is also consumed by framework and runtime overhead, temporary workspace, activations or model-specific runtime state such as the KV cache, and the headroom needed to absorb variability without triggering out-of-memory failures. Increasing batch size or context length can expand some of these allocations even when the model weights remain unchanged. The example is primarily inference-oriented; during training, gradients, optimizer state, and additional saved activations introduce further memory demands.

The composition of GPU memory also changes between training and inference. Training commonly requires model parameters together with gradients, optimizer state, saved activations, temporary workspace, and batch data. Inference removes the optimizer and gradient requirements but introduces serving-specific allocations, which may include batched-request state and, for transformer models, a KV cache that can grow as sequences become longer or more concurrent. Memory planning should therefore begin with the execution mode rather than assuming that model weights alone determine the required capacity.

Memory capacity defines what can run; memory bandwidth and compute throughput influence how quickly it runs. Precision support can improve both throughput and memory efficiency.

Consider precision and software optimization

Lower-precision formats can reduce memory use and increase Tensor Core throughput. The A100 supports mixed-precision workflows associated with the Ampere generation. The H100 adds FP8 capabilities. The B200 introduces FP4 support in the discussion. The L40S supports precision modes suited to enterprise inference and AI-graphics workloads.

A precision capability is only valuable when the software stack and model can use it safely. Training frameworks, libraries, TensorRT, and quantization methods must produce an execution path that preserves acceptable model quality. Infrastructure selection should therefore be coordinated with the model and platform teams rather than based on peak marketing figures alone.

Optimized containers and validated framework versions can make these features easier to adopt. NGC assets, CUDA libraries, and TensorRT reduce the amount of custom integration required to reach the hardware capability.

The final filters concern how the GPU connects to the rest of the system and how the resource will be shared.

Account for interconnect, graphics, and tenancy

A multi-GPU training job benefits from high-bandwidth, low-latency communication. NVLink and NVSwitch are therefore important in systems that distribute one workload across several GPUs. In contrast, a single-GPU inference service may care more about device memory, batching, and request latency than about GPU-to-GPU links.

Graphics capability can be decisive for digital twins, rendering, VDI, and simulation. The L40S is designed to combine these visual workloads with AI inference. Selecting a training-focused accelerator for a mixed graphics environment may provide the wrong balance of features.

Tenancy also matters. A large GPU assigned to a small workload can be expensive and underutilized. MIG on supported A100 and H100 systems allows hardware-partitioned sharing. vGPU, discussed later in the book, enables hypervisor-based sharing for virtual machines and other enterprise environments.

The following decision table summarizes a workload-oriented selection process:

Scenario signal	Capability to prioritize	Best-fit direction
Large transformer or foundation-model training	High memory bandwidth, Tensor Core throughput, large memory, and strong multi-GPU communication	H100, with B200 representing the next-generation direction for the largest workloads
Mixed enterprise training and inference with resource sharing	Mature software support, flexible performance, and MIG	A100
Low-latency inference combined with rendering, VDI, or visualization	Inference throughput plus graphics capability	L40S
Very large generative or multimodal AI with newer low-precision execution	Maximum memory and FP4-oriented next-generation acceleration	B200
Several smaller isolated workloads on one physical GPU	Hardware partitioning and right-sized memory profiles	A100 or H100 with MIG

Table 3.2: Workload signals, capability priorities, and candidate GPU-selection directions

Tip

A scenario may point to more than one technically capable GPU. The correct decision then depends on operational factors such as installed platform, software validation, procurement, energy, and cost. At associate level, the priority is to identify the differentiating capability that the scenario is testing.

This selection method connects architecture to operations. A selection tree should narrow the set of plausible GPUs rather than convert one workload characteristic directly into a product choice. Once a candidate has been identified, verify that its exact configuration supports the required memory capacity, interconnect, MIG or virtualization mode, software stack, power envelope, and cooling design. The next chapter will examine how supported GPUs can be partitioned, monitored, and scheduled so that their capabilities remain available and efficiently used in production.

Figure 3.8 turns these workload characteristics into a repeatable selection process, beginning with the primary workload and narrowing the choice through memory, latency, scaling, sharing, and platform requirements.

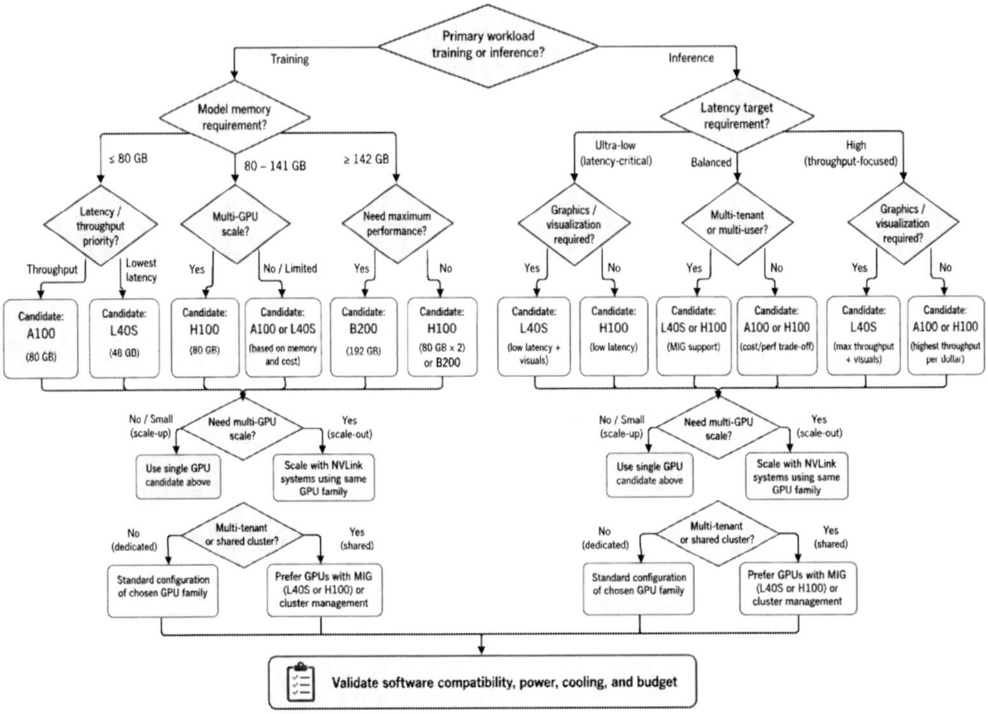

Figure 3.8: A repeatable GPU-selection decision tree

Figure 3.8 combines the chapter's selection criteria into a sequence of questions rather than treating one specification as decisive. The first distinction is whether the workload is dominated by training or inference. Memory requirements, latency and throughput goals, graphics needs, multi-GPU scaling, and multi-tenant operation then narrow the possible platforms. The final step is deliberately outside the GPU itself: a candidate device must still be validated against software compatibility, power, cooling, availability, and budget. The outputs of the tree are therefore candidates for evaluation, not guaranteed answers based on a single requirement.

GPU selection is ultimately a system-level decision: the chosen accelerator must fit the server architecture, available power and cooling, interconnect topology, software support, and operational budget.

The architecture and product comparison have now been converted into a workload-driven selection process. You are ready to move from choosing a GPU to operating it as a shared, observable data center resource.

Summary

This chapter examined the GPU as an AI compute engine. Streaming multiprocessors schedule and execute large numbers of CUDA threads, Tensor Cores accelerate supported matrix operations, and NVLink provides high-bandwidth communication for multi-GPU systems. These capabilities work together to support workloads that exceed the performance or memory of one general-purpose processor.

We then compared the A100, H100, L40S, and B200. The A100 is a mature and flexible accelerator with MIG support. The H100 targets demanding large-model and distributed workloads with Hopper-generation features such as FP8. The L40S combines enterprise inference with graphics and visualization. The B200 represents the Blackwell direction toward larger memory and newer low-precision generative AI performance.

The chapter objective was to match architectural capabilities to workload needs. You can now begin with training or inference, evaluate memory and precision, consider interconnect and graphics requirements, and account for sharing. This approach is more durable than memorizing a list of specifications because it explains why one platform fits a scenario better than another.

The next chapter focuses on GPU utilization in practice through MIG partitioning, DCGM fleet management, observability with Prometheus and Grafana, and workload scheduling with Kubernetes and Slurm.

Chapter review questions

Choose the single best answer for each question. The answer key and explanations follow the complete set for this chapter.

1. What is the main role of a streaming multiprocessor in an NVIDIA GPU?
    a. Store long-term model artifacts
    b. Schedule and execute groups of parallel threads
    c. Manage virtual-machine licensing
    d. Provide external network routing
2. Which operation is a Tensor Core designed to accelerate?
    a. Matrix multiply-accumulate used in AI

   b. File-system permission checks
   c. VM snapshot creation
   d. DNS name resolution

3. What is the primary purpose of NVLink?
   a. Replace CUDA with a programming language
   b. Provide high-bandwidth communication between supported GPUs and related components
   c. Track experiments in a model registry
   d. Create a virtual desktop session

4. Which GPU is most closely associated with a mature, flexible Ampere platform and optional MIG-based partitioning?
   a. B200
   b. A100
   c. L40S
   d. BlueField-3

5. Which feature most clearly distinguishes the H100 for demanding transformer and foundation-model work?
   a. A requirement to run without CUDA
   b. No support for multi-GPU communication
   c. Hopper architecture with high-bandwidth memory and FP8-capable Tensor Cores
   d. A focus on office graphics only

6. Which workload is the strongest fit for an L40S?
   a. A storage array with no compute requirement
   b. A firewall that performs no AI computation
   c. A CPU-only database backup
   d. A mixed enterprise workload requiring AI inference and visual/graphics capability

7. Which characteristic is associated with the B200 in the book's comparison?
   a. Blackwell architecture and very large-memory, low-precision generative-AI capability
   b. A design limited to virtual desktop graphics

   c. A requirement for 32-bit-only inference
   d. No Tensor Core support

8. Why must GPU selection consider model memory in addition to raw compute performance?
   a. Model size affects only network cabling.
   b. A model that does not fit cannot use the available compute effectively.
   c. GPU memory is used only for display output.
   d. Compute performance automatically increases host RAM.
9. A team needs to train a model across several GPUs in one server with frequent tensor exchange. Which capability deserves special attention?
   a. High-bandwidth GPU interconnect topology
   b. Virtual desktop display resolution
   c. The number of review flashcards
   d. A public DNS record
10. What is the best overall GPU-selection method?
    a. Always choose the newest GPU.
    b. Choose by architecture name alone.
    c. Select whichever device has the most marketing material.
    d. Map workload type, memory, precision, communication, tenancy, software, and facility constraints to candidate GPUs.

Answer key and explanations

Use the explanations to verify both the correct choice and the layer of the stack being tested.

1. B. SMs are the primary parallel execution engines inside the GPU. They contain execution resources, registers, caches, and scheduling logic.
2. A. Tensor Cores specialize in matrix-heavy operations central to neural-network training and inference.
3. B. NVLink provides a faster GPU-to-GPU path than a conventional PCIe-only route in supported systems.
4. B. The A100 is an Ampere data center GPU used broadly for training, inference, and analytics, with MIG support on applicable configurations.
5. C. The H100 targets demanding AI with high memory bandwidth, fourth-generation Tensor Cores, and FP8 support.

6. D. The L40S is positioned for enterprise inference, rendering, virtual workstations, and mixed AI-graphics workloads.
7. A. The B200 represents the Blackwell generation, with increased memory and low-precision capabilities aimed at large generative-AI workloads.
8. B. Weights, activations, runtime workspace, and batch or context state must fit in device memory with operating headroom.
9. A. Multi-GPU efficiency depends strongly on how quickly participating devices communicate, so NVLink/NVSwitch topology matters.
10. D. A defensible selection process begins with requirements and validates the whole platform, not a single specification or generation.

Part 2

Building and Operating GPU Infrastructure

The second part of this book moves from understanding accelerated computing to building an environment in which GPU resources can be used efficiently and reliably. You will learn how MIG divides supported GPUs into isolated resources, how DCGM and observability tools expose health and utilization, and how Kubernetes and Slurm place workloads across available accelerators. You will then widen the infrastructure boundary to examine storage and network performance, RDMA and GPUDirect technologies, GPU virtualization, and DPU-based offload.

By the end of this part, you will understand that GPU performance depends on much more than the accelerator itself. You will be able to reason about resource sharing, scheduling, storage and network bottlenecks, multi-tenant delivery, and the role of BlueField DPUs and DOCA in moving infrastructure work away from the host CPU.

This part contains the following chapters:

- *Chapter 4, Sharing, Monitoring, and Scheduling GPU Resources*
- *Chapter 5, Building High-Throughput Storage and Network Paths*
- *Chapter 6, Virtualized GPU Infrastructure and DPU Offload*

4

Sharing, Monitoring, and Scheduling GPU Resources

> Note
>
> A production GPU is valuable only when its capacity is allocated correctly, its health is visible, and workloads can be placed without conflict or waste.

GPU operations extend beyond installing a device and launching a model. Shared environments must divide resources among users and services, observe utilization and health, detect faults, and schedule work predictably. **NVIDIA Multi-Instance GPU** and **Data Center GPU Manager** address the device layer, while **Prometheus**, **Grafana**, **Kubernetes**, and **Slurm** connect GPU state to cluster operations.

This chapter begins with MIG, which partitions a supported physical GPU into isolated instances for smaller or multi-tenant workloads. It then examines DCGM as the monitoring and management foundation for GPU fleets. The final section connects DCGM telemetry to observability platforms and compares Kubernetes and Slurm as schedulers for cloud-native and high-performance computing environments.

By the end of the chapter, you will be able to describe how a GPU can be shared safely, which signals an operator should monitor, and how a scheduler assigns workloads to full GPUs or MIG instances. The objective is to turn accelerator hardware into a controlled service rather than an unmanaged collection of devices.

We will be covering the following main topics in this chapter:

- Partitioning GPUs with MIG

- Operating GPU fleets with DCGM
- Observability and workload scheduling

The operational journey begins with allocation, because the first source of waste in a shared cluster is often assigning an entire GPU to a workload that needs only a fraction of it.

Partitioning GPUs with MIG

Multi-Instance GPU, or **MIG**, is a hardware partitioning feature available on supported NVIDIA data center GPUs, including the A100 and H100 discussed in *Chapter 3*. MIG divides one physical GPU into several isolated GPU instances. Each instance behaves as an independent accelerator from the perspective of the assigned workload.

Why GPU partitioning is needed

Traditional GPU allocation often assigns one physical device to one process, container, or virtual machine. This model is simple, but it can waste capacity when the workload uses only part of the available compute or memory. The unused portion remains unavailable to other jobs even though it is idle.

Figure 4.1 illustrates this utilization problem by contrasting a lightly used full GPU with the same physical device divided into several right-sized MIG instances.

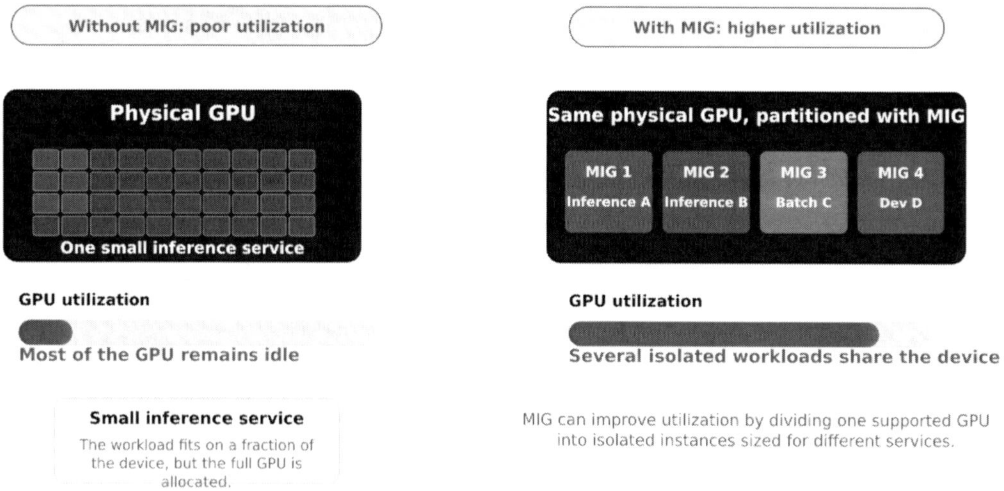

Figure 4.1: Utilization problem that MIG addresses

Figure 4.1 shows the difference between allocation and actual use. On the left, one small inference service receives the entire physical GPU even though it consumes only a fraction of its capacity, leaving the remaining resources unavailable to other workloads. On the right, MIG partitions the same GPU into isolated instances that can be assigned to several services independently. The objective is not simply to make the utilization percentage higher; it is to allocate the device at a granularity that better matches the workloads using it.

This problem is common in development environments, inference platforms, hosted notebooks, and AI-as-a-service offerings. Several small models may each need reliable GPU access but not the performance of a full A100 or H100. Buying and dedicating a physical device to every workload increases cost and lowers utilization.

MIG addresses the problem by creating right-sized hardware partitions. A cluster can place different workloads on separate instances of the same GPU while preserving boundaries between them. This brings GPU allocation closer to the way modern data centers already share CPU and memory capacity.

The value of MIG depends on the strength of its isolation, which is built into the hardware resource layout rather than implemented only as a software scheduling rule.

Hardware-isolated GPU instances

A MIG instance receives a defined portion of GPU compute and memory resources. This involves dedicated streaming multiprocessors, cache, memory controllers, and memory capacity for each instance. Error and performance isolation help one workload operate without consuming the resources assigned to another instance. *Figure 4.2* shows how this isolation is implemented conceptually by assigning separate compute, cache, and memory resources to individual MIG instances within the same physical GPU.

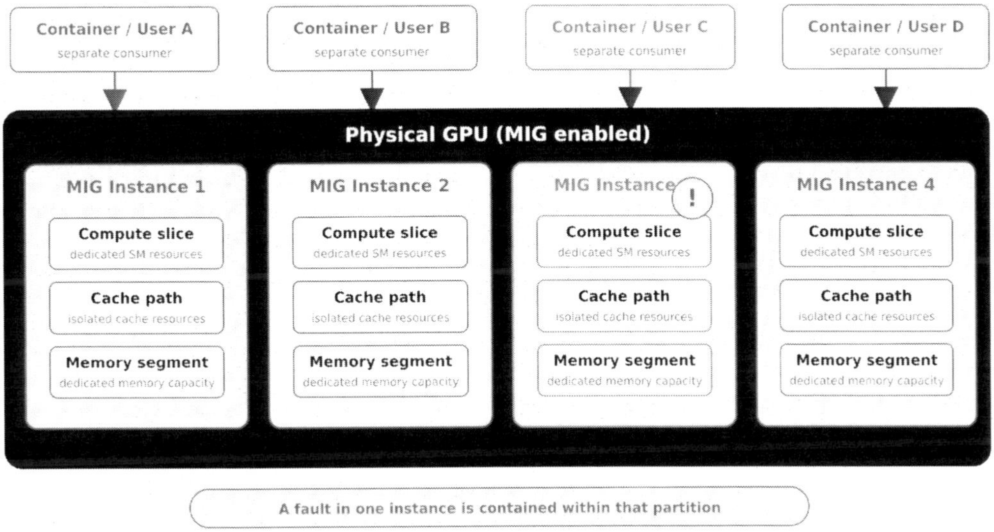

Figure 4.2: Hardware-level isolation inside a MIG-capable GPU

The partitions in *Figure 4.2* illustrate why MIG differs from software-only sharing. Each instance receives defined compute resources together with an isolated path through portions of the memory system, so activity in one instance does not simply consume the resources assigned to another. The fault symbol in the third instance also represents the isolation objective: a problem associated with one partition should remain contained rather than automatically disrupting neighboring instances. This provides the predictable resource boundaries needed for multi-tenant and service-oriented environments.

It should be noted that a supported GPU can be divided into as many as seven instances, depending on the device and selected profile. Because the instances are predefined rather than arbitrary, administrators choose from supported combinations of compute slices and memory.

This hardware-level division is important for multi-tenant environments. A noisy workload cannot simply take all available GPU memory or scheduling time from a neighboring MIG instance. The resulting predictability is useful for service-level objectives, chargeback, quotas, and security boundaries.

Isolation alone is not enough; the partition must also be sized to the model. MIG profiles express the amount of compute and memory assigned to each instance.

Understanding MIG profiles

A MIG profile name identifies the resource shape allocated to an instance. This book uses examples such as **1g.5gb**, **2g.10gb**, and **3g.20gb**. The first number represents the number of GPU compute slices, while the second value represents the approximate memory capacity assigned by that profile on the relevant GPU configuration.

MIG profile names are specific to the GPU configuration. For example, the `1g.5gb`, `2g.10gb`, and `3g.20gb` names used here correspond to profile naming on an A100 40 GB configuration. An A100 80 GB configuration uses different memory values for comparable compute-slice counts, such as `1g.10gb` and `2g.20gb`. Other MIG-capable GPU generations provide their own supported profile sets. Always discover and select from the profiles supported by the installed GPU rather than assuming that a profile name is portable across devices.

A small profile can support a lightweight inference service, notebook, or development workload. A larger profile can support a model with greater memory and compute requirements. The administrator must select a profile that fits the workload because a model that exceeds the instance memory will fail even if unused capacity exists elsewhere on the physical GPU.

Profile selection also affects packing efficiency. Several small profiles may increase workload density, while fewer large profiles provide more resources to each job. The correct configuration depends on the service catalog and demand pattern rather than on a goal of always creating the maximum number of instances.

The following table illustrates the interpretation used in this book. Available profile names and capacities depend on the exact GPU and software version.

Illustrative profile	**Compute allocation**	**Memory allocation**	**Possible use**
1g.5gb	One compute slice	Approximately 5 GB on the referenced configuration	Small inference service, development job, or light notebook workload
2g.10gb	Two compute slices	Approximately 10 GB on the referenced configuration	Larger inference model or moderate isolated workload
3g.20gb	Three compute slices	Approximately 20 GB on the referenced configuration	More demanding model that still does not require a full GPU

Table 4.1: Illustrative MIG profile names, resource allocations, and workload uses

Figure 4.3 makes the profile notation easier to interpret by separating its compute and memory components and showing how predefined profiles represent different resource shapes on a supported GPU.

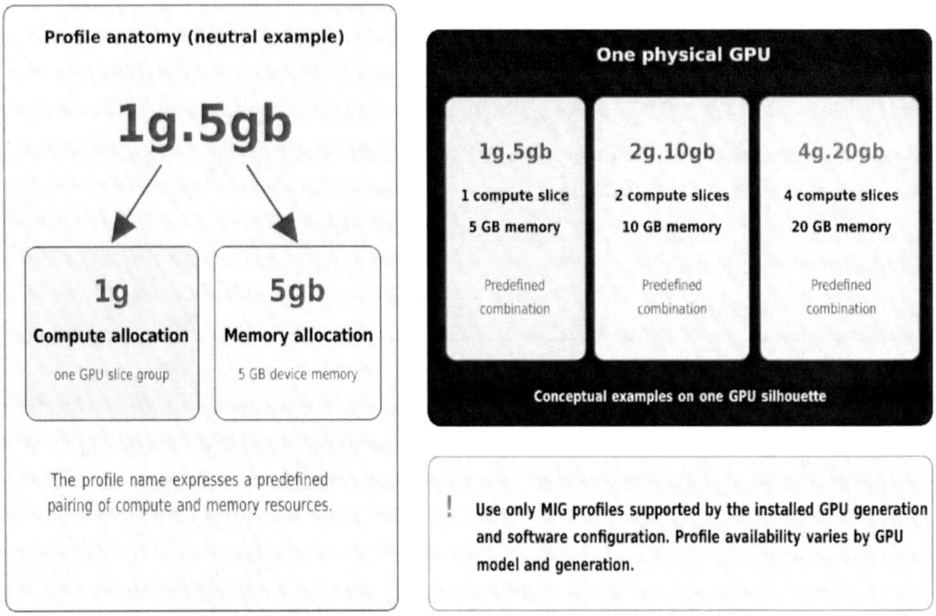

Figure 4.3: Reading a MIG profile and using predefined combinations

Figure 4.3 shows that a MIG profile is a predefined resource shape rather than an arbitrary percentage of a GPU. In the example, the g portion indicates the compute allocation while the memory suffix identifies the memory capacity associated with that profile on the referenced GPU. Larger profiles combine more compute and memory resources. Administrators therefore select from configurations supported by the installed GPU instead of independently choosing any desired number of SMs or gigabytes of memory.

The profile is a capacity contract. Schedulers and platform teams can use that contract to offer specific GPU service tiers rather than an undifferentiated full-device request.

This service model becomes most useful when connected to containers, Kubernetes, and monitoring.

MIG in multi-tenant and inference environments

MIG is especially well suited to inference workloads that do not need an entire GPU. Several chatbot models, image classifiers, or small services can run on separate instances. Each workload receives predictable resources, and the physical device achieves higher aggregate utilization.

Before Kubernetes can schedule MIG resources, the node must first be configured with an appropriate MIG geometry. In NVIDIA GPU Operator environments, MIG Manager can manage this node-level configuration. Once the instances exist, the NVIDIA device plugin advertises the available accelerator resources to Kubernetes so that workloads can request them. In other words, MIG configuration creates the resource shape; the device plugin exposes it; and the Kubernetes scheduler places workloads against the advertised capacity.

Kubernetes can expose MIG instances as schedulable resources through the NVIDIA software stack. A pod requests a supported resource type, and the scheduler places it on a node with an available instance. This preserves the declarative resource model used for CPU and memory while adding accelerator-specific capacity.

Cloud and internal platform teams can also use MIG to create standardized offerings. Users request a small, medium, or large instance rather than choosing a physical GPU. Usage can be measured per instance, and quotas can limit how much capacity each team consumes.

MIG is not supported on every GPU and requires compatible drivers, CUDA components, and management tools. It also does not solve every sharing problem. Virtual machines and graphics-oriented environments may use vGPU, which is discussed in *Chapter 6*. MIG is most compelling when strict hardware partitioning and predictable compute isolation are required. *Figure 4.4* extends this resource model into Kubernetes, showing how MIG instances can be advertised to the cluster and assigned to pods that request an available accelerator resource.

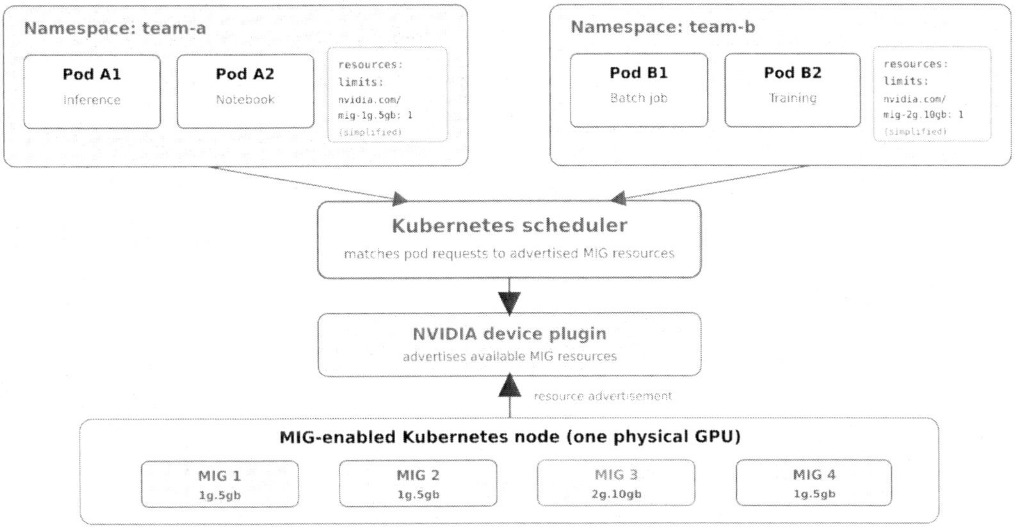

Figure 4.4: MIG instances as schedulable Kubernetes resources

Figure 4.4 separates two responsibilities in the Kubernetes path. NVIDIA software makes the configured MIG devices available as Kubernetes accelerator resources, and the Kubernetes scheduler then matches a pod's request with capacity advertised by an appropriate node. The namespaces at the top show how separate teams can request accelerator resources while Kubernetes maintains the allocation record. MIG provides the hardware resource boundary; Kubernetes determines where the workload that consumes that resource should run.

The exact Kubernetes resource name depends on how the NVIDIA device plugin is configured. A mixed MIG strategy can expose profile-specific resources such as `nvidia.com/mig-1g.5gb`, whereas other strategies can present MIG-backed capacity differently. Treat the resource names in *Figure 4.4* as one configuration example rather than a universal Kubernetes syntax.

MIG establishes how GPU capacity can be divided, but partitioning creates more resources to observe. The next section introduces DCGM, which provides the health and telemetry needed to operate both full GPUs and MIG instances at scale.

Operating GPU fleets with DCGM

NVIDIA Data Center GPU Manager, or **DCGM**, is an enterprise toolkit for managing and monitoring NVIDIA GPUs. It provides real-time telemetry, health information, diagnostics, and interfaces that can be integrated into automation and observability platforms. DCGM supports single nodes, larger clusters, containerized deployments, and MIG-enabled systems.

DCGM components and operating model

DCGM includes a background service that collects device data, a command-line interface named `dcgmi`, and programming interfaces that applications or monitoring agents can use. Exporters make the metrics available to platforms such as Prometheus. This modular design allows the same underlying telemetry to support interactive diagnosis, automated policy, and dashboards. *Figure 4.5* brings the major DCGM components together to show how device telemetry, health information, policy, and diagnostics move from the GPU fleet to management and monitoring interfaces.

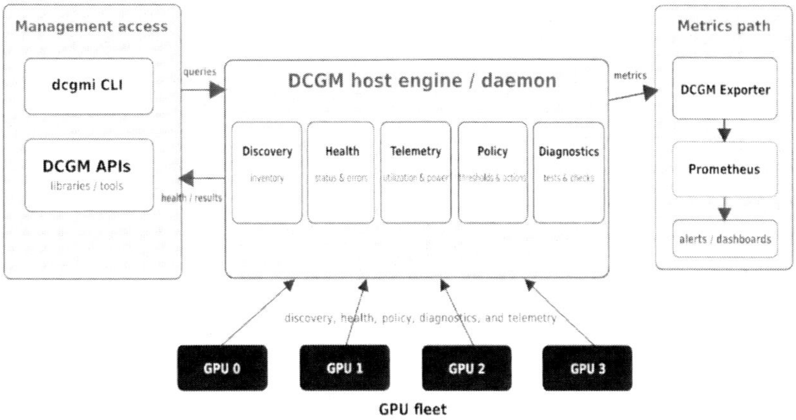

Figure 4.5: DCGM components and operating data flow

Figure 4.5 places the DCGM host engine at the center of GPU operations. The engine gathers information from the GPU fleet and makes services such as discovery, health monitoring, telemetry, policy, and diagnostics available to management clients. Administrators can interact through `dcgmi` or APIs, while DCGM Exporter exposes selected telemetry in a Prometheus-compatible form for longer-term monitoring. The same underlying device information can therefore support interactive troubleshooting, automated management, and fleet-wide observability.

On a single server, an administrator can use the command-line interface to discover devices and inspect health. In a Kubernetes cluster, DCGM components can run across nodes so that metrics from the GPU fleet are gathered consistently. MIG-aware monitoring can report activity for individual instances as well as the parent device.

The key operational benefit is a common view of accelerator state. Without a standardized management layer, teams may depend on application logs or occasional command output. DCGM provides continuous data that can be stored, trended, and correlated with workload behavior.

The value of that data becomes clearer when the metrics are grouped into performance, health, and efficiency signals.

Telemetry for utilization and capacity planning

DCGM can report GPU utilization, memory usage, temperature, power draw, and other performance metrics. These signals help operators determine whether a workload is compute-bound, memory-constrained, idle, or approaching a thermal or power limit.

Utilization data supports capacity planning. A cluster in which GPUs remain near saturation may need more devices or better workload distribution. A cluster with consistently low utilization may be overprovisioned, may have poorly configured jobs, or may be limited by storage, networking, or CPU preprocessing.

Memory metrics are equally important. A job can show moderate compute utilization while consuming nearly all device memory. In that condition, another process cannot be placed safely even if arithmetic capacity appears available. MIG profiles make the relationship explicit by assigning fixed memory to each instance.

Figure 4.6 demonstrates why these metrics should be interpreted together by comparing several operational patterns that would be difficult to diagnose from GPU utilization alone.

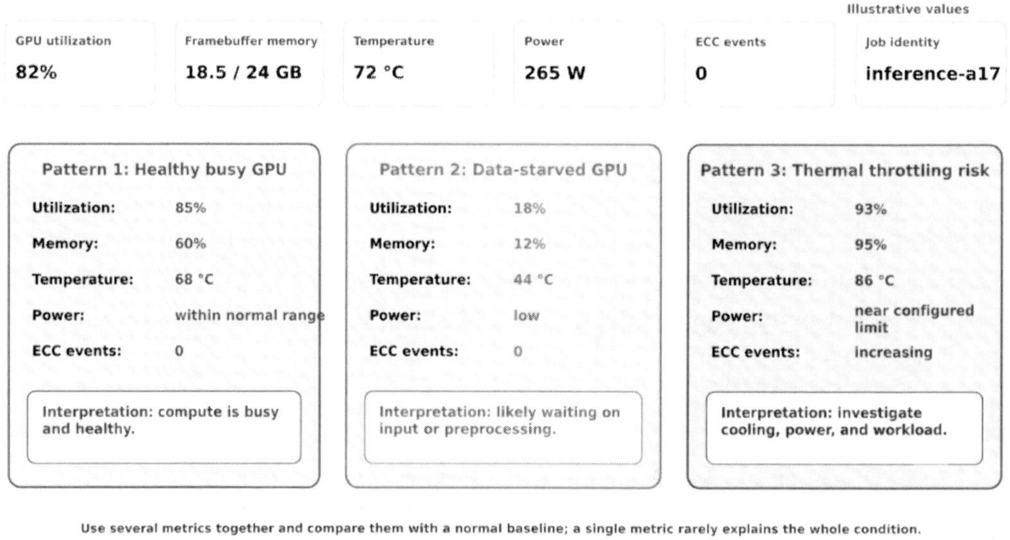

Figure 4.6: Interpreting GPU telemetry as a combined operational picture

Figure 4.6 illustrates that similar workloads can produce very different combinations of signals. A healthy busy GPU combines high utilization with values that remain within an expected operating baseline. A GPU with low utilization, low memory use, and low power may be waiting for input or preprocessing rather than suffering from inadequate accelerator performance. High temperature and power near configured limits, meanwhile, can justify investigation for thermal or power-related throttling. The values in the figure are illustrative; operators should compare several signals with the known baseline for the particular GPU, node, and workload before diagnosing a problem.

Trends are more informative than isolated snapshots. Sustained temperature increases, recurring power limits, or gradually changing utilization can reveal environmental or workload patterns that a one-time inspection would miss.

Performance metrics explain how resources are being used. Health and error data explain whether the device can continue to provide reliable service.

Health checks, errors, and policy

DCGM records health-related events such as ECC errors, XID events, page faults, and other conditions that may indicate hardware, driver, or workload problems. Automated health checks can evaluate GPUs for instability or failure before a production job is assigned.

Two error categories deserve special attention. **Error-correcting code** (**ECC**) memory protects GPU memory against certain bit errors; an increasing error count or an uncorrectable error can indicate a memory-reliability problem that requires investigation. An XID is a driver-reported GPU error event written to the operating-system log. Different XID values represent different conditions, and an XID does not automatically mean that the physical GPU has failed—it may point to hardware, driver, system, or application behavior. Operators should interpret the specific error code together with DCGM health information and workload logs.

Policy rules can trigger alerts or other responses when thresholds are crossed. An operator may want notification when temperature exceeds an acceptable level, when repeated errors occur, or when power behavior changes unexpectedly. The exact remediation depends on the environment, but early detection provides time to drain workloads or investigate before a larger failure occurs.

Health information is also useful after a job failure. If a training run stops unexpectedly, the team can compare application logs with DCGM events from the same period. This correlation helps separate a model or container error from a device or node problem.

In shared environments, the monitoring system should preserve context. Operators need to know which node, physical GPU, MIG instance, and workload were active when the event occurred. DCGM supplies the device data, while the scheduler and observability platform supply the workload identity.

The command-line interface provides a direct way to explore these capabilities during administration and troubleshooting.

Working with the dcgmi command-line interface

The exact `dcgmi` flags vary by DCGM release and operation, so production procedures should use the help output and the documentation installed with the environment. The following command patterns show a safe starting point for discovery and command exploration.

```
dcgmi discovery -l
dcgmi health -help
dcgmi stats --help
```

The `discovery` command lists GPUs visible to DCGM. The `health` and `stats help` commands show the syntax supported by the installed version before an administrator targets a group or device. This habit is preferable to copying commands from a different release without validation.

The CLI can also be used in scripts and operational runbooks. A scheduled health check can record results, a diagnostic workflow can gather device state after a failure, and an automation system can query metrics before placing or moving workloads.

DCGM is most powerful when its data is not isolated in a terminal. Exporting metrics to Prometheus and presenting them in Grafana turns device telemetry into a shared operational view. DCGM distinguishes passive health monitoring from active diagnostics. Health monitoring observes telemetry collected during normal operation and evaluates it for evidence of problems in areas such as memory, PCIe, thermal and power behavior, drivers, and NVLink. It does not deliberately load the GPU. Active diagnostics, invoked through dcgmi diag, run tests designed to validate GPU and system behavior under controlled work. A useful operational rule is to use health monitoring for continuous observation and incident context, then use diagnostics when the node can be tested more actively.

DCGM in Kubernetes and automation workflows

In Kubernetes, DCGM monitoring components can be deployed across GPU nodes so that every device is observed. This book describes a daemon-style deployment, which is appropriate because each node needs local access to its GPUs. Metrics can then be exposed to the cluster monitoring system.

Prometheus scrapes and stores the time-series data. Grafana displays dashboards and can support alerting. The platform team can compare GPU utilization with pod placement, job duration, node health, and service latency. MIG instances can be tracked individually, making it possible to see whether a particular partition is overloaded or idle.

Automation can use the same data for operational decisions. A platform may identify persistent underutilization, shift workloads, or increase capacity when thresholds are reached.

These actions require careful policy, but DCGM supplies the measurements needed to make them evidence-based.

DCGM therefore acts as an operations enabler rather than only a monitoring utility. It connects device state to capacity planning, incident response, policy, and scheduler behavior.

You have now seen how DCGM discovers GPUs, collects telemetry, reports health, and integrates with automated platforms. The final section connects those metrics to dashboards and explains how Kubernetes and Slurm schedule accelerator workloads.

Observability and workload scheduling

Monitoring and scheduling are complementary. Monitoring shows what the GPU fleet is doing and whether it is healthy. Scheduling decides where a workload should run and which accelerator resources it may consume. A production platform needs both functions to prevent failures and reduce waste.

Prometheus and Grafana for GPU observability

Prometheus is a time-series monitoring system that collects metrics from exporters and endpoints. In a GPU environment, a DCGM exporter can expose device utilization, memory consumption, temperature, power, and other signals. Prometheus stores those values with timestamps and labels so that they can be queried over time.

Grafana provides the visualization layer. Dashboards can show fleet-wide status, per-node utilization, MIG instance activity, temperature trends, and workload-specific views. Alerts can notify operators when a threshold is crossed or when a pattern suggests a developing problem.

In environments that use Prometheus alerting, **Alertmanager** commonly handles the notification stage. Prometheus evaluates alerting rules and forwards firing alerts to Alertmanager, which can group, suppress, and route them to configured receivers such as an on-call or messaging system. Grafana remains the primary dashboard and visualization layer in the architecture shown here.

Figure 4.7 follows this telemetry beyond the individual node, showing how GPU metrics and workload context move through the observability stack before reaching dashboards, alerts, and operators.

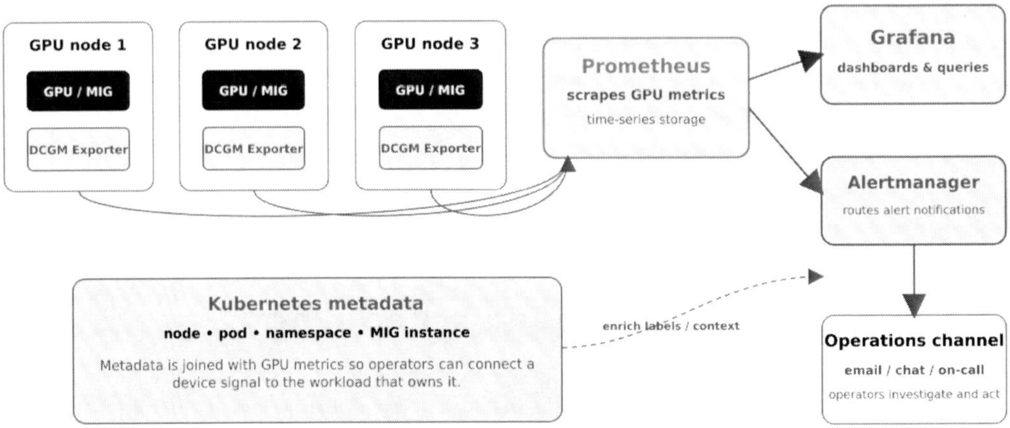

Figure 4.7: GPU observability pipeline from device metrics to operators

Figure 4.7 shows the observability path from each GPU node to the operations team. DCGM Exporter exposes GPU telemetry from the nodes, Prometheus collects and stores the resulting time-series data, and Grafana provides a dashboarding and query layer. Workload metadata adds context such as the node, pod, namespace, or MIG instance so that a device signal can be associated with the workload responsible for it. In the alerting path shown here, Prometheus can evaluate alert rules and send firing alerts to Alertmanager, which then routes notifications to the appropriate operations channel.

The combination supports both reactive and proactive operations. During an incident, the team can examine the time window around a failure. During capacity planning, it can review weeks of utilization. During optimization, it can identify devices that remain idle while other nodes are congested.

A useful dashboard should connect metrics to an action. A red temperature panel matters because the runbook explains whether to drain the node, inspect cooling, or reduce load. A low-utilization panel matters because the team can investigate data bottlenecks or allocation policy. Observability is valuable when it leads to a decision.

Kubernetes uses a different set of mechanisms to turn available GPU capacity into pod placement.

Scheduling GPUs with Kubernetes

Kubernetes treats hardware resources as part of a pod specification. With the NVIDIA device plugin and related components, full GPUs or supported MIG resources can be advertised by a node. A pod requests the resource, and the scheduler places the pod only where the requested capacity is available.

This model provides isolation and repeatability. The resource request becomes part of the workload definition rather than an informal instruction to an operator. Kubernetes can combine GPU requests with CPU, memory, storage, and networking requirements.

Labels, node selectors, affinity rules, and taints can control placement. A team may label nodes by GPU model, memory size, or workload tier. Taints can reserve expensive GPU nodes for approved workloads. Quotas can limit how many accelerator resources a namespace or team may consume.

MIG adds more granular resource types. A pod can request an instance profile rather than a full physical device, assuming the cluster has been configured to advertise that profile. This allows multiple pods to use isolated portions of one GPU while the scheduler maintains a consistent allocation record.

Metrics can also support scaling decisions. A service may increase the number of pods when demand rises and decrease it when demand falls, although GPU-aware autoscaling must account for model load time, device availability, and the cost of additional replicas. Kubernetes is strongest when AI workloads are packaged as cloud-native services or containerized jobs.

Research and high-performance computing environments often use Slurm instead, where the scheduling model is built around queued jobs and shared clusters.

Scheduling batch and research workloads with Slurm

Slurm is a workload manager widely used in high-performance computing and research environments. Users submit jobs, request resources, and wait in a queue until suitable nodes and GPUs are available. Policies can control priority, fairness, reservations, and maximum resource use.

Interactive work can be started with `srun`, batch jobs can be submitted with `sbatch`, and the queue can be viewed with `squeue`. The following patterns show the role of each command without assuming one site-specific resource configuration.

```
srun <resource-options> <command>
sbatch <job-script>
squeue
```

A Slurm job can request one or more GPUs and can be constrained to nodes with particular capabilities. Environments may also expose MIG resources, use node features and constraints to control placement, or enforce job priorities. Slurm can integrate with NVIDIA management interfaces and DCGM data to support monitoring and policy.

Slurm commonly represents GPUs as **Generic RESources**, or **GRES**. A job requests the required GPU resources, and Slurm includes those resources when determining where the job can run.

MIG devices can also be represented as GPU GRES when the cluster is configured for them. Node features and constraints can then narrow placement to systems with required characteristics such as a particular GPU class.

The queued-job model fits long-running training, simulation, and research workloads. Kubernetes can run batch jobs as well, and Slurm can support services through additional tooling, but their common deployment patterns differ. The infrastructure team should select or integrate schedulers according to the workload and organizational operating model.

The tools can now be compared as parts of one operational workflow.

Bringing monitoring and scheduling together

A well-operated GPU cluster follows a continuous loop. The scheduler assigns a full GPU or MIG instance. DCGM collects device and instance telemetry. Prometheus stores the metrics. Grafana and alerting reveal trends or faults. Operators or automation then adjust placement, capacity, policy, or workload configuration.

The following table summarizes the primary roles of the tools introduced in the chapter:

Tool or feature	Primary role	Typical question it answers
MIG	Hardware-level GPU partitioning	How can several isolated workloads share one supported physical GPU?
DCGM	GPU fleet health, telemetry, diagnostics, and management interfaces	Are the GPUs and MIG instances healthy, busy, memory-constrained, hot, or reporting errors?
Prometheus	Time-series metric collection and query	How has GPU behavior changed over time, and which labels identify the affected node or workload?
Grafana	Dashboards and alert presentation	What does the fleet look like now, and which conditions require attention?
Kubernetes	Container orchestration and declarative resource scheduling	Where should a pod run, and which full GPU or MIG resource should it receive?

Tool or feature	Primary role	Typical question it answers
Slurm	Queued job scheduling for HPC and research clusters	When and where can a batch or interactive job obtain the requested accelerator resources?

Table 4.2: Roles of GPU sharing, monitoring, observability, and scheduling components

Figure 4.8 turns the scheduler comparison into a workload-oriented decision aid, highlighting the operating patterns that commonly favor Kubernetes or Slurm while preserving a shared monitoring foundation.

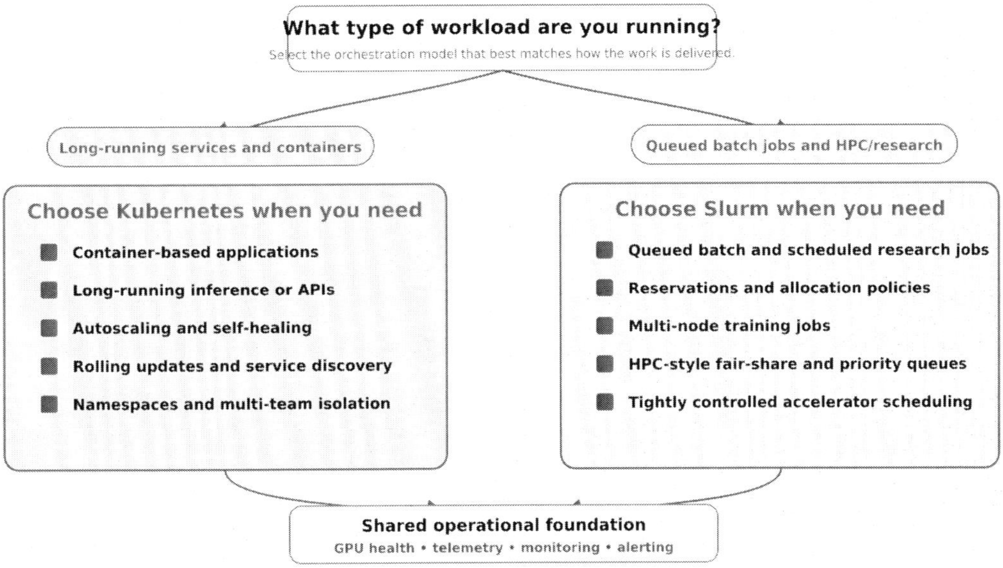

Figure 4.8: Choosing Kubernetes or Slurm for GPU workloads

Figure 4.8 presents Kubernetes and Slurm as different scheduling models rather than mutually exclusive capabilities. Kubernetes commonly fits containerized services that require features such as long-running deployment, scaling, self-healing, rolling updates, and namespace-based organization. Slurm commonly fits queued HPC, research, and distributed-training jobs that rely on reservations, priorities, and controlled batch allocation. Both still depend on accurate GPU inventory, health information, telemetry, and operational policy, which is why the two branches converge on a common monitoring foundation.

The loop also supports cost efficiency. High utilization is not the only goal; useful and predictable utilization is. A GPU at 100 percent because of a misbehaving job is not healthy capacity. A lightly used MIG instance may be correct if it meets a latency objective. The platform must interpret metrics in the context of workload intent.

> **Tip**
>
> For certification scenarios, look for the function being tested. A question about hardware-isolated sharing points to MIG. A question about temperature, ECC errors, or fleet telemetry points to DCGM. A question about dashboards points to Prometheus and Grafana. A question about pod placement points to Kubernetes, while a queued research job points to Slurm.

The chapter has now connected allocation, telemetry, dashboards, and scheduling into one GPU operations model. The next chapter widens the system boundary to the storage and network paths that keep those scheduled GPUs supplied with data.

Summary

This chapter turned GPU hardware into an operational service. MIG partitions supported GPUs, including the A100 and H100 examples used in this chapter, into isolated instances with defined compute and memory profiles. This improves utilization and allows several workloads or tenants to share one physical device without competing for the same assigned resources.

DCGM provides the monitoring and management foundation. It discovers devices, collects utilization and health data, records errors, supports diagnostics and policy, and exposes information through a CLI, APIs, and exporters. In Kubernetes, DCGM metrics can be collected across nodes and linked to MIG instances and workloads.

Prometheus and Grafana store, visualize, and alert on the telemetry. Kubernetes schedules containerized services and jobs using full GPU or MIG resource requests, while Slurm manages queued batch and research workloads. The chapter goal was to explain how sharing, monitoring, and scheduling work together. You can now map each tool to its operational function and place it in a continuous allocation-and-observation loop.

The next chapter examines the data path beyond the GPU, including accelerated storage, Ethernet and InfiniBand, RDMA, and GPUDirect Storage.

Chapter review questions

Choose the single best answer for each question. The answer key and explanations follow the complete set for this chapter.

1. What problem is MIG designed to solve?
   a. Connect separate data centers over the internet
   b. Partition a supported physical GPU into isolated hardware instances
   c. Convert a PyTorch model to ONNX
   d. Track model experiments
2. Why is MIG useful for multi-tenant inference?
   a. MIG removes the need for a driver.
   b. Every tenant receives the entire physical GPU.
   c. Each tenant can receive an isolated instance with defined compute and memory resources.
   d. MIG turns a GPU into a DPU.
3. What does a MIG profile describe?
   a. A model-training dataset
   b. A network-routing policy
   c. A predefined combination of GPU compute and memory resources
   d. A Kubernetes user password
4. Which tool is NVIDIA's purpose-built platform for data-center GPU health, telemetry, diagnostics, and policy?
   a. DCGM
   b. Airflow
   c. ONNX
   d. Helm
5. A GPU shows low utilization while memory use is moderate and the job remains active. What should an operator do first?
   a. Increase the model's numerical precision without measurement.
   b. Assume the GPU has failed and replace it immediately.
   c. Disable all monitoring.
   d. Correlate GPU metrics with input throughput, CPU activity, and job behavior.

6. Which DCGM signal most directly supports hardware-reliability investigation?
    a. ECC or XID error events
    b. Model-registry stage name
    c. HTTP response body size
    d. Git commit count
7. How do Prometheus and Grafana commonly work together for GPU observability?
    a. Both tools partition a GPU into MIG instances.
    b. Grafana collects raw GPU metrics while Prometheus schedules pods.
    c. Prometheus replaces the NVIDIA driver.
    d. Prometheus stores scraped time-series metrics, and Grafana presents dashboards and alerts.
8. What enables Kubernetes to recognize NVIDIA GPUs as schedulable resources?
    a. An ONNX export file
    b. MLflow Tracking
    c. TensorRT calibration
    d. The NVIDIA device plugin
9. Which environment is most strongly associated with Slurm?
    a. Browser-based image editing
    b. Model-format conversion only
    c. Queued HPC and research batch workloads
    d. DPU firmware development only
10. Why should scheduling data be correlated with GPU telemetry?
    a. To determine which job, pod, or tenant produced a utilization or health pattern
    b. To remove the need for quotas
    c. To ensure every GPU always runs at maximum temperature
    d. To convert all models into TensorRT engines

Answer key and explanations

Use the explanations to verify both the correct choice and the layer of the stack being tested.

1. B. MIG provides hardware-partitioned GPU instances for predictable sharing and better utilization on supported GPUs.

2. C. MIG isolates resources at the hardware level so several smaller services can share one GPU with predictable boundaries.
3. C. Profiles define supported instance sizes. Administrators choose profiles that match workload capacity requirements.
4. A. DCGM provides fleet-oriented GPU discovery, health checks, metrics, diagnostics, and integrations.
5. D. Low utilization is a symptom, not a diagnosis. The workload may be data-starved, synchronization-bound, or incorrectly configured.
6. A. ECC and XID events can indicate GPU hardware or driver-level problems and should be correlated with health checks and logs.
7. D. Prometheus handles metric collection/storage, while Grafana provides visualization and dashboarding.
8. D. The device plugin registers GPU resources with Kubernetes so pods can request them explicitly.
9. C. Slurm is a workload manager widely used for scheduled batch jobs and multi-node HPC/AI training.
10. A. Resource identity gives operational meaning to metrics. It allows teams to attribute inefficiency or failures to the correct workload.

5

Building High-Throughput Storage and Network Paths

> **Note**
>
> The fastest GPU cannot deliver useful performance when data arrives slowly, takes unnecessary copies, or waits in a congested network.

AI infrastructure is a data-movement system as well as a compute system. Training jobs read large datasets, distributed models exchange gradients and parameters, inference services receive streams of requests, and storage systems must keep accelerators supplied. When the data path is inefficient, GPUs spend expensive cycles waiting rather than computing.

This chapter begins with GPU-accelerated storage and the bottlenecks created by the traditional CPU-centered I/O path. It then compares Ethernet and InfiniBand as data center interconnects for AI workloads. The final section examines Remote Direct Memory Access and GPUDirect Storage, which reduce CPU involvement and memory copies when data moves between storage, networks, and GPU memory.

By the end of the chapter, you will be able to identify whether a workload is limited by storage, network latency, or unnecessary data movement, and you will be able to select the corresponding relevant technology. The objective is to see the infrastructure as one end-to-end pipeline rather than treating the GPU as an isolated component.

We will be covering the following main topics:

- GPU-accelerated storage
- Choosing Ethernet or InfiniBand
- GPUDirect Storage and RDMA

The discussion begins at the point where data leaves storage, because a traditional path can make the CPU an unintended middleman between fast devices.

GPU-accelerated storage

GPU-accelerated storage is an architecture and technology set designed to deliver data to GPUs with less CPU overhead and fewer unnecessary copies. The aim is not to make the storage device itself a GPU. It is to build an I/O path that matches the throughput of accelerated compute.

The traditional CPU-centered data path

In a conventional architecture, an application reads data from storage through the CPU and system memory. The CPU may load files, decode or preprocess data, place it in host memory, and then copy it to GPU memory. Each stage consumes time, memory bandwidth, and CPU cycles.

Figure 5.1 traces these handoffs through a traditional storage-to-GPU path, making the additional copies, latency, and CPU involvement visible before the data reaches GPU computation.

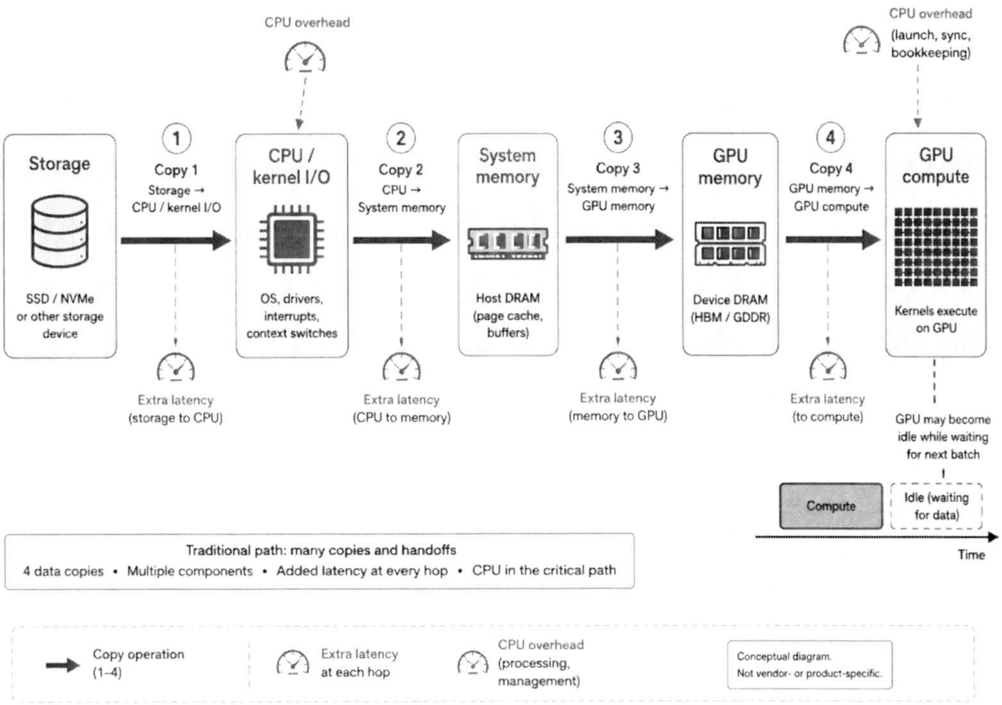

Figure 5.1: Traditional CPU-centered storage-to-GPU data path

The figure above shows how the traditional path introduces several handoffs before useful GPU computation begins. Data moves from storage through CPU and kernel I/O, into system memory, then into GPU memory before the GPU can process it. Each copy or software stage can add latency and consume CPU or memory-bandwidth resources. If these stages cannot supply data as quickly as the GPU consumes it, the accelerator can spend part of its time idle while waiting for the next batch.

This pattern can work for modest datasets and workloads, but it becomes a bottleneck when the GPU can process data faster than the host path can supply it. High-resolution images, video, audio, and large unstructured datasets are especially demanding. The accelerator finishes one batch and then waits for the next batch to arrive.

Idle GPU time reduces return on investment. The organization has purchased parallel compute, but the system is operating at the rate of the slowest data stage. Increasing GPU count can make the imbalance worse because more accelerators compete for the same CPU, memory, storage, or network path.

The bottleneck may also be inconsistent. A job can show bursts of high utilization followed by gaps while the data loader catches up. This is why a time-series view from DCGM and application profiling is more useful than one utilization snapshot.

GPU-accelerated storage changes the path so that data can move more directly and processing can overlap with I/O.

Moving data closer to the GPU

GPU-accelerated storage is a design in which data can travel from storage toward GPU memory without relying on the CPU as the central transfer point. PCIe topology, DMA-capable storage or network devices, compatible drivers, and the GPUDirect Storage software stack support this direct path.

A direct path reduces the number of copies between devices. It also reduces CPU interrupts and software processing associated with moving each block of data. The CPU remains responsible for application control and coordination, but it no longer needs to touch every byte before the GPU can use it. *Figure 5.2* contrasts this traditional multi-stage route with an accelerated path in which supported storage can move data toward GPU memory with less CPU involvement and fewer intermediate copies.

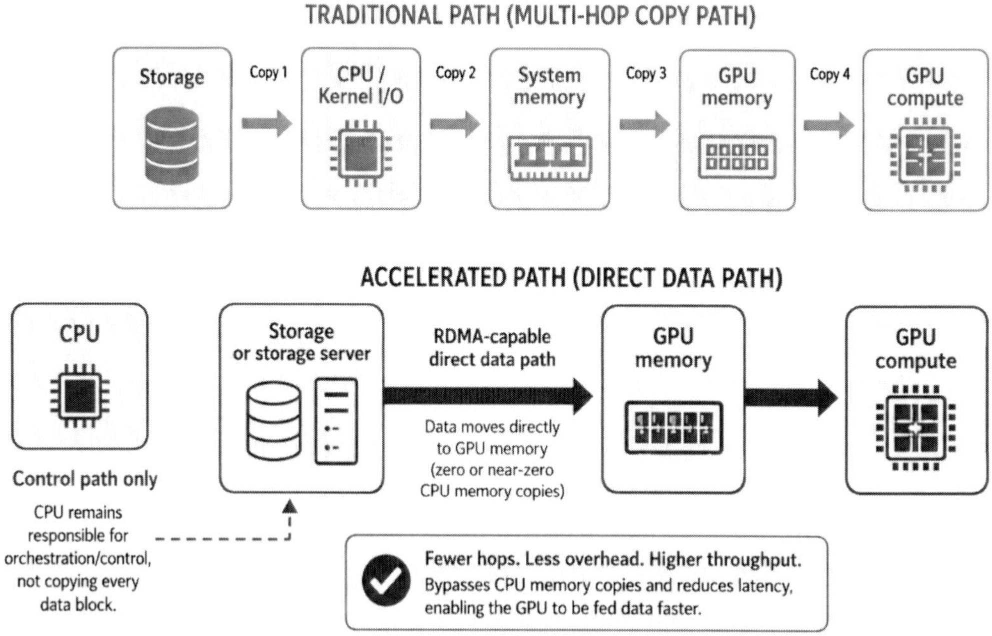

Figure 5.2: Accelerated path versus Traditional path

The comparison in the above figure separates the control path from the bulk data path. In the traditional route, data is repeatedly staged through CPU-managed memory before reaching GPU memory. In the accelerated path, the CPU continues to orchestrate the operation, but supported DMA mechanisms allow the bulk data to move toward GPU memory without using host memory as an unnecessary intermediate staging area. The result can be fewer handoffs, lower CPU overhead, and a data path better matched to the rate of GPU computation.

A direct data path does not remove the CPU from the system. The application still runs control logic on the host, establishes the I/O operation, manages permissions and synchronization, and responds to completion. The optimization concerns the bulk data itself: supported DMA engines can transfer it without repeatedly staging it through CPU-managed memory. This distinction is useful whenever a technology is described as bypassing the CPU.

The GPU can also process one portion of data while another portion is being loaded. This overlap increases pipeline efficiency because compute and I/O do not have to occur as completely separate phases. The result is more consistent utilization and lower end-to-end latency.

The design is particularly valuable when time-to-data is critical, including large-scale training, live video analytics, streaming inference, and accelerated data analytics. In each case, compute performance depends on sustained delivery rather than a one-time transfer speed.

The benefits can be grouped into throughput, latency, CPU efficiency, and scaling behavior.

Operational benefits of an accelerated storage path

The first benefit is **higher throughput into the GPU**. When storage can deliver batches at the rate the model consumes them, the accelerator spends more time on useful computation. Training completes sooner, and a fixed GPU fleet can process more work.

The second benefit is **lower latency**. Removing host-memory copies and reducing CPU involvement shortens the path between data and computation. In streaming systems, even small delays can accumulate across a pipeline, so reducing I/O latency can improve the response of the complete application.

The third benefit is **lower CPU overhead**. The host processor can focus on orchestration, application logic, and tasks that actually require general-purpose execution. An organization may also avoid adding CPU capacity solely to move data for GPUs.

The fourth benefit is **more predictable scaling**. A storage architecture that performs well for one GPU may fail when eight GPUs request data simultaneously. High-throughput NVMe, parallel file systems, NVMe over Fabrics, and direct data paths help the storage system scale with the accelerator count.

Figure 5.3 shows how improving input throughput and overlapping data movement with computation can translate into more consistent GPU utilization over time:

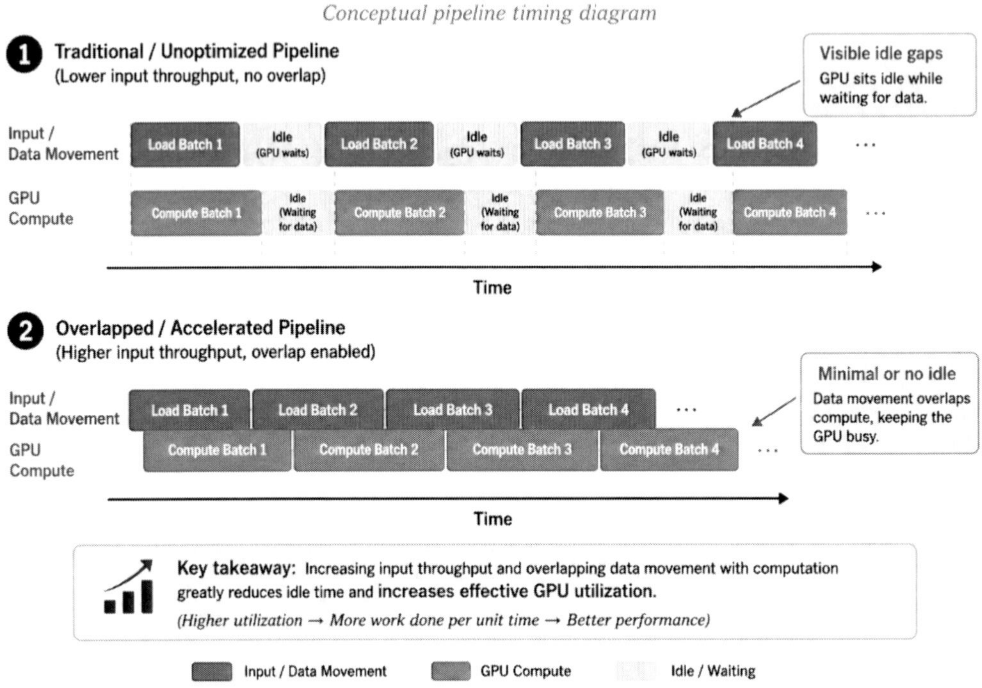

Figure 5.3: Input throughput and effective GPU utilization

Figure 5.3 shows that effective GPU utilization depends on timing as well as raw transfer speed. In the upper pipeline, the GPU repeatedly finishes computation and waits while the next batch is loaded. In the lower pipeline, data movement for a later batch overlaps with computation on the current batch, reducing those idle gaps. The improvement therefore comes from keeping the pipeline supplied and coordinating I/O with computation rather than from making the GPU itself execute arithmetic faster.

Storage performance is not represented by one throughput number. Large sequential reads may be limited primarily by sustained bandwidth, while workloads that access many small files can be sensitive to I/O operations per second, latency, and metadata performance. Concurrent GPU workers also increase pressure on the shared storage system. For this reason, the same storage platform can perform well for one dataset layout and poorly for another even when its advertised peak bandwidth is unchanged.

The benefits discussed in this section depend on several technologies working together rather than on one product name.

Technologies that support GPU-accelerated storage

GPUDirect Storage, or **GDS**, is the most important technology for direct storage-to-GPU data movement. It enables direct memory access between supported storage and GPU memory, reducing the need to route data through CPU memory.

NVMe devices provide high-performance local storage. NVMe over Fabrics extends NVMe access across a network, allowing remote storage to deliver data over Ethernet or InfiniBand. Parallel file systems and NFS environments can also participate when the required software and network capabilities are present.

NVIDIA DALI, the **Data Loading Library**, accelerates data loading and preprocessing for image, video, and related pipelines. It can move transformations closer to the GPU so that a CPU-based input pipeline does not become the limiting stage.

BlueField DPUs can offload storage and network processing at the infrastructure layer. By handling data movement, security, and I/O services, the DPU helps preserve CPU cycles and contributes to a more direct path between remote data and GPU computation.

The technology choice should follow the bottleneck. A job limited by file decoding may benefit from accelerated data loading. A job limited by repeated host copies may benefit from GDS. A multi-node job reading remote data may need NVMe over Fabrics, RDMA, and a network designed for sustained throughput.

The storage path explains how data reaches a GPU within or across a node.

It is useful to keep the technologies in this section at different layers. NVMe provides high-performance local storage, while NVMe over Fabrics provides remote access to NVMe storage across a network. DALI focuses on loading and preprocessing data for accelerated applications. RDMA is a general mechanism for direct memory access across networked systems. GPUDirect RDMA extends direct network or peer-device access to GPU memory, while GPUDirect Storage focuses specifically on moving data between supported storage and GPU memory. These technologies can be combined, but they do not solve the same problem.

The next section focuses on the network fabric that connects compute nodes, storage systems, and distributed accelerators.

Choosing Ethernet or InfiniBand

As AI workloads scale beyond one device or one server, the network becomes a performance-critical component. It carries training data, model parameters, gradients, storage traffic, service requests, and orchestration messages. Ethernet and InfiniBand can both support AI infrastructure, but they offer different operational and performance characteristics. *Figure 5.4* places the network in the middle of the AI performance path, showing how storage delivery, distributed GPU communication, and inference traffic all depend on the underlying fabric.

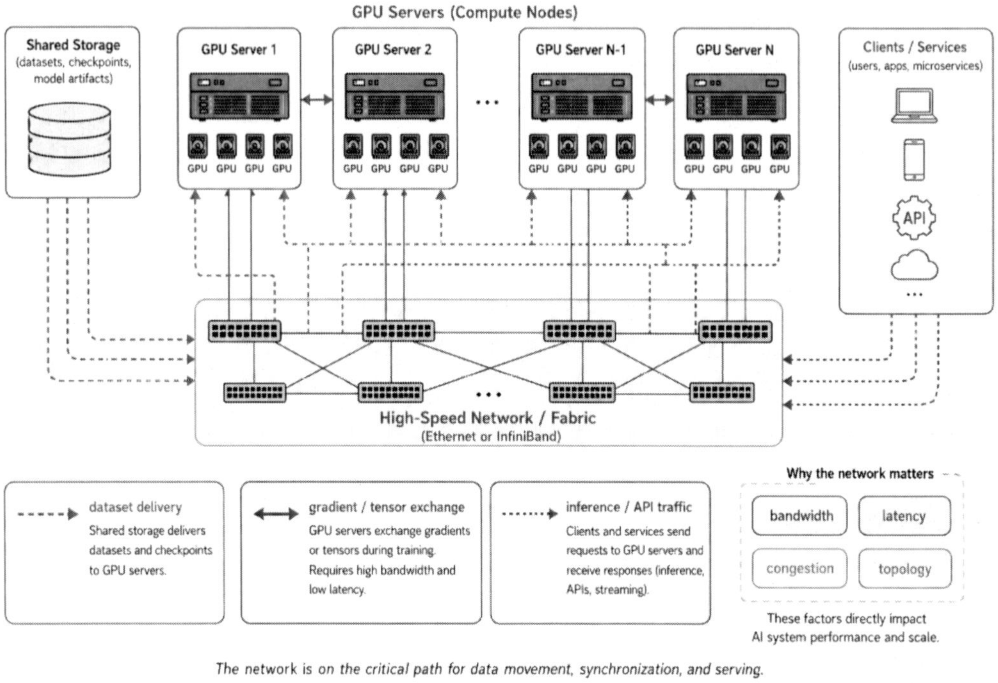

Figure 5.4: The network as part of the AI performance path

Figure 5.4 shows that the network carries several kinds of AI traffic at the same time. Shared storage supplies datasets and checkpoints to GPU servers, distributed workloads exchange gradients or tensors among compute nodes, and client applications send inference and API traffic to running services. Bandwidth, latency, congestion, and topology can therefore affect different stages of the workload in different ways. A problem in the fabric can leave powerful GPUs waiting even when the compute nodes themselves are healthy.

Why distributed AI is sensitive to the network

Distributed training divides a model, data, or both across several GPUs. At synchronization points, the devices exchange information before the next step can proceed. If one transfer is delayed, other GPUs may wait even though their local computation is complete.

Four network characteristics appear repeatedly in AI infrastructure discussions. **Bandwidth** describes how much data the fabric can carry over time. **Latency** describes how long a transfer takes to make progress from one endpoint to another. **Jitter** is variation in that latency, while congestion occurs when competing traffic exceeds the capacity available along part of the path. **Topology** describes how endpoints and switches are connected and therefore which links different flows must share. Distributed AI can be sensitive to all of these characteristics because participating workers frequently need to reach synchronization points together.

Large language models and large vision workloads can generate substantial communication. The network must provide not only high bandwidth but also low and predictable latency. Packet loss, congestion, and jitter can reduce scaling efficiency because tightly coordinated processes progress at the speed of the slowest participant.

Storage traffic adds another source of load. A cluster may read training data from a shared file system while GPUs exchange gradients on the same fabric. Network design must account for these traffic classes or separate them so that one does not disrupt the other.

Inference is often less synchronized than training, but it can still depend on the network for request handling, feature retrieval, remote storage, and service-to-service communication. The correct fabric depends on the scale and latency sensitivity of the workload.

Ethernet is the most familiar option and offers broad compatibility across enterprise environments.

Ethernet for compatibility and flexibility

Ethernet is widely used in data centers, enterprise networks, cloud platforms, and general-purpose infrastructure. Modern Ethernet spans multiple high-speed generations, and AI fabrics may use increasingly high link rates according to cluster scale and platform generation. For infrastructure planning, the more important considerations are whether the network provides sufficient effective bandwidth, predictable latency, and appropriate congestion management for the target workload.

Its strengths include broad vendor support, familiar operational tooling, and compatibility with many services and devices. Teams already understand Ethernet routing, switching, monitoring, and security. This can reduce deployment complexity and make it easier to integrate AI systems with existing infrastructure.

Ethernet is well suited to inference services, APIs, management traffic, general-purpose storage, and training environments that do not require the lowest possible latency. It can also support RDMA through RoCE when the network is configured for the necessary lossless or congestion-managed behavior.

Conventional Ethernet can experience higher latency, packet loss, and jitter under heavy load. These characteristics become important when many GPUs must synchronize frequently. A network that performs well for ordinary application traffic may not provide the consistency required by large distributed training.

Ethernet should not be interpreted as suitable only for general-purpose or lightly synchronized workloads. AI-optimized Ethernet fabrics can combine high link speeds, RDMA through RoCE, congestion control, telemetry, and topology-aware operation to support large distributed AI environments. InfiniBand remains a purpose-built high-performance computing fabric with native RDMA, but the selection should be based on the characteristics and design of the complete network rather than on the Ethernet name alone.

InfiniBand is designed around the high-performance communication needs of clustered computing.

InfiniBand for high-performance AI and HPC

InfiniBand is a high-bandwidth, low-latency interconnect widely used in high-performance computing and large AI clusters. It has evolved through multiple high-speed generations, including HDR, NDR, and XDR, but infrastructure selection should focus on the effective bandwidth, latency, topology, and RDMA capabilities required by the workload rather than on a particular link-speed threshold.

A defining capability is native support for Remote Direct Memory Access. RDMA allows data to move between device memory spaces with minimal CPU and operating-system involvement. This reduces interrupts, context switches, and copies, which lowers latency and CPU overhead.

These properties make InfiniBand well suited to distributed deep learning, model parallelism, scientific computing, and tightly synchronized multi-node workloads. NVIDIA DGX and HGX environments and major AI supercomputers use high-performance fabrics for this reason.

InfiniBand requires specialized adapters, switches, and operational knowledge. It may cost more and fit less naturally into an existing enterprise network than Ethernet. The performance benefit must therefore be evaluated against workload scale, budget, and team capability.

The choice is often not exclusive. Many AI data centers use different fabrics for different traffic types.

Hybrid network designs

A hybrid design can use Ethernet for management, orchestration, user access, and general service traffic while using InfiniBand for GPU-to-GPU communication and demanding storage paths. This approach assigns each network the traffic pattern that best matches its strengths.

Separation can also improve predictability. Distributed training traffic may be isolated from general application bursts, while management access remains available through the standard enterprise network. The design adds complexity, but that complexity can be justified in large clusters where communication efficiency has a direct effect on expensive GPU utilization.

The following table summarizes the comparison.

Characteristic	Ethernet	InfiniBand
Primary advantage	Compatibility, familiarity, flexibility, and broad ecosystem support	Very low latency, high throughput, and native high-performance cluster communication
Common AI use	Inference services, APIs, management, storage, and less synchronization-sensitive training	Distributed training, model parallelism, HPC, and frequent GPU synchronization
RDMA	Available through technologies such as RoCE when the network is configured appropriately	A foundational capability of the fabric
Operational trade-off	Easier integration with existing data center practice but can face jitter or loss under load	Higher-performance specialization with additional hardware and operational requirements
Typical design role	General-purpose or service network	Dedicated compute interconnect in high-end clusters

Table 5.1: Operational comparison of Ethernet and InfiniBand for AI data center networking

Figure 5.5 turns this comparison into an operational view, highlighting the different strengths of Ethernet and InfiniBand as well as the design requirements that both fabrics share.

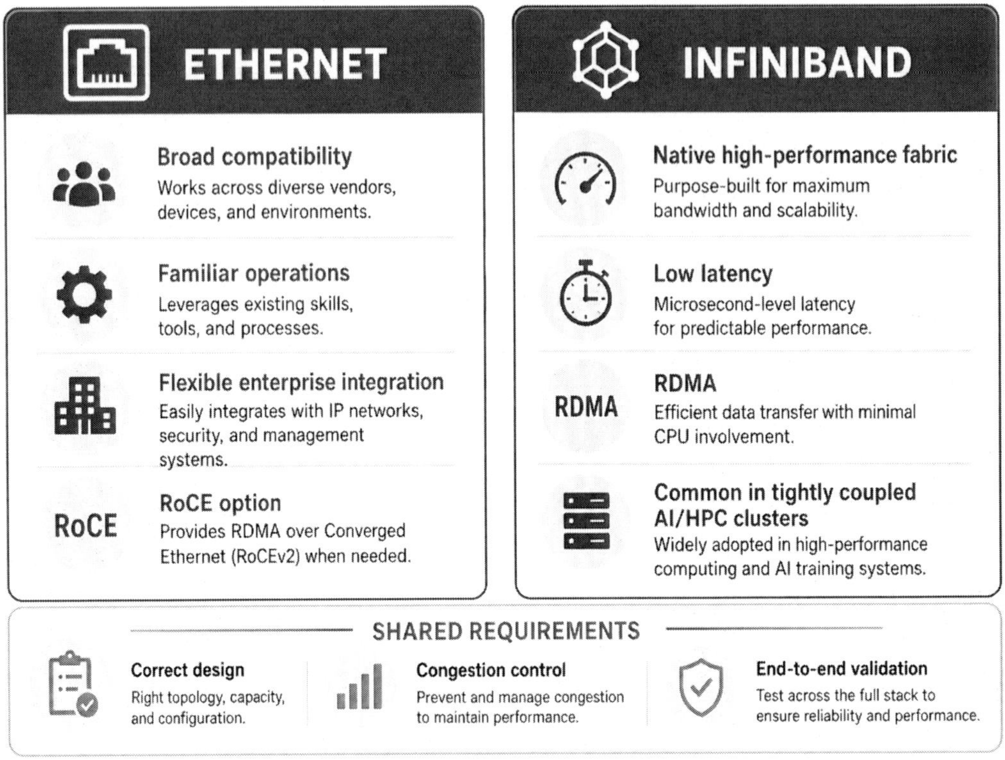

Figure 5.5: Practical tradeoffs: Ethernet and InfiniBand

Figure 5.5 emphasizes that the choice is not simply between a slow general-purpose network and a fast specialized network. Ethernet offers broad interoperability, familiar operations, and the ability to support RDMA through appropriately designed RoCE environments, while InfiniBand is purpose-built for high-performance clustered communication and provides RDMA as a fundamental capability. Both still require correct topology, capacity planning, congestion management, and end-to-end validation. The workload and operating environment determine which fabric is the better fit.

A scenario that emphasizes cost, general compatibility, and inference may point toward Ethernet. A scenario that emphasizes multi-node training, frequent synchronization, and the lowest possible latency may point toward InfiniBand. A large production platform may use both.

RDMA provides the mechanism that makes direct, low-overhead transfers possible across these high-performance paths. GPUDirect extends that principle to NVIDIA GPU memory.

You have now compared the network fabrics used to connect AI systems. The final section looks beneath the fabric choice to the data-movement mechanisms that bypass the CPU and reduce copies.

GPUDirect Storage and RDMA

Remote Direct Memory Access and GPUDirect Storage are designed to remove unnecessary software and memory stages from the data path. These technologies are sometimes described using the term zero-copy, but this does not mean that data is never copied or transferred. The important point is that the bulk data can avoid unnecessary intermediate copies through CPU-managed host memory, reducing CPU involvement and shortening the data path.

The cost of copies and CPU involvement

In a traditional transfer, data may move from a storage device to host memory, be processed by the CPU or kernel, and then be copied into GPU memory. A network transfer may similarly involve kernel buffers, interrupts, and context switches before the receiving application can use the data.

Each step adds latency and consumes host memory bandwidth. The CPU must coordinate work that does not contribute directly to model computation. At small scale, this overhead may be acceptable. At AI scale, repeated copies across large datasets or many nodes can become a dominant bottleneck.

The following comparison shows the logical difference between the two paths. It is a conceptual view rather than a complete physical topology.

Traditional path	Direct path
Storage or remote device -> CPU/kernel -> host memory -> GPU memory	Storage or RDMA-capable device -> direct memory access -> GPU memory
Multiple software stages and memory copies	Reduced CPU involvement and fewer copies
Higher host overhead and potential jitter	Lower latency and more consistent throughput when correctly configured

Table 5.2: Traditional CPU-staged data movement compared with a direct DMA-based path to GPU memory

The direct path still requires control logic, drivers, permissions, and compatible hardware. Zero-copy does not mean zero software. It means the bulk data avoids unnecessary staging through the CPU data path.

RDMA is the general network mechanism that enables direct transfer between memory regions.

Remote Direct Memory Access

RDMA allows one device to read from or write to the memory of another system with minimal involvement from the remote CPU and operating-system kernel. The endpoints establish and authorize memory regions, and the network adapter transfers the data directly. *Figure 5.6* makes the effect of RDMA clearer by contrasting a conventional network path that involves the operating-system and CPU data path with a more direct memory-to-memory transfer.

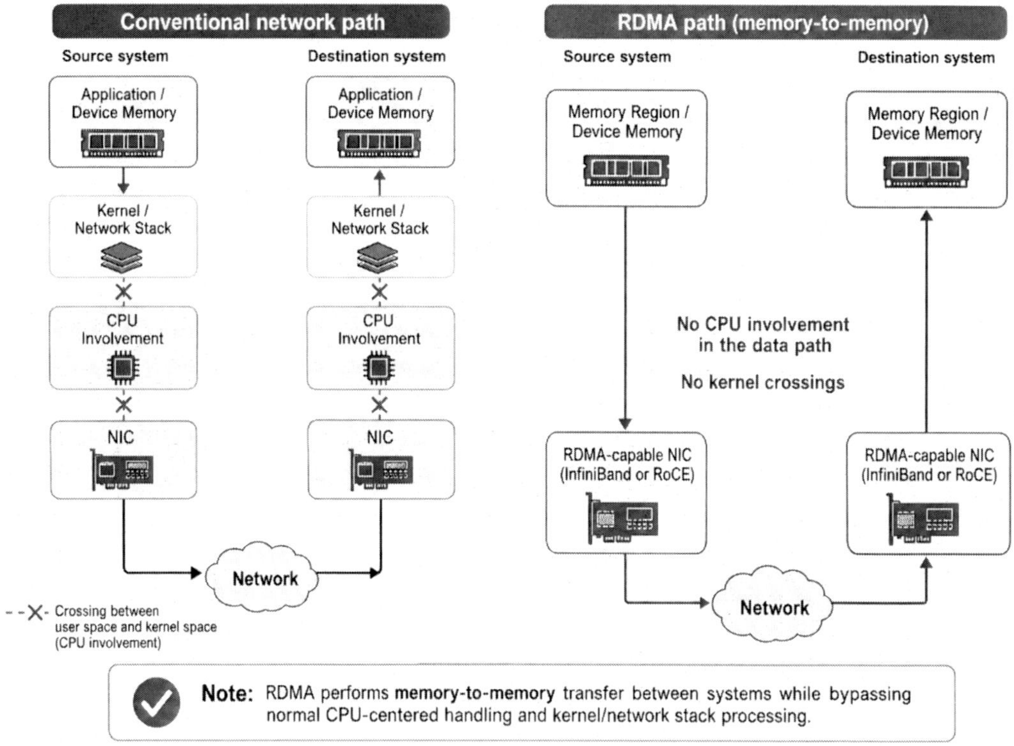

Figure 5.6: RDMA compared with a conventional network path

The above figure highlights where RDMA removes work from the conventional data path. In the traditional route, network traffic crosses the operating-system networking stack and involves CPU processing before reaching application memory on each endpoint. With RDMA, the participating memory regions are prepared in advance and RDMA-capable network adapters perform the bulk transfer directly between them. The CPU is still involved in setup and control, but it does not have to process every transferred data block through the normal network stack.

Avoiding repeated kernel transitions and CPU copies lowers latency, reduces jitter, and preserves host cycles. These properties are valuable in distributed training, where many devices exchange data at synchronization points, and in remote storage, where large datasets must be delivered consistently.

InfiniBand provides RDMA as a native capability. RDMA over Converged Ethernet, or RoCE, brings RDMA semantics to suitably configured Ethernet environments. The network must be engineered to manage congestion and packet behavior because the performance goal depends on predictable delivery.

RDMA is not limited to GPUs. It is a general direct-memory transport. GPUDirect technologies use the principle to create efficient paths specifically to and from NVIDIA GPU memory.

RDMA is the general mechanism: an RDMA-capable network transfers data directly between registered memory regions with minimal CPU involvement in the bulk data path. GPUDirect RDMA is the NVIDIA capability that allows a compatible peer device, commonly a network adapter, to access GPU memory directly rather than staging the data through host memory. GPUDirect Storage applies direct-memory access to the storage path, allowing supported local or remote storage to transfer data directly to or from GPU memory. Remote GDS configurations may themselves depend on RDMA-capable networking to preserve the direct path from the network adapter to GPU memory.

The storage-focused implementation is GPUDirect Storage.

How GPUDirect Storage changes the I/O path

GPUDirect Storage allows supported storage systems to transfer data directly into GPU memory through direct memory access. Local NVMe drives, remote NFS or parallel file systems, and RDMA-capable storage paths can participate when the hardware and software requirements are met. *Figure 5.7* separates two related GPUDirect use cases, showing how GPUDirect RDMA addresses network-oriented transfers while GPUDirect Storage addresses storage-to-GPU data movement.

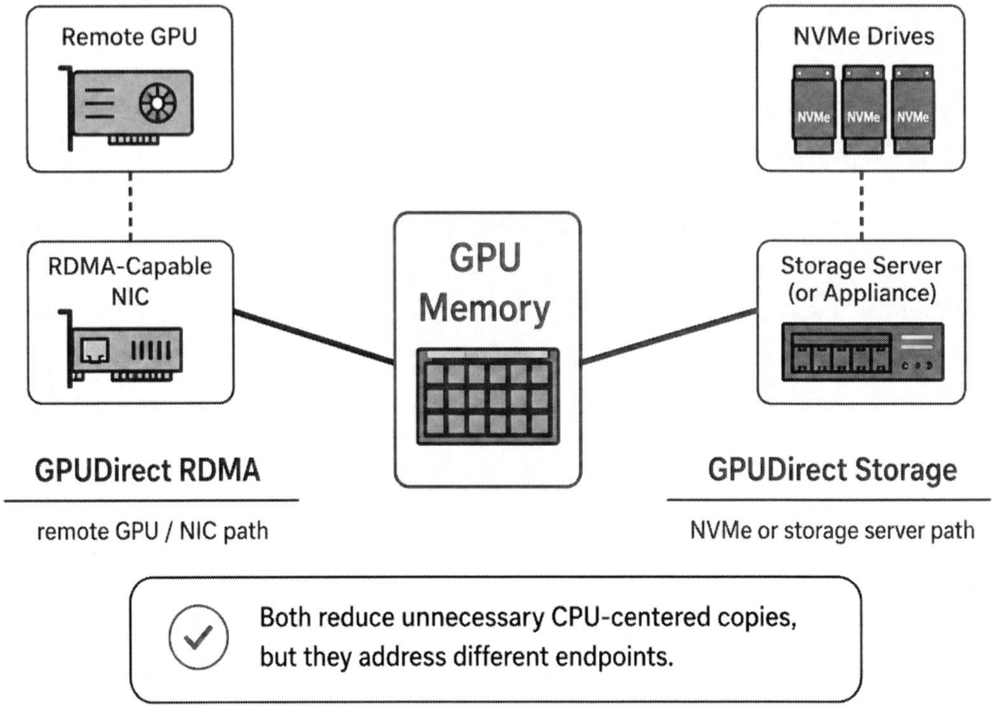

Figure 5.7: GPUDirect RDMA and GPUDirect Storage

Figure 5.7 distinguishes two GPUDirect paths by the device at the other end of the transfer. GPUDirect RDMA allows an RDMA-capable network or peer device to exchange data directly with GPU memory without staging the bulk data through host memory. GPUDirect Storage applies the same objective to storage, allowing supported local or remote storage paths to transfer data directly to or from GPU memory. Both reduce unnecessary CPU-centered staging, but they address different endpoints and should not be treated as interchangeable technologies.

The CPU initiates and coordinates the operation but does not need to copy the complete data through host memory. This reduces CPU utilization and memory traffic. The GPU receives data sooner and can maintain higher utilization, especially when large datasets are read repeatedly.

The cuFile API, the CUDA runtime, and NVIDIA DALI are software components associated with the path. cuFile provides interfaces for direct file I/O to GPU memory. DALI can accelerate loading and transformations. The exact stack depends on the application and storage environment.

BlueField DPUs can strengthen the architecture by offloading network and storage processing. A DPU can handle parts of the remote I/O, security, and data-plane path while the host CPU focuses on application control and the GPU focuses on AI computation.

The performance benefit appears only when the complete path is compatible, so implementation requires attention to prerequisites.

Compatibility and deployment requirements

GPUDirect Storage requires a supported NVIDIA GPU and a compatible end-to-end storage, driver, filesystem, and software configuration. Because support evolves across GPU and platform generations, deployment should be validated against the current GDS support documentation. The environment also needs compatible drivers, a suitable CUDA and cuFile software stack, supported storage devices or file systems, and a PCIe or network topology that can provide the direct path.

Using the cuFile API does not by itself guarantee that every transfer is using the optimized GPUDirect Storage path. When the required hardware, filesystem, driver, or topology conditions are not available, the software may use a compatibility path in which data is staged through host memory instead. Operators should therefore validate the effective data path and measure end-to-end performance rather than assuming that an application is using direct storage-to-GPU transfers simply because it uses cuFile.

Remote designs may require RDMA-capable network adapters and a fabric configured for the necessary throughput and latency. Local designs require NVMe and system topology that allow efficient peer or direct memory access. Security and access controls must authorize the transfer without exposing memory or storage inappropriately.

Using the cuFile API does not by itself guarantee that every transfer is using the optimized GDS path. The required storage, filesystem, driver, topology, and software conditions must be satisfied. In supported configurations, cuFile can also operate through a compatibility path when a direct GDS route is unavailable. Operators should therefore validate the effective I/O path and measure end-to-end performance rather than assuming that the presence of the API proves that host-memory staging has been eliminated.

Validation should measure end-to-end behavior rather than only device specifications. Storage bandwidth, file size, access pattern, data decoding, CPU use, GPU utilization, and network congestion all influence results. A direct path cannot compensate for a slow source or a workload that performs tiny, irregular reads inefficiently.

Operational monitoring should include both sides of the path. DCGM shows whether the GPU remains active and whether memory is constrained. Storage and network telemetry show whether data is delivered consistently. Application profiling reveals gaps between I/O and compute.

When these requirements are met, RDMA and GPUDirect technologies produce several important benefits.

Workloads that benefit most

Large-scale training benefits because datasets can be loaded at higher throughput and CPU resources are preserved. Multi-node training benefits because gradients, parameters, and data can move with lower latency. Streaming inference benefits because input can reach the GPU with fewer stages. Video analytics benefits because large frame streams can be decoded, transformed, and processed without a CPU-centered bottleneck.

The largest gains appear when data movement is already the limiting factor. A compute-bound model may not improve simply because GDS is enabled. The infrastructure team must confirm that the GPU is waiting on I/O and that the application can use the direct path.

These technologies shift the architecture from CPU-constrained movement toward GPU-optimized throughput. The CPU still orchestrates, but storage and network devices can communicate with GPU memory through a path designed for the rate of accelerated computation.

> **Tip**
>
> For exam scenarios, identify the unwanted middle stage. If the CPU and host memory are bottlenecks during storage-to-GPU transfer, GPUDirect Storage is the key concept. If the question concerns direct memory transfer across nodes with low CPU overhead, RDMA is the key concept. If the scenario asks for the network most closely associated with high-performance RDMA clusters, InfiniBand is the likely focus.

A practical diagnosis should begin with evidence rather than a technology choice. First confirm whether the GPU is actually underutilized over time. Next determine whether the workload is waiting on input, distributed synchronization, available device memory, or its own execution pattern. Correlate DCGM data with storage throughput and latency, network or collective-communication metrics, CPU activity, and application profiling. Change the suspected bottleneck one layer at a time and measure the workload again against the same baseline.

Figure 5.8 turns these recurring symptoms into a diagnostic workflow for investigating low GPU utilization before deciding which infrastructure layer requires attention.

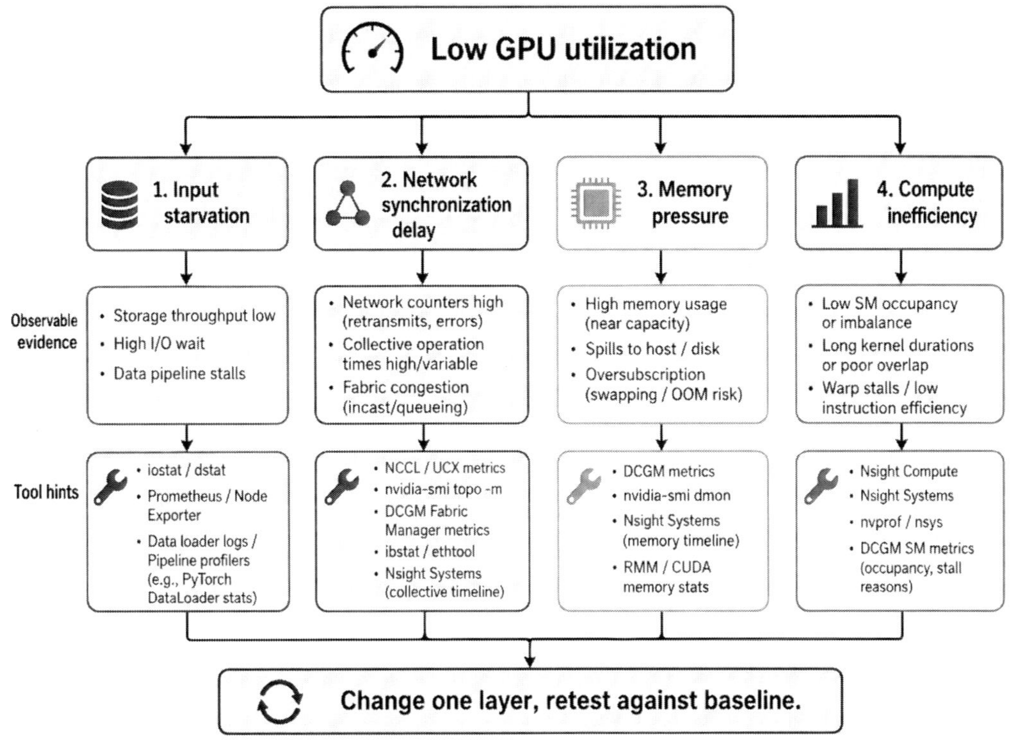

Figure 5.8: Bottleneck diagnosis flow for data and communication paths

Figure 5.8 reinforces the principle that low GPU utilization is a symptom rather than a diagnosis. Input starvation points toward the storage or data-loading pipeline, synchronization delays point toward the network and distributed communication path, memory pressure requires examination of device capacity and allocation, and inefficient GPU execution calls for application-level profiling. The correct response is to gather evidence at the relevant layers, change one suspected constraint at a time, and compare the result with the original baseline.

The chapter has now connected storage, fabric choice, RDMA, and GPUDirect into one high-throughput data path. The next chapter examines how the resulting infrastructure can be shared through vGPU and protected and accelerated through BlueField DPUs.

Summary

This chapter showed that GPU performance depends on data delivery. A traditional storage path routes data through the CPU and host memory, creating copies, latency, and CPU overhead. GPU-accelerated storage reduces those stages and helps the accelerator remain supplied with input.

You compared Ethernet and InfiniBand. Ethernet offers familiarity, compatibility, and flexibility for general-purpose, service, and less synchronization-sensitive workloads. InfiniBand is designed for low-latency, high-throughput clustered communication and is especially suited to distributed training and HPC. Hybrid designs can assign different traffic classes to different fabrics.

RDMA enables direct memory transfer with minimal CPU and kernel involvement, while GPUDirect Storage applies direct access to storage-to-GPU paths. cuFile, CUDA, DALI, NVMe, NVMe over Fabrics, RDMA-capable adapters, and BlueField DPUs can participate in the complete solution. The chapter goal was to identify data-path bottlenecks and connect them to the appropriate technology. You can now reason from idle GPUs, copy overhead, synchronization delay, or storage latency to the relevant infrastructure response.

The next chapter focuses on shared and programmable infrastructure through NVIDIA vGPU, the distinction between vGPU and MIG, and the CPU-GPU-DPU architecture enabled by BlueField and DOCA.

Chapter review questions

Choose the single best answer for each question. The answer key and explanations follow the complete set for this chapter.

1. In a traditional storage-to-GPU path, why can the CPU become a bottleneck?
    a. Data may pass through the kernel and system memory before being copied to GPU memory.
    b. The CPU always performs the GPU's matrix multiplication.
    c. Storage data cannot be represented in memory.
    d. The CPU controls the temperature of every storage device.
2. What is the primary objective of GPUDirect Storage?
    a. Partition a GPU into virtual machines
    b. Create a Kubernetes namespace
    c. Enable a more direct data path between compatible storage and GPU memory
    d. Track inference requests in MLflow
3. What does RDMA provide?
    a. Direct memory access across compatible network endpoints with reduced CPU/kernel involvement

   b. A method for creating MIG profiles
   c. A tool for editing Helm values
   d. A new deep-learning model format

4. Which fabric is most commonly selected for tightly coupled, latency-sensitive multi-node AI training?
   a. InfiniBand
   b. Bluetooth
   c. A low-speed home Wi-Fi network
   d. A serial console cable

5. What is RoCE?
   a. A TensorRT precision format
   b. A DPU programming language
   c. RDMA over Converged Ethernet
   d. A GPU model registry

6. A distributed training job spends substantial time synchronizing gradients between nodes. Which infrastructure area should be investigated first?
   a. The badge-sharing policy
   b. Inter-node network latency, bandwidth, congestion, and topology
   c. The number of VM desktop icons
   d. The document font used for the model card

7. A GPU is idle because high-resolution images cannot be loaded quickly enough. Which improvement most directly addresses the symptom?
   a. Increase sustained storage and data-pipeline throughput
   b. Disable batching
   c. Move the workload to a slower disk
   d. Add more model-registry stages

8. Which statement about GPUDirect Storage deployment is correct?
   a. It works on every system without configuration.
   b. It is used only for virtual desktops.
   c. It removes the need for a file system or application.
   d. It requires a compatible combination of GPU, storage or network path, drivers, and software.

9. When is Ethernet a reasonable choice for AI infrastructure?

   a. Never; Ethernet cannot carry AI traffic

   b. When compatibility, operational familiarity, and broad enterprise integration outweigh the need for the most specialized low-latency fabric

   c. Only for model training inside one GPU

   d. Only when no GPUs are installed

10. What is the best diagnostic principle for a suspected data-path bottleneck?

   a. Ignore the application's input pipeline.

   b. Replace every component at once.

   c. Measure storage, network, CPU, memory, and GPU behavior against a known baseline.

   d. Assume low GPU utilization always means a faulty GPU.

Answer key and explanations

Use the explanations to verify both the correct choice and the layer of the stack being tested.

1. A. Multiple copies and CPU/kernel involvement add latency and consume host resources before data reaches the accelerator.
2. C. GDS reduces unnecessary CPU-centered copies so data can reach GPU memory more efficiently.
3. A. RDMA reduces copy, interrupt, and context-switch overhead for high-throughput, low-latency data movement.
4. A. InfiniBand is designed for high-performance, low-latency communication and native RDMA, making it common in large AI/HPC clusters.
5. C. RoCE carries RDMA semantics over an appropriately designed Ethernet fabric.
6. B. Frequent synchronization makes distributed training highly sensitive to the network fabric and placement of participating GPUs.
7. A. The compute resource is input-starved. Improving the end-to-end data path is more relevant than adding GPU arithmetic capacity.
8. D. Direct-data technologies depend on end-to-end support. Compatibility and validation are part of the design.
9. B. Ethernet supports many inference, storage, and training environments, especially when designed with sufficient bandwidth and congestion controls.
10. C. End-to-end measurement identifies the constrained layer and avoids changing unrelated components.

6

Virtualized GPU Infrastructure and DPU Offload

> **Note**
>
> Modern AI platforms share expensive accelerators across tenants while moving networking, storage, and security work away from the host CPU.

AI infrastructure must serve more than one team, model, or application. **Virtualization** makes it possible to share physical GPU capacity across virtual machines and users, while maintaining control over resource allocation and isolation. At the same time, data processing units move networking, storage, and security work away from the host CPU so that the complete platform can scale more efficiently.

This chapter first explains NVIDIA vGPU and the software components that present portions of a physical GPU to virtualized workloads. It then compares vGPU with MIG, clarifying the different layers at which they operate and the use cases each one serves. The final section introduces DPUs, NVIDIA BlueField, and the DOCA SDK as a programmable infrastructure layer for data movement, offload, observability, and zero-trust security.

By the end of the chapter, you will be able to choose between vGPU and MIG for a multi-tenant scenario and explain how a DPU complements the CPU and GPU. The objective is to understand shared AI infrastructure as a combination of compute allocation and data-plane offload rather than as GPU hardware alone.

- NVIDIA vGPU and multi-tenancy
- Choosing between MIG and vGPU
- DPUs and NVIDIA BlueField

The chapter begins at the virtualization layer, where one physical GPU can be presented to several virtual machines or users as separately managed resources.

NVIDIA vGPU and multi-tenancy

GPU virtualization divides the capacity of a physical GPU into virtual GPU resources that can be assigned to virtual machines, users, or workloads. Each virtual GPU appears to the guest environment as an available accelerator with an assigned share of compute and memory. The goal is to improve utilization without requiring every tenant to receive a dedicated physical device.

Why virtualize GPU resources

A dedicated-GPU model provides simple isolation but often wastes capacity. A development user, classroom exercise, virtual desktop, or small inference model may use only part of the device. When the remaining capacity cannot be allocated elsewhere, the organization pays for idle hardware. *Figure 6.1* shows the basic vGPU architecture, separating the physical host components from the guest virtual machines that consume individually assigned virtual GPU resources.

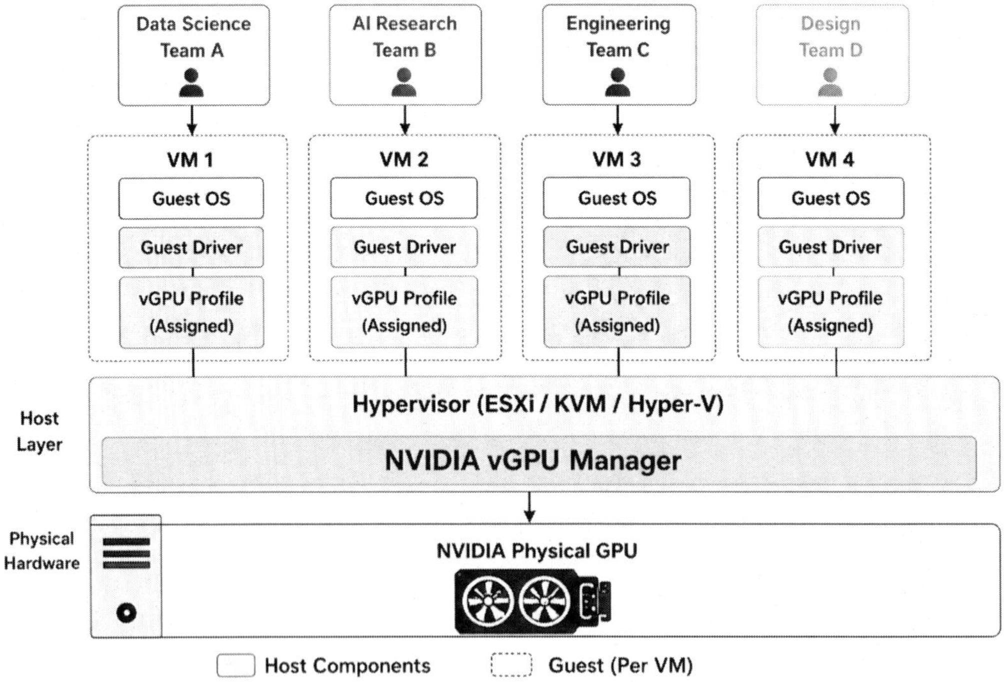

Figure 6.1: vGPU architecture multi tenancy

This figure above separates the architecture into host and guest layers. The physical GPU remains under the control of the hypervisor and NVIDIA vGPU Manager, while each virtual machine contains its own guest operating system, NVIDIA guest driver, and assigned vGPU resource. From the tenant's perspective, that assigned resource appears as a GPU available inside the VM; from the operator's perspective, the underlying physical device remains centrally managed and can support multiple tenants.

vGPU enables more granular allocation. Several virtual machines can share one physical GPU according to configured profiles and scheduling policies. Each tenant receives an environment that behaves like a dedicated accelerator from within the virtual machine, while the platform controls the physical resource underneath.

This model supports public and private cloud services, AI training labs, virtual desktop infrastructure, hosted development environments, and multi-team enterprise platforms. It can also simplify migration and lifecycle management because the GPU resource is attached to a virtual machine rather than tied directly to one bare-metal operating system installation.

Sharing introduces concerns about predictability, fairness, and monitoring. NVIDIA vGPU therefore includes more than a device driver; it is a software platform integrated with the hypervisor and management environment.

The NVIDIA vGPU software platform

NVIDIA vGPU is a platform that includes host and guest drivers, hypervisor integration, licensing services, scheduling controls, and telemetry. These components coordinate access to the physical GPU and expose the assigned virtual resource to each workload.

The vGPU Manager operates at the virtualization-host layer and coordinates the physical GPU resources made available to guest VMs. Inside each VM, the NVIDIA guest driver allows applications to use the assigned virtual GPU much as they would use an accelerator installed directly in the system. This host-versus-guest distinction is useful when troubleshooting: a problem affecting the physical GPU or vGPU Manager belongs to the virtualization host, while a guest-driver problem belongs inside the VM.

Major enterprise virtualization environments are supported, including platforms based on VMware vSphere, Citrix technologies, Red Hat virtualization, and KVM. The exact support matrix depends on the GPU, hypervisor, vGPU release, and guest operating system, so deployments should use a validated combination.

vGPU profiles define the amount of framebuffer memory and the class of capability made available to the virtual machine. Scheduling policies determine how time on the physical device is shared. Quality-of-service controls and telemetry help administrators enforce fair allocation and identify workloads that are consuming more than expected.

For time-sliced vGPUs, scheduling determines how GPU processing cycles are shared among the VMs using the same physical resource. NVIDIA vGPU supports scheduling policies including best effort, equal share, and fixed share on supported configurations. Best effort allows unused processing capacity to be consumed by other vGPUs, while equal-share and fixed-share approaches impose stronger limits on how processing time is distributed. Time-slice configuration also creates a trade-off: shorter slices can favor responsiveness, while longer slices can reduce switching overhead and favor throughput.

Figure 6.2 makes this profile-based allocation model more concrete by showing how portions of one physical GPU can be offered as conceptual service tiers for workloads with different resource requirements.

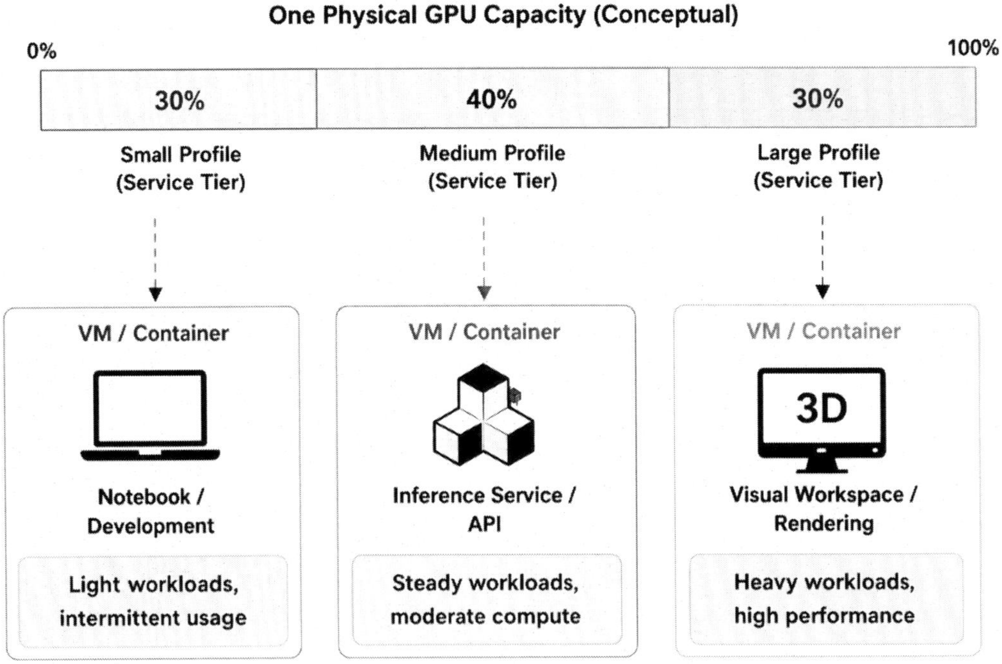

Figure 6.2: vGPU profiles create service tiers

Figure 6.2 illustrates the service-provider view of vGPU profiles. Instead of exposing one undifferentiated physical accelerator, the platform can offer differently sized resource tiers suited to lighter development work, steady inference services, or more demanding virtual workloads. The sizes shown are conceptual rather than official NVIDIA profile names; in a real deployment, administrators select profiles supported by the specific GPU, vGPU release, licensing model, and workload requirements.

The platform supports both compute-oriented and graphics-oriented use cases on suitable GPUs. This versatility is important in enterprises that run AI inference, virtual workstations, visualization, and virtual desktop workloads on the same physical infrastructure.

From the tenant perspective, the most important requirement is isolation: one user should not be able to interfere with another user's memory or workload. From the operator perspective, the additional requirements are policy, accounting, and lifecycle control.

Isolation, quotas, and service delivery

A multi-tenant platform must control who can access GPU capacity, how much each tenant receives, and what happens when demand exceeds supply. vGPU profiles and virtual machine assignments create the basic allocation boundary. Platform quotas can limit the number or size of GPU-enabled virtual machines a team may create.

Licensing is also part of the service boundary. NVIDIA vGPU software products require the appropriate licensing configuration for their supported feature set. A licensing problem can therefore appear as an operational problem even when the VM, guest driver, and physical GPU are otherwise functioning correctly. Infrastructure teams should treat license availability and connectivity as part of the validated vGPU platform rather than as an administrative detail added after deployment.

Telemetry supports usage reporting and chargeback. An internal cloud team may measure how long a virtual GPU is assigned, how much memory it uses, and whether the workload is active. This information can be used to reclaim idle assignments, plan capacity, or allocate cost to business units.

Quality-of-service controls improve predictability when several virtual GPUs share one device. The scheduling model should prevent one tenant from monopolizing the accelerator. The exact behavior depends on the selected vGPU mode and platform configuration, so testing must reflect the real workload mix.

Security also extends beyond GPU memory. The virtual machine boundary, hypervisor, driver stack, network, storage, and identity controls all contribute to tenant separation. vGPU is one layer in a broader multi-tenant architecture rather than a complete security solution by itself. *Figure 6.3* brings these controls together to show how profiles, quotas, licensing, placement, monitoring, and metering surround the actual delivery of vGPU resources to tenant virtual machines.

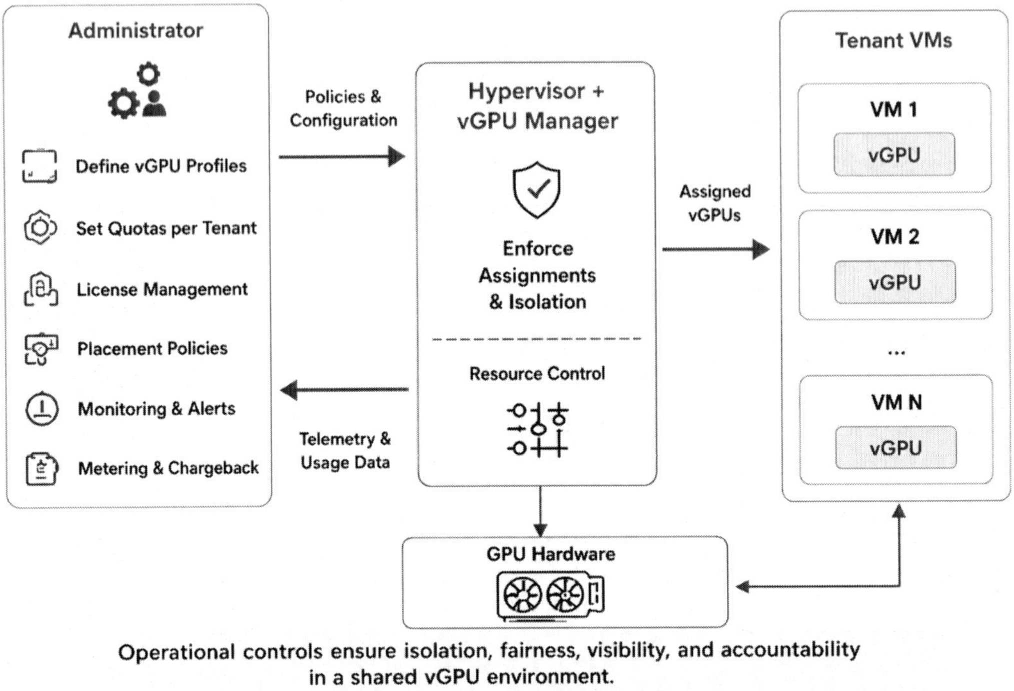

Figure 6.3: vGPU service delivery and operational controls

Figure 6.3 shows that operating a shared vGPU environment involves more than attaching a virtual accelerator to a VM. Administrators define the available profiles and quotas, control licensing and placement, and monitor resource consumption, while the hypervisor and vGPU software enforce the assignments presented to tenant VMs. Telemetry and usage information then return to the management layer for monitoring, capacity planning, and chargeback. The result is a managed GPU service rather than unmanaged time sharing of a physical device.

The technology is especially useful when the workload already lives in a virtual machine or requires graphics and desktop integration.

Common vGPU use cases

Virtual desktop infrastructure is a traditional vGPU use case. Engineers, designers, analysts, and developers can receive GPU-accelerated desktops without a workstation at every desk. The same infrastructure can support remote graphics, visualization, simulation, and AI-enabled applications.

AI development labs use vGPU to provide isolated virtual machines to students or teams. Each user receives a reproducible operating system and software environment with controlled accelerator access. The platform can reset, snapshot, or migrate the virtual machines according to enterprise practice.

Cloud and MLOps platforms can use vGPU for tenant-specific training or inference environments. A user requests a virtual machine with a defined GPU profile, and the platform enforces allocation and licensing. This is valuable when existing governance, backup, and access processes are built around virtual machines.

Workloads that need an entire physical GPU can still receive one. Virtualization is not an obligation to divide every device; it is a way to offer several resource shapes from the same infrastructure pool. The operator chooses between dedicated assignment and shared profiles according to performance and isolation requirements.

MIG solves a related sharing problem, but it does so through hardware partitioning rather than the hypervisor-centered model used by vGPU.

You have now seen how vGPU creates managed accelerator resources for virtual machines and enterprise tenants. The next section compares that software-defined approach with MIG hardware partitioning so that the correct sharing model can be selected.

Choosing between MIG and vGPU

MIG and vGPU both improve GPU utilization by allowing multiple workloads to use one physical device, but they operate at different layers. Confusing them can lead to an unsuitable design. MIG partitions the GPU hardware into isolated instances. vGPU virtualizes GPU access through a hypervisor and software platform.

Hardware partitioning with MIG

MIG creates predefined hardware instances on supported GPUs such as the A100 and H100. Each instance receives dedicated compute slices, memory, cache, and related resources. A container, process, or supported virtualized workload can be assigned to that instance as if it were a smaller GPU.

The strength of MIG is predictable hardware isolation. One instance cannot simply consume the memory or compute assigned to another. This makes MIG appropriate for containerized inference, bare-metal multi-user environments, and cloud-native services that need guaranteed resource boundaries.

MIG profiles are constrained by the physical architecture. Administrators select from supported shapes rather than defining an arbitrary percentage. Reconfiguration also needs operational planning because changing the instance layout affects the resources available on the device.

The design is closely connected to Kubernetes resource scheduling and DCGM monitoring. A cluster can advertise a MIG profile, schedule a pod to it, and track the instance separately.

vGPU emphasizes virtual machines and software-defined allocation at the hypervisor layer.

Hypervisor-based sharing with vGPU

vGPU allows several virtual machines to share a physical GPU through the NVIDIA vGPU software stack and the hypervisor. Each VM loads a guest driver and receives a virtual GPU profile. The host components schedule access and enforce the configured resource model.

This approach fits organizations that already use virtualization as the standard delivery platform. Identity, network policy, storage, templates, lifecycle management, and user access can remain aligned with the virtual machine environment. vGPU also serves graphics and VDI workloads that are not the primary target of MIG-only container sharing.

The isolation and performance model depends on the selected vGPU configuration. It is software-defined and connected to the hypervisor, whereas MIG creates separate hardware resource partitions. This difference is the central concept for exam questions that ask which technology operates at which layer.

The two approaches can appear in the same broader environment. A platform may use vGPU for virtual desktops and tenant VMs while using MIG-backed Kubernetes nodes for containerized inference services.

A direct comparison makes the selection criteria clearer.

Criterion	MIG	vGPU
Partitioning layer	Hardware-level partitioning on supported GPUs	Software and hypervisor-based GPU virtualization
Primary resource boundary	Dedicated GPU compute slices, memory, cache, and related hardware resources	Virtual GPU profile assigned to a guest VM or virtualized workload
Common environment	Bare metal, containers, Kubernetes, and isolated inference services	Virtual machines, VDI, enterprise virtualization, and hosted tenant environments
Strength	Strong, predictable hardware isolation and right-sized accelerator instances	Integration with VM lifecycle, graphics, enterprise controls, and flexible virtual service delivery

Criterion	MIG	vGPU
Management focus	MIG profiles, device configuration, DCGM, and scheduler resource types	Hypervisor integration, vGPU drivers, licensing, profiles, QoS, and VM management
Typical exam signal	Several isolated container workloads share an A100 or H100	Several virtual machines or desktops require shared GPU acceleration

Table 6.1: Comparison of MIG and vGPU resource-sharing models

Figure 6.4 places MIG and vGPU side by side so that the difference between hardware partitioning and hypervisor-based virtual GPU delivery can be seen at the infrastructure layer where each operates.

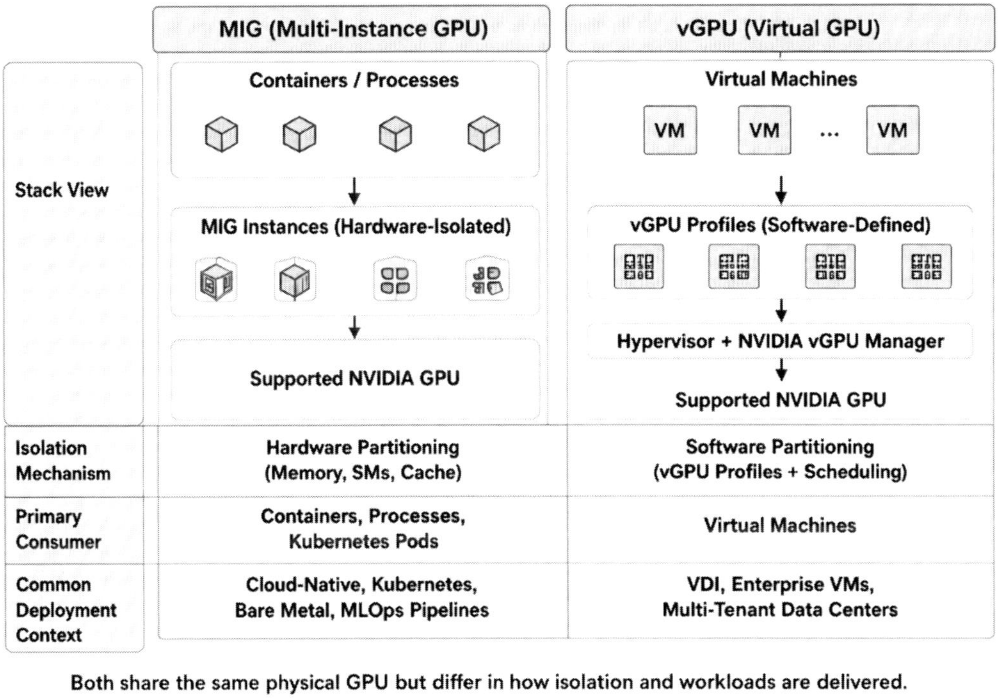

Figure 6.4: MIG vs GPU: Architectural comparison

Figure 6.4 highlights the primary architectural distinction. MIG begins by partitioning a supported GPU into hardware-isolated instances, which can then be consumed by processes, containers, or other supported workloads. vGPU begins at the virtualization layer, where the hypervisor and NVIDIA vGPU software present GPU resources to virtual machines.

> **Tip**
>
> For exam reasoning, the useful question is therefore whether the requirement is fundamentally about hardware partitioning or about delivering accelerator resources through a VM and hypervisor environment.

The distinction between MIG and vGPU describes two different layers, but the technologies are not always mutually exclusive. On supported GPUs and virtualization platforms, NVIDIA vGPU can be backed by a MIG instance. In that design, MIG first supplies the hardware-isolated GPU partition, while the vGPU software and hypervisor present accelerator access from that partition to a virtual machine. For exam reasoning, first identify which layer the question is testing: MIG describes the hardware partition, whereas vGPU describes how GPU capacity is delivered through the virtualization stack.

The decision should begin with the workload boundary. If the unit of delivery is a Kubernetes pod or bare-metal service that needs a guaranteed hardware slice, MIG is a strong fit. If the unit of delivery is a virtual machine that must integrate with a hypervisor and enterprise VDI or cloud operations, vGPU is the stronger fit.

Performance requirements may still justify a dedicated physical GPU. Sharing is beneficial only when workloads can coexist without violating latency, throughput, or memory requirements.

Scenario-based selection

Consider a platform hosting seven small inference microservices on one supported data center GPU. Each service needs predictable compute and memory but does not need a virtual machine. MIG aligns with this requirement because the device can be divided into hardware-isolated instances and scheduled through Kubernetes.

Now consider a university lab that gives each student a separate virtual machine with a desktop, development tools, and GPU access. vGPU aligns with the virtual machine delivery model and allows the institution to manage images, access, and resource profiles through its virtualization platform.

A cloud provider may need both. It can offer vGPU-backed VM instance types to customers and operate MIG-enabled container services internally. The technologies solve different layers of the sharing problem, so a mixed design is not contradictory.

Tip

An exam question may include words such as hypervisor, VM, VDI, or virtual workstation; these point toward vGPU. Words such as hardware isolation, GPU slice, MIG profile, or Kubernetes pod point toward MIG. The workload and management boundary are more reliable clues than the general phrase GPU sharing.

Once compute capacity has been allocated, the infrastructure still needs to move data, enforce security, and process network and storage traffic. DPUs address those data-plane responsibilities. *Figure 6.5* turns these distinctions into a practical selection process by starting with the workload boundary and then considering isolation, sharing, compatibility, licensing, and performance requirements.

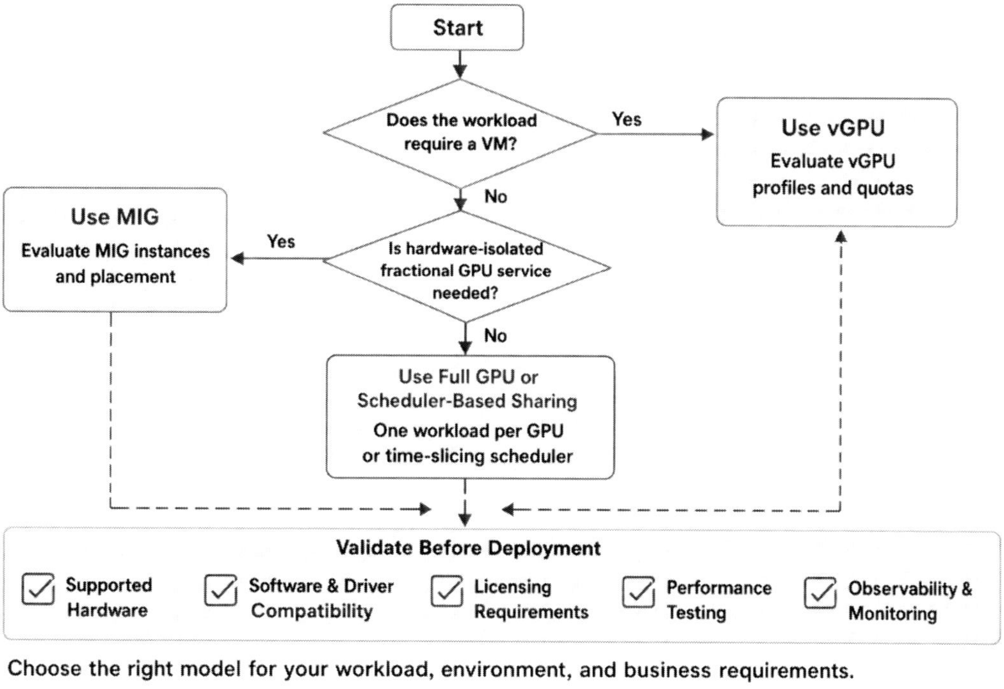

Figure 6.5: Choosing between Full GOPU, MIG, and vGPU

Figure 6.5 shows that the first decision is the delivery model rather than the GPU product name. A workload that requires a VM naturally directs attention toward vGPU, while a non-VM workload that needs hardware-isolated fractional GPU capacity points toward MIG on supported hardware. If neither condition applies, a full GPU or another supported sharing mechanism may be appropriate. Whichever path is selected, the final design still requires validation of hardware support, software and driver compatibility, licensing, performance, and observability.

The difference between MIG and vGPU is now clear: one partitions hardware, while the other virtualizes accelerator access through the hypervisor. The final section introduces the DPU as the third processor in the accelerated data center.

DPUs and NVIDIA BlueField

A data processing unit, or DPU, is a programmable processor designed for infrastructure data-plane work. It handles operations such as packet processing, storage I/O, encryption, compression, virtualization, and telemetry. By offloading these functions from the host CPU, a DPU preserves CPU resources for application control and helps keep GPUs focused on AI computation.

The DPU as an infrastructure processor

A CPU is optimized for general-purpose logic and orchestration. A GPU is optimized for highly parallel computation. A DPU is optimized for moving, transforming, securing, and observing data as it enters and leaves a system. This specialization creates a three-processor architecture in modern accelerated data centers.

The terms control plane and data plane help explain this separation. The control plane makes decisions about how the system should operate—for example, orchestration, configuration, policy, and scheduling. The data plane performs the high-volume work required to carry out those decisions, such as moving packets, transferring storage data, applying encryption, and enforcing traffic rules. A DPU is designed primarily to accelerate and isolate this data-plane work while the CPU continues to coordinate the broader system.

Figure 6.6 places the DPU alongside the CPU and GPU to show how control, AI computation, and infrastructure data-plane processing can be divided across specialized processors within the same server.

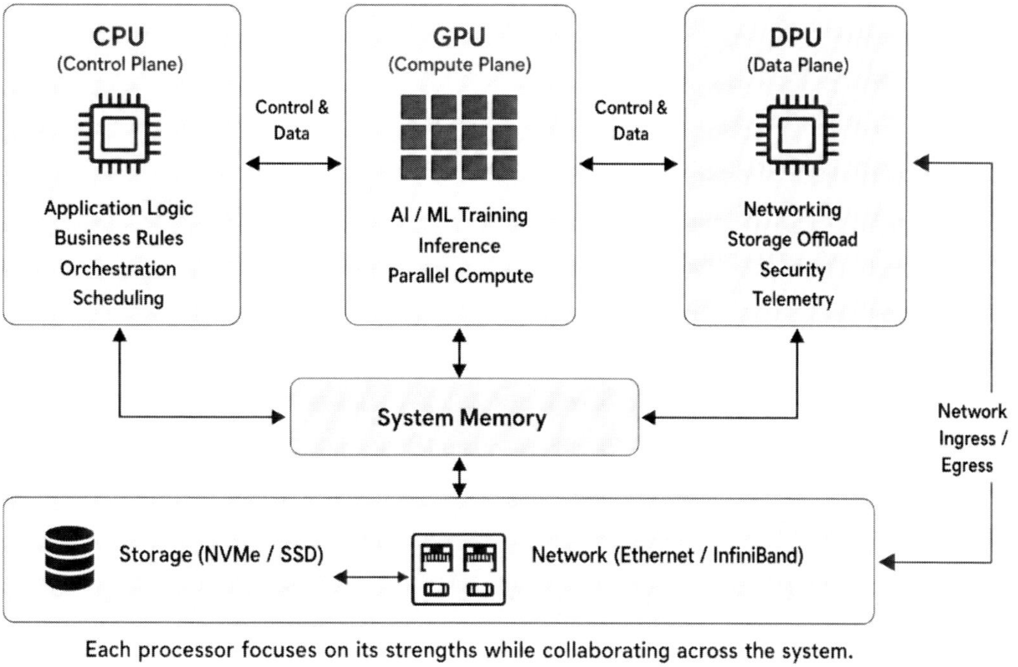

Figure 6.6: CPU, GPU, and DPU in the server data path

Figure 6.6 shows the three processors performing complementary roles across one system. The CPU handles application logic, orchestration, and other control-oriented work; the GPU handles the parallel computation required for training and inference; and the DPU sits close to the network and storage data path, where it can offload infrastructure processing such as networking, security, storage services, and telemetry. System memory, storage, and networking connect these responsibilities, so useful work frequently crosses more than one processor class.

Networking tasks can include routing, switching, firewall enforcement, network address translation, load balancing, and packet inspection. Storage tasks can include NVMe access, data replication, compression, and remote I/O processing. Security tasks can include encryption, access control, and policy enforcement.

When the CPU performs all these functions, infrastructure traffic competes with the application for cores, memory bandwidth, and interrupts. A DPU moves selected tasks to dedicated hardware and embedded processing resources. The host sees a service rather than performing every packet and storage operation itself.

This offload can improve consistency as well as throughput. Infrastructure functions continue to run even when the host is heavily loaded. The DPU can also create a security boundary that is controlled independently of the tenant operating system.

NVIDIA BlueField is the DPU platform discussed in this book.

BlueField architecture and capabilities

A BlueField DPU combines high-speed network interfaces, Arm CPU cores, memory, and hardware accelerators for functions such as encryption, compression, and packet processing. It can support Ethernet and InfiniBand connectivity, allowing the same platform family to participate in different AI data center fabrics. *Figure 6.7* looks inside a BlueField DPU conceptually, showing how embedded processing, memory, high-speed networking, and acceleration resources support its infrastructure role.

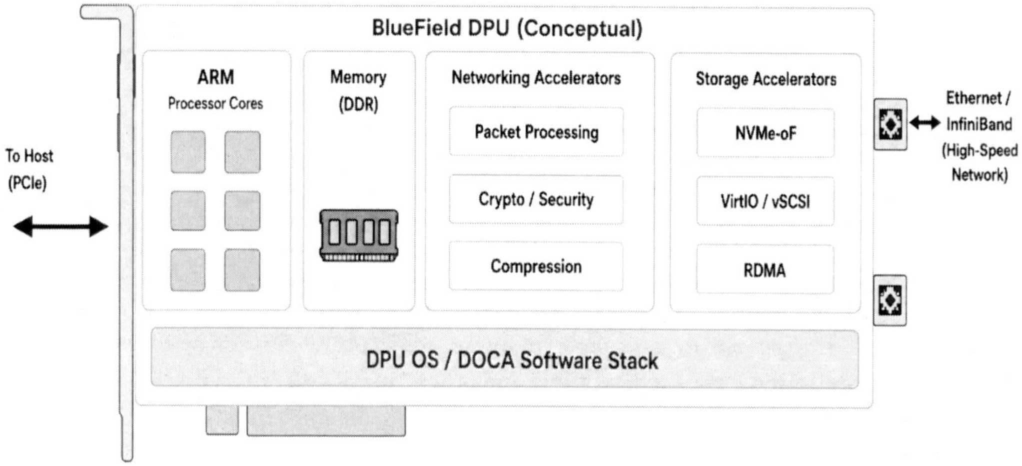

Figure 6.7: BlueField DPU architecture (conceptual)

Figure 6.7 shows why BlueField is more than a conventional network interface. Its embedded Arm processing resources can run infrastructure software, while high-speed network interfaces and hardware acceleration blocks support networking, storage, security, and data-movement functions. The host connects to the DPU through PCIe, while the external interfaces connect the server to the Ethernet or InfiniBand fabric supported by the particular platform. This combination allows selected infrastructure services to execute close to the data path instead of consuming host CPU resources.

When operating in DPU mode, BlueField activates its embedded Arm processing environment and can host infrastructure services separately from the main server CPU. This allows selected networking, storage, security, and management functions to remain under DPU control rather than relying entirely on software running on the host. This independence allows networking, storage, security, and telemetry functions to continue at the DPU layer even when the host workload changes.

BlueField can be deployed in accelerated servers and data center platforms, as well as in cloud-native, edge, and multi-tenant infrastructure. In these environments, the DPU is valuable when networking, storage, security, or telemetry functions need to remain fast, isolated, and close to the data path. In each case, the DPU handles work that must be fast, isolated, and close to the network or storage path.

A high-speed interface alone would make BlueField a smart adapter. Its programmable environment turns it into an infrastructure platform. The DOCA SDK exposes that environment to developers and operators.

Programming the data plane with DOCA

NVIDIA DOCA is the software framework for developing and operating accelerated services on BlueField and related NVIDIA networking platforms. It includes SDK libraries and APIs together with drivers, tools, and supporting software for networking, storage, security, telemetry, and infrastructure acceleration.

With DOCA, a team can implement functions such as deep observability, microsegmentation, encryption, packet filtering, and data-path control at the DPU layer. The DPU becomes programmable in the same general sense that CUDA makes the GPU programmable, although the workloads and APIs are different.

This programmability supports software-defined infrastructure. Instead of relying only on fixed adapter behavior, the organization can deploy and update infrastructure services according to policy. A security agent can inspect traffic at the node boundary. A telemetry service can report network behavior. A storage service can accelerate or control remote access.

The development model must be governed carefully. Code running on the DPU can affect critical network and storage paths, so version control, testing, security review, and staged deployment are essential. The value of programmability comes with operational responsibility.

The most visible benefits appear in offload, isolation, and zero-trust architecture.

Offloading networking, storage, and security

Network offload allows routing, firewall rules, load balancing, and other packet operations to be processed without consuming host CPU cycles for every packet. Storage offload can accelerate NVMe access, compression, replication, and remote data movement. Security offload can apply encryption and access policy close to the point where traffic enters the server.

This placement is valuable in a multi-tenant system. A tenant operating system should not be able to disable the infrastructure security controls that separate it from other tenants. When the policy is enforced by the DPU, the boundary remains outside the host workload.

BlueField can also collect telemetry about network traffic, application usage, and infrastructure behavior. Because the DPU observes the data path directly, it can provide visibility that complements GPU metrics from DCGM and host metrics from the operating system.

The offload does not mean the CPU is idle or unimportant. The CPU continues to run the operating system, scheduler agents, application logic, and control plane. The DPU reduces the volume of infrastructure work that competes with those tasks. The GPU remains dedicated to model computation.

The following table summarizes the three-processor model.

Processor	Primary domain	Representative work
CPU	Control plane and general-purpose application processing	Operating system, orchestration, scheduling, application logic, and sequential tasks
GPU	Parallel AI and accelerated computation	Training, tensor operations, model inference, simulation, and analytics
DPU	Infrastructure data plane and offload	Networking, storage I/O, encryption, compression, firewalling, telemetry, and isolation

Table 6.2: Complementary roles of the CPU, GPU, and DPU in accelerated infrastructure

When each processor is used for its intended domain, the platform can deliver more predictable application performance and stronger infrastructure separation.

BlueField in secure, multi-tenant AI infrastructure

BlueField complements MIG and vGPU. MIG isolates portions of GPU hardware. vGPU separates accelerator access through the hypervisor. BlueField can enforce network, storage, and security policy around those tenants. Together, the technologies address different layers of the shared platform.

The DPU also supports GPUDirect and accelerated I/O paths introduced in Chapter 5. It can participate in moving data efficiently between storage, the network, and GPU memory while applying security and telemetry. This combination helps reduce latency and CPU overhead in real-time inference and large data pipelines.

Zero-trust infrastructure assumes that no workload should be trusted simply because it runs inside the data center. Policy should be enforced at multiple boundaries, and access should be explicit. A DPU can provide a node-level enforcement point that remains separate from the tenant OS, supporting microsegmentation and continuous observation.

Microsegmentation applies this principle by dividing the infrastructure into smaller security zones and controlling which workloads or services may communicate across those boundaries. Enforcing such policy at the DPU layer can keep the control outside the tenant operating system, reducing the ability of a compromised or misconfigured host workload to bypass the infrastructure boundary.

Composable infrastructure is another concept associated with DPUs. Compute, storage, and networking resources can be assigned and connected dynamically rather than fixed permanently to one workload. The DPU helps create and secure those data paths as resources are disaggregated or reallocated.

The important idea is disaggregation. Instead of assuming that every workload permanently owns the compute, storage, and network devices installed in one server, a composable platform can expose selected resources as services and connect them to workloads according to current demand. The DPU can help establish, accelerate, secure, and observe those dynamically created data paths.

Tip

For exam scenarios, look for infrastructure offload, network and storage acceleration, zero-trust enforcement, microsegmentation, or programmable data-plane services. These signals point to a DPU, BlueField, and DOCA rather than to a GPU feature alone.

Figure 6.8 brings these capabilities into a multi-tenant environment, showing how BlueField and DOCA can place networking, storage, security, and telemetry services at a boundary outside the tenant workloads themselves.

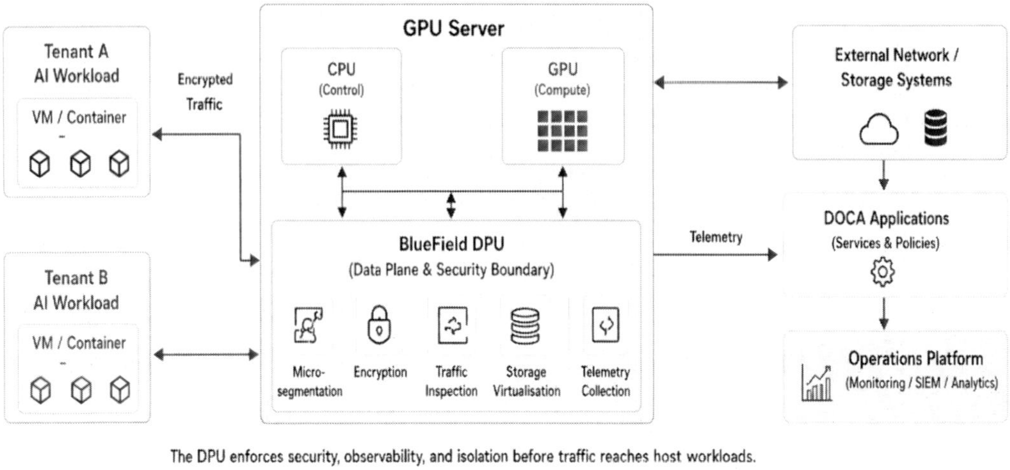

Figure 6.8: BlueField + DOCA for zero-trust, multi-tenant AI infrastructure

Figure 6.8 illustrates how the DPU can become an infrastructure boundary around tenant workloads. Traffic entering or leaving the server can pass through services that apply segmentation, encryption, inspection, storage controls, and telemetry before relying on the tenant operating system to enforce those policies. DOCA-based applications provide the programmable software layer for these services, while telemetry can be exported to an operations platform for monitoring and analysis. The design therefore complements GPU sharing by protecting and observing the network and storage paths surrounding the workload.

The chapter has now connected virtual GPU sharing with programmable infrastructure offload. The CPU, GPU, and DPU can be treated as complementary pillars that control applications, accelerate AI, and operate the data plane.

Summary

This chapter examined two parts of shared AI infrastructure. NVIDIA vGPU virtualizes physical GPU capacity through a hypervisor and software platform so that virtual machines, virtual desktops, and tenant environments can receive managed accelerator profiles. The platform includes drivers, hypervisor integration, licensing, scheduling controls, and telemetry.

MIG and vGPU both improve utilization, but they solve the problem at different layers. MIG creates hardware-isolated instances with dedicated compute and memory on supported GPUs. vGPU presents virtual accelerator resources to guest environments through the hypervisor. The chapter objective was to choose between them according to the workload boundary, and you can now distinguish a container-oriented hardware slice from a VM-oriented virtual GPU.

The chapter also introduced the DPU as a third processor alongside the CPU and GPU. NVIDIA BlueField combines Arm cores, high-speed networking, memory, and accelerators for infrastructure work. The DOCA SDK makes the data plane programmable, enabling networking, storage, security, observability, and zero-trust services to run at the DPU layer. Offload preserves host resources and strengthens tenant separation while supporting accelerated data movement.

The next chapter follows AI projects from development and training through deployment and monitoring, introducing the MLOps lifecycle and tools such as Airflow, MLflow, and Kubeflow.

Chapter review questions

Choose the single best answer for each question. The answer key and explanations follow the complete set for this chapter.

1. What is NVIDIA vGPU designed to provide?
    a. A. Hardware-only partitioning for bare-metal processes without a hypervisor
    b. B. GPU resources assigned to virtual machines through a supported virtualization stack
    c. C. A time-series database for GPU metrics
    d. D. Direct model export to ONNX
2. Where does the NVIDIA vGPU Manager operate?
    a. Inside the InfiniBand cable
    b. In the MLflow experiment database
    c. In the virtualization host or hypervisor layer
    d. Inside an ONNX model file
3. Which statement best distinguishes MIG from vGPU?
    a. MIG uses hardware partitioning on supported GPUs; vGPU provides GPU resources through a hypervisor to VMs.
    b. They are identical names for the same implementation.
    c. MIG is a network protocol; vGPU is a storage protocol.
    d. MIG tracks experiments; vGPU serves models.
4. What is the primary role of a DPU in an AI server?
    a. Offload infrastructure work such as networking, storage, security, and telemetry
    b. Provide a desktop display connector

   c. Replace every GPU matrix operation
   d. Train only natural-language models

5. Which component combination best describes NVIDIA BlueField?
   a. ARM processor cores, a high-performance NIC, and hardware accelerators
   b. A GPU model format and registry
   c. A CPU compiler with no network interface
   d. Only a passive Ethernet cable
6. What is DOCA?
   a. A hypervisor license file
   b. A replacement for CUDA on GPUs
   c. A distributed training algorithm
   d. The software framework and SDK for building applications and services that use BlueField DPUs
7. Why is a DPU useful in a zero-trust architecture?
   a. It can enforce and observe network and security policy at the infrastructure boundary, separately from the host workload.
   b. It prevents all telemetry collection.
   c. It allows every tenant unrestricted access.
   d. It removes encryption from the data path.
8. Which task is a strong candidate for DPU offload?
   a. Encryption, packet inspection, storage virtualization, or telemetry processing
   b. Model experiment approval in MLflow
   c. Writing an Airflow DAG
   d. Neural-network weight optimization inside TensorRT
9. A university needs isolated GPU-enabled virtual machines for many students. Which technology is the most direct fit?
   a. vGPU on a supported hypervisor stack
   b. cuBLAS only

   c. NVSwitch only
   d. GPUDirect Storage only

10. A GPU server is losing substantial CPU capacity to packet processing and encryption. What is the most relevant architectural response?
    a. Increase only the number of flashcards
    b. Evaluate BlueField DPU offload
    c. Disable network security controls
    d. Convert the model to a different natural language

Answer key and explanations

Use the explanations to verify both the correct choice and the layer of the stack being tested.

1. B. vGPU integrates physical GPU resources with a hypervisor so multiple VMs can receive defined GPU service profiles.
2. C. The vGPU Manager is a host-side component that coordinates physical GPU resources for guest VMs.
3. A. Both support sharing, but they operate at different layers and serve different deployment models.
4. A. A DPU handles data-centric infrastructure functions so CPU and GPU resources can focus on application logic and AI computation.
5. A. BlueField combines programmable processing, network connectivity, and specialized accelerators in a DPU platform.
6. D. DOCA provides APIs, libraries, runtimes, and development tools for DPU-accelerated infrastructure functions.
7. A. Policy and inspection close to the network boundary improve isolation and reduce reliance on the potentially compromised host.
8. A. These are infrastructure data-path functions aligned with the DPU's purpose.
9. A. The requirement explicitly centers on VMs, making vGPU the relevant sharing model.
10. B. A DPU can move infrastructure processing away from host CPU cores while preserving policy and observability.

Part 3

Production AI Platforms and Exam Readiness

The third part of this book brings the infrastructure components together into the workflows and platforms used to operate AI in production. You will follow a model from development and training through deployment and monitoring, learn how Airflow, MLflow, Kubeflow, ONNX, TensorRT, and Triton support that lifecycle, and then examine how NGC, Kubernetes, the GPU Operator, and NVIDIA monitoring and troubleshooting tools turn individual workloads into an operable platform.

The part concludes by shifting from platform operation to certification readiness. You will learn how to recognize the technology layer being tested in an NCA-AIIO scenario, eliminate plausible but incorrect answers, manage your exam time, and use the certification as a foundation for further hands-on development.

This part contains the following chapters:

7

Operating the AI Lifecycle with MLOps and Inference

> **Note**
>
> Production AI is a continuous operating cycle in which experiments become trained artifacts, deployed services, monitored systems, and new development work.

An AI model becomes useful only when a complete operating path surrounds it. The model must be developed, trained, packaged, deployed, observed, and improved as conditions change. Each stage places a different demand on infrastructure: experimentation favors fast access to flexible environments, training favors scalable GPU compute, deployment favors predictable latency and availability, and monitoring favors reliable telemetry and feedback loops.

This chapter follows that path in the order an AI project normally encounters it. It begins with the four-stage lifecycle of development, training, deployment, and monitoring. It then introduces MLOps as the discipline that makes the lifecycle repeatable, using Airflow for workflow orchestration, MLflow for experiment and model management, and Kubeflow for Kubernetes-based machine learning pipelines. The final section turns to production inference through NVIDIA Triton Inference Server, ONNX, and TensorRT.

By the end of the chapter, you will be able to map each lifecycle stage to its infrastructure needs, select the appropriate MLOps tool for a given operational problem, and explain how a trained model is converted into a scalable inference service. The objective is to see production AI as one connected system rather than as a collection of unrelated development and operations tools.

- Moving an AI project from development to monitoring

- Building reproducible workflows with Airflow, MLflow, and Kubeflow
- Serving and optimizing models with Triton, ONNX, and TensorRT

The lifecycle provides the organizing model for the chapter, so the first step is to follow an AI project from its earliest prototype to the feedback that starts the next iteration.

Moving an AI project from development to monitoring

The AI lifecycle comprises four connected stages: development, training, deployment, and monitoring. The sequence is useful because it clarifies the changing purpose of infrastructure. It should not, however, be read as a one-way production line. Models are revised, data changes, performance targets move, and monitoring frequently sends the team back to development or training.

The following table establishes the operating focus of each stage before the chapter examines the stages in more detail.

Lifecycle stage	**Primary objective**	**Typical infrastructure emphasis**	**Representative output**
Development	Turn an idea into a working prototype	Interactive notebooks or IDEs, local or hosted GPUs, small datasets, version control	A script or notebook that defines an initial model pipeline
Training	Learn model parameters from production-scale data	Multi-GPU systems, distributed compute, containers, orchestration, experiment tracking	A trained model artifact, checkpoints, metrics, and logs
Deployment	Make the model available to applications	Inference servers, containers, APIs, optimization, load balancing, and high availability	A versioned real-time or batch inference service

Lifecycle stage	Primary objective	Typical infrastructure emphasis	Representative output
Monitoring	Keep the service reliable and useful over time	Metrics, logs, dashboards, alerts, drift detection, and retraining triggers	Operational evidence and feedback for the next iteration

Table 7.1: Lifecycle stages, infrastructure priorities, and outputs of a production AI project

Figure 7.1 makes this iterative relationship explicit by showing development, training, deployment, and monitoring as a continuous lifecycle rather than a one-way sequence.

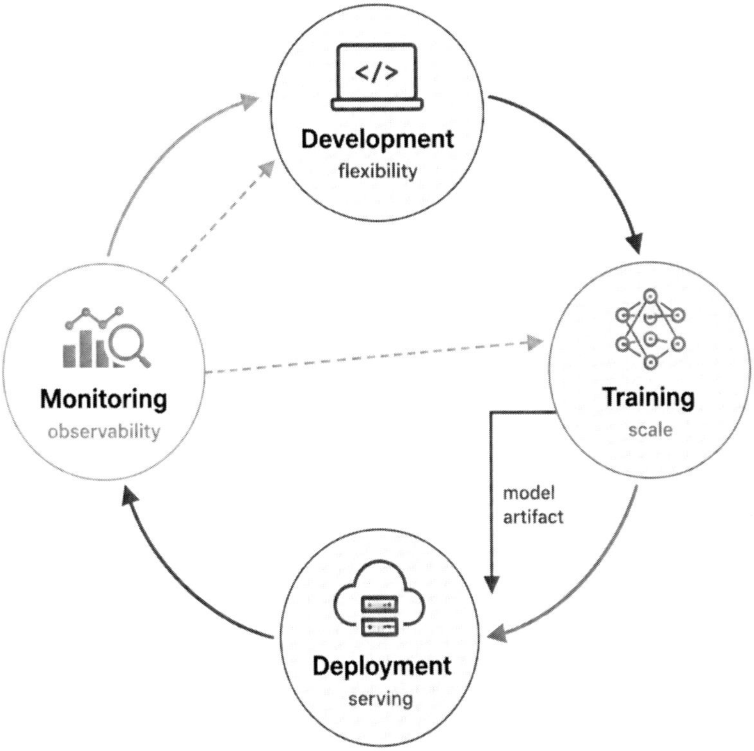

Figure 7.1: The AI lifecycle as an iterative development-to-monitoring feedback loop

Figure 7.1 shows the four lifecycle stages as connected activities with different infrastructure priorities. Development emphasizes flexibility, training emphasizes scale, deployment emphasizes serving, and monitoring emphasizes observability. The feedback paths from monitoring to development and training show how production evidence can trigger a new experiment or retraining cycle, while the trained model artifact moves forward into deployment.

With the four stages positioned, the next task is to understand why the cycle must remain iterative rather than rigidly linear.

The lifecycle as an iterative operating model

Development, training, deployment, and monitoring are often drawn in a straight line because the order is easy to remember. In practice, the lifecycle behaves as a loop. A monitoring alert may reveal that input data has changed. A deployment test may show that a model is accurate but too slow. A training run may expose a data-quality problem that requires another development pass. Each result can redirect the project to an earlier stage.

This iterative behavior changes the infrastructure requirement. Teams need environments that can reproduce an earlier experiment, preserve model and data versions, and promote a known artifact into production. They also need a traceable relationship among code, configuration, training data, metrics, and deployed versions. Without that relationship, a team may know that a model is failing but not be able to recreate the conditions that produced it.

The lifecycle is therefore both technical and collaborative. Data scientists need fast experimentation, platform teams need controlled environments, and operations teams need stable services. MLOps connects those interests by turning handoffs into managed workflows. Before examining those workflows, the chapter follows the infrastructure needs of each stage, beginning with development.

Development: Fast and controlled experimentation

During development, data scientists and machine learning engineers explore ideas, prepare data, choose model structures, and tune early parameters. Jupyter Notebooks and integrated development environments are common because they shorten the distance between a hypothesis and a result. Frameworks such as PyTorch and TensorFlow provide the model-building environment, while a local GPU, Google Colab session, or cloud GPU environment using suitable NVIDIA software assets can supply acceleration for prototypes.

The development stage values flexibility more than maximum throughput. Small datasets and short runs allow a team to reject weak ideas quickly. The environment should be easy to reset, modify, and share. A large distributed cluster may be unnecessary at this point because the objective is not yet to complete the final training run. It is to produce a working pipeline that proves the model and data can be processed as intended.

Speed does not remove the need for control. Code and datasets should be versioned from the beginning so that a promising result can be reproduced later. Git is used for source control and DVC or similar tooling for data versioning. Those records become more important when the prototype moves into a larger training environment, where a small configuration difference can produce a different model.

The output of development is normally a script or notebook that captures the initial pipeline. Once the team has a defensible prototype, infrastructure priorities shift from rapid interaction to repeatable execution at scale.

Training: Scaling compute and preserving evidence

Training takes the prototype and applies it to larger, production-scale datasets. The increase in data and model size may require a multi-GPU server, distributed training across several nodes, or cloud-based compute. The central infrastructure question becomes how to provide enough compute, memory, storage throughput, and interconnect bandwidth without losing control of the experiment.

Containers help by placing the framework, CUDA libraries, and dependencies into a consistent runtime. Kubernetes or Slurm can then schedule the training job onto appropriate GPU resources. The training platform must also preserve checkpoints so that a long run can recover from interruption and must capture logs and metrics so that different runs can be compared rather than judged from memory.

Experiment-tracking tools such as MLflow, Weights and Biases, or TensorBoard record parameters, metrics, and artifacts. This evidence matters for both model quality and infrastructure cost. A model that gains a small accuracy improvement while consuming substantially more GPU time may not be the best production choice. Training operations therefore balance model performance with duration, capacity, and cost.

At the end of training, the team should have more than a model file. It should have a versioned artifact accompanied by checkpoints, metrics, logs, and enough configuration information to explain how the artifact was produced. That package becomes the input to deployment.

Deployment: turning an artifact into a service

Deployment changes the perspective from model creation to model consumption. The trained artifact must be packaged and exposed so that another application can request predictions. The service may respond to real-time requests, as in a chatbot or recommendation system, or process batches in an offline pipeline. The infrastructure must match the response pattern.

Real-time inference emphasizes low latency, consistent response time, and high availability. Batch inference emphasizes throughput and efficient use of resources over a larger collection of records. In either case, the model may be converted to an efficient format and placed behind an inference server. NVIDIA Triton Inference Server, TensorRT, and ONNX are central tools in this stage.

The model does not always need a GPU in production. A small or infrequently used service may meet its target on a CPU, while a high-volume or latency-sensitive service may require one or more GPUs. The correct choice depends on the workload, service-level objective, and cost constraint rather than on the assumption that every trained GPU model must remain on a GPU.

Deployment also introduces versioning, rollback, traffic management, and health checking. The model becomes part of a wider application, so its availability and behavior must be observable. That requirement leads directly to the monitoring stage.

Monitoring: reliability, drift, and feedback

Monitoring keeps an AI service useful after deployment. Infrastructure teams track operational signals such as latency, errors, throughput, resource usage, and availability. Model owners may also track accuracy or business-quality signals. These two views must be connected because a service can be operationally healthy while its predictions become less useful, or it can remain accurate while failing to meet latency targets.

Data drift, concept drift, and changing user behavior are reasons a model may degrade. Data drift occurs when the characteristics of incoming data move away from the data used during training. Concept drift occurs when the relationship between inputs and the desired outcome changes. In either case, the model may require new data, retraining, or a design change.

Logs and dashboards help teams detect anomalies and performance bottlenecks. Alerts can notify an administrator or trigger an automated workflow. In a mature MLOps pipeline, the monitoring stage can start a retraining process, validate a new model, and return the result to a controlled deployment path. Monitoring therefore closes the lifecycle loop rather than acting as its final destination.

Figure 7.2 expands this lifecycle view by comparing the users, tools, compute patterns, controls, and outputs associated with each stage.

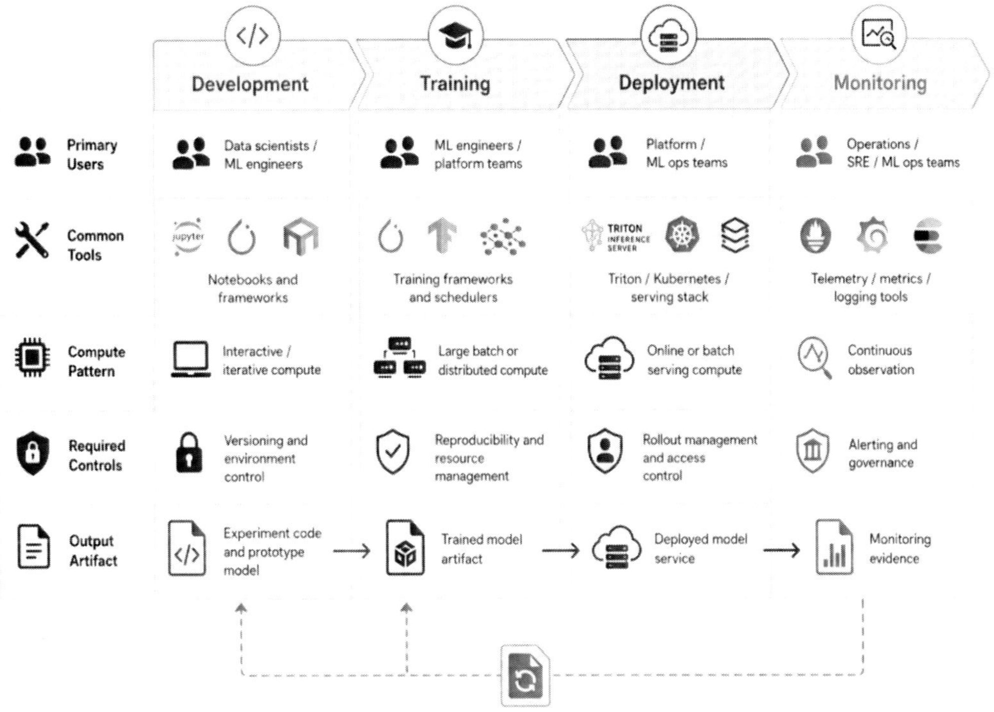

Figure 7.2: Users, tools, controls, compute patterns, and artifacts across the AI lifecycle

Figure 7.2 shows how responsibility and infrastructure change as the project moves from development to production. Data scientists work interactively during development, training shifts toward larger compute environments, deployment introduces controlled serving, and operations teams continuously observe the running service. The model artifact moves forward through the lifecycle, while monitoring evidence feeds back into development and training when another iteration is required.

The lifecycle section has established what each stage needs and why evidence must move with the model. The next section introduces the tools that orchestrate those movements and make them reproducible.

Building reproducible workflows with Airflow, MLflow, and Kubeflow

MLOps applies operational discipline to the machine learning lifecycle. It addresses the fact that an AI system includes more than application code: data pipelines, training configurations, model artifacts, approval decisions, deployment environments, monitoring signals, and retraining loops all have to work together. Reproducibility and traceability are therefore core requirements rather than optional documentation tasks.

Airflow, MLflow, and Kubeflow solve different parts of this problem. The following comparison provides a quick placement before each tool is examined in depth.

Tool	Primary role	Typical objects or capabilities	Best-fit scenario signal
Apache Airflow	Workflow orchestration and scheduling	Python-defined DAGs, dependencies, retries, schedules, task status	A sequence of recurring tasks must run in the correct order
MLflow	Experiment and model lifecycle management	Run tracking, parameters, metrics, artifacts, model registry, version promotion	A team must compare, register, approve, or roll back models
Kubeflow	End-to-end ML workflows on Kubernetes	Pipeline components, notebook integration, training jobs, tuning, deployment	The organization needs scalable, reproducible ML pipelines on Kubernetes

Table 7.2: Operational roles of Airflow, MLflow, and Kubeflow in MLOps

The table shows that the tools are complementary, and *Figure 7.3* makes their different responsibilities and areas of integration clearer.

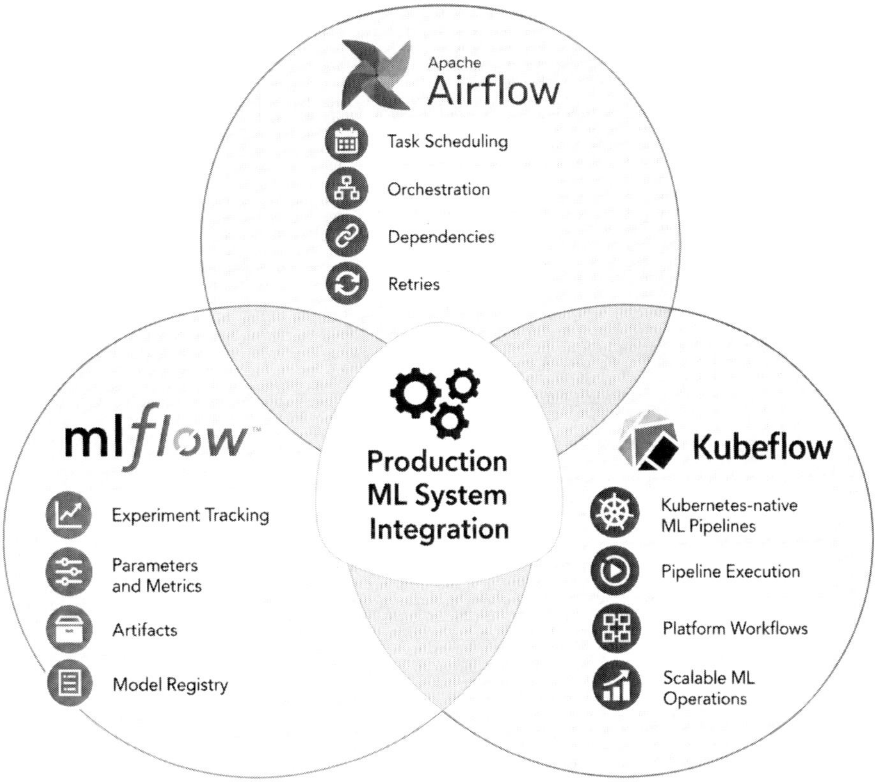

Figure 7.3: Complementary roles of Airflow, MLflow, and Kubeflow in a production ML system

Figure 7.3 separates the primary responsibility of each tool while showing that they can participate in the same production system. Airflow focuses on task scheduling, dependencies, and retries; MLflow records experiments, artifacts, and model versions; and Kubeflow provides Kubernetes-native machine learning pipelines and platform workflows. Their overlap represents integration rather than duplication, with each tool addressing a different operational requirement.

Understanding MLOps itself makes their boundaries easier to remember.

MLOps as an operational discipline

MLOps extends DevOps ideas into a domain where data and models change independently of application code. A conventional deployment can often be reproduced from a source repository and build definition. An AI deployment may also depend on a particular dataset version, feature transformation, model configuration, checkpoint, framework version, and hardware environment.

The discipline therefore emphasizes version control, reproducibility, audit trails, and consistent promotion across environments. A team should be able to answer which code and data produced a model, which metrics justified its promotion, which version is serving production traffic, and how to roll back if the deployment fails. These questions require records that span development and operations.

Automation reduces the chance that an undocumented manual step will break that chain. A pipeline can ingest data, validate it, train a model, record metrics, run tests, register an artifact, and deploy it only after approval. Monitoring can later start the same pipeline with new data. The tools in the remainder of this section implement different parts of that operating model.

Apache Airflow for task orchestration

Apache Airflow orchestrates workflows that contain ordered and dependent tasks. A workflow is represented as a directed acyclic graph, or DAG. Each node represents work such as data ingestion, cleaning, model training, evaluation, batch inference, or report generation. The directed edges define which tasks must finish before another task can begin.

The acyclic property prevents a workflow from creating an endless dependency loop. Repetition is handled through scheduling rather than by connecting a task back to itself. Airflow can run a DAG on a timetable, monitor task status, retry failures, and expose the execution history so that operators can see where a pipeline stopped.

Figure 7.4 makes the DAG structure concrete by following a retraining workflow from data ingestion through validation, training, evaluation, model registration, and notification.

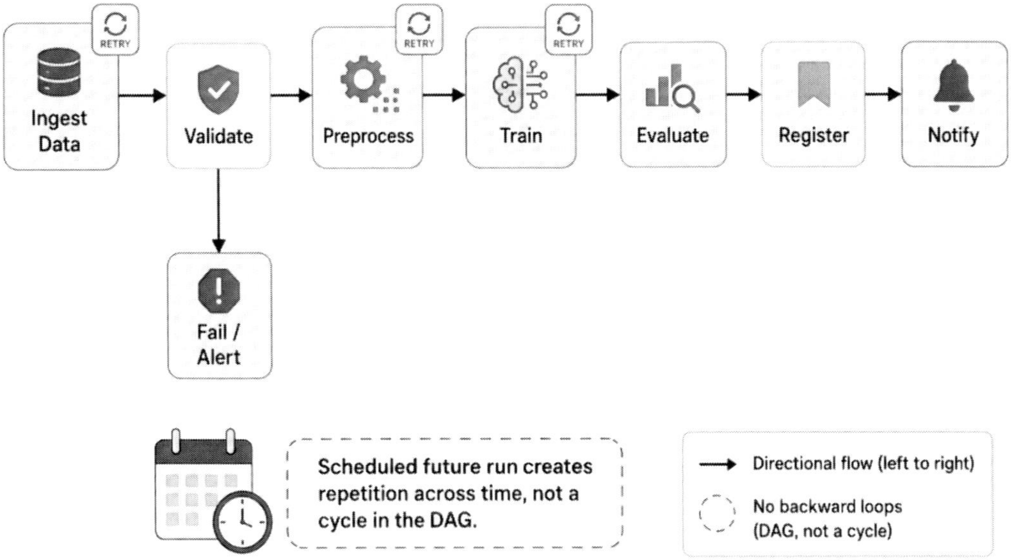

Figure 7.4: A retraining DAG with validation, retries, and scheduled repetition

Figure 7.4 shows that task dependencies move forward through the DAG rather than looping backward. Validation can stop the workflow when input is unacceptable, while selected tasks can be retried after transient failures. A later scheduled run starts the DAG again from the beginning; this repetition is created by scheduling and does not turn the DAG itself into a cycle.

In AI infrastructure, Airflow is useful when the main problem is coordination. A nightly retraining process may first pull new data, validate the dataset, launch a training job, compare metrics, and notify a reviewer. Airflow ensures the sequence runs in the correct order and that a failed validation prevents later tasks from using bad input.

Airflow can integrate with cloud storage, Docker, and Kubernetes, so an orchestration task does not have to execute all work on the Airflow host. It can trigger a container or cluster job and then monitor the result. Once the execution path is controlled, another tool can preserve the details of each experiment.

MLflow for experiments and the model registry

MLflow manages evidence about machine learning runs and models. During experimentation or training, it can log hyperparameters, metrics, artifacts, configuration values, and source-code versions. Those records allow teams to compare runs using more than a final model name or a screenshot of a graph.

The model registry extends tracking into deployment governance. A trained model can be registered and assigned a version so that the team can identify exactly which artifact is being evaluated or deployed. Current MLflow workflows can use aliases and tags to identify versions by deployment role or status, such as a candidate version or the version currently serving production traffic. If a new version performs poorly, the registry helps the team identify and restore an earlier approved artifact. This makes rollback a controlled model-lifecycle action rather than an improvised file replacement.

Figure 7.5 connects experiment tracking with model governance by showing how evidence from individual runs can be associated with registered model versions and controlled deployment decisions.

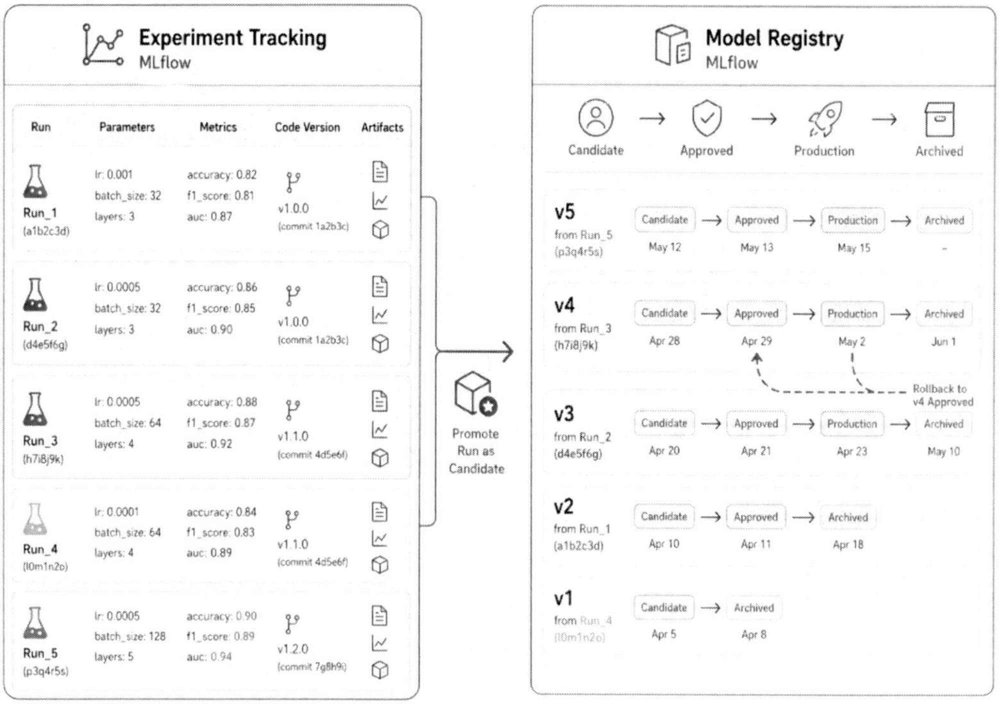

Figure 7.5: Experiment tracking and controlled model-version management with MLflow

Figure 7.5 shows two related responsibilities. Experiment tracking records the parameters, metrics, code version, and artifacts associated with individual runs, while the model registry preserves identifiable model versions that can be reviewed and selected for deployment. The promotion states shown in the workflow should be understood conceptually: current MLflow workflows use model aliases and tags to identify deployment status and selected versions, while fixed Model Registry stages are deprecated.

MLflow is framework agnostic, so the same operating process can record models produced with PyTorch, TensorFlow, XGBoost, and other frameworks. This is connected with questions about lineage, versioning, approval, and rollback. When the scenario asks which tool preserves the history of experiments or manages model versions, MLflow is the direct fit.

Tracking and registry functions do not by themselves create a scalable Kubernetes machine learning platform. That wider role belongs to Kubeflow.

Kubeflow for Kubernetes-based ML pipelines

Kubeflow is designed to run machine learning workflows on Kubernetes. A pipeline can include data preprocessing, model training, hyperparameter tuning, evaluation, and deployment. Each stage runs as a Kubernetes job or pod, which gives the workflow the scheduling, isolation, and scaling behavior of the underlying cluster.

Figure 7.6 shows how this pipeline model maps onto Kubernetes by running individual machine learning stages as separately scheduled workloads inside a controlled namespace.

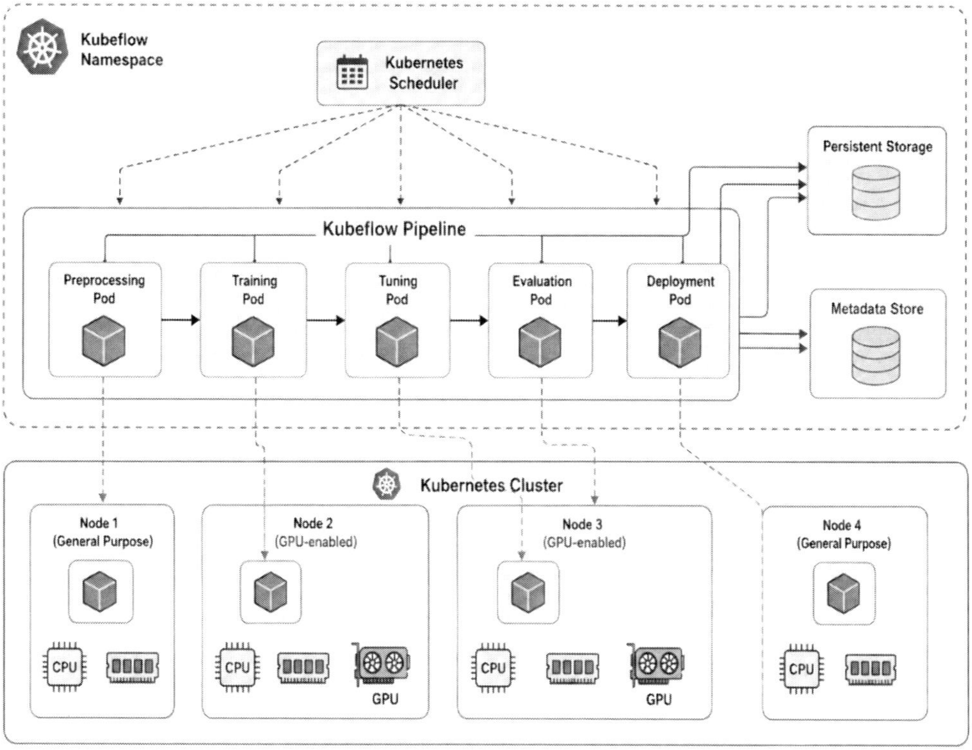

Figure 7.6: Mapping Kubeflow pipeline stages to Kubernetes resources

Figure 7.6 shows preprocessing, training, tuning, evaluation, and deployment as separate pipeline components managed through Kubernetes. The scheduler places these workloads on suitable nodes, including GPU-enabled nodes when acceleration is required, while persistent storage and the metadata store preserve data and execution information across stages. This allows the machine learning workflow to inherit Kubernetes capabilities for scheduling, isolation, and resource management.

This design supports reproducibility because a pipeline component can be packaged with its dependencies and executed in the same way across environments. It also supports scale because Kubernetes can place work on GPU-enabled nodes, recover failed pods, and manage several users or teams. Notebook environments can be connected to the same platform so that development and pipeline execution share a consistent infrastructure foundation.

Kubeflow supports common frameworks and integrates with NVIDIA GPUs. This is connected with NGC Helm charts, which can simplify deployment of GPU-optimized components. In exam scenarios, Kubeflow is the strongest answer when the requirement is a complete machine learning platform built on Kubernetes rather than a scheduler alone or an experiment registry alone.

Because Kubeflow contains many lifecycle capabilities, it may overlap with other tools. The correct design depends on whether a team wants an integrated platform or a combination of focused services.

Combining the tools in one production workflow

Airflow, MLflow, and Kubeflow are not mutually exclusive. An enterprise platform may use Airflow to schedule data ingestion and start a Kubeflow pipeline. The Kubeflow pipeline may run preprocessing and distributed training on Kubernetes. Each training component may log parameters and artifacts to MLflow, and the selected model may enter the MLflow registry before deployment.

The distinction is easiest to remember by asking three questions. What must run, and in what order? That is an orchestration problem suited to Airflow. What happened during each experiment, and which model version is approved? That is a tracking and registry problem suited to MLflow. Where should an end-to-end machine learning pipeline execute at Kubernetes scale? That is a Kubeflow problem.

A well-designed MLOps platform uses each tool to remove a specific manual or ambiguous handoff. The result is not automation for its own sake. It is a lifecycle in which the team can reproduce a result, explain a deployment, recover from failure, and respond when monitoring indicates that the model must change.

The workflow is now reproducible and governed. The next section focuses on the runtime that exposes the resulting model to applications and the optimization path that improves inference performance.

Serving and optimizing models with Triton, ONNX, and TensorRT

A trained and registered model still needs a production runtime. NVIDIA Triton Inference Server provides a unified service for model execution, while ONNX provides a portable representation and TensorRT creates GPU-optimized inference engines. Together, the three tools separate model development from the operational concerns of serving, compatibility, and performance.

The following table summarizes the role of each component before the chapter follows the deployment path.

Component	Primary purpose	Operational value	Representative exam cue
Triton Inference Server	Serve one or more models through a consistent inference interface	Batching, concurrency, versioning, metrics, CPU/GPU execution, REST and gRPC access	Scalable, observable, multi-framework production inference
ONNX	Represent models in an interoperable format	Separates the training framework from the deployment runtime	Portability or conversion between frameworks and runtimes
TensorRT	Optimize and execute inference on NVIDIA GPUs	Lower latency, higher throughput, reduced memory through precision and graph optimization	GPU-specific inference optimization for production

Table 7.3: Roles of Triton, ONNX, and TensorRT in production inference

Triton is the serving layer, so it is the natural starting point for the production path.

Triton as a unified inference runtime

NVIDIA Triton Inference Server is an open-source inference server designed to deploy models on GPUs or CPUs. It supports models produced by several frameworks and runtimes, including TensorFlow, PyTorch, ONNX Runtime, TensorRT, and XGBoost. This allows an infrastructure team to offer one serving pattern even when model teams use different development frameworks.

A unified runtime simplifies operations. Applications can send inference requests through REST or gRPC rather than integrating separately with every framework. The infrastructure team can standardize containers, health checks, metrics, and deployment patterns around Triton while model teams preserve the tools that fit their training work.

Figure 7.7 places Triton between the stored model artifacts and the client applications that consume inference results, making its serving role within the production architecture explicit.

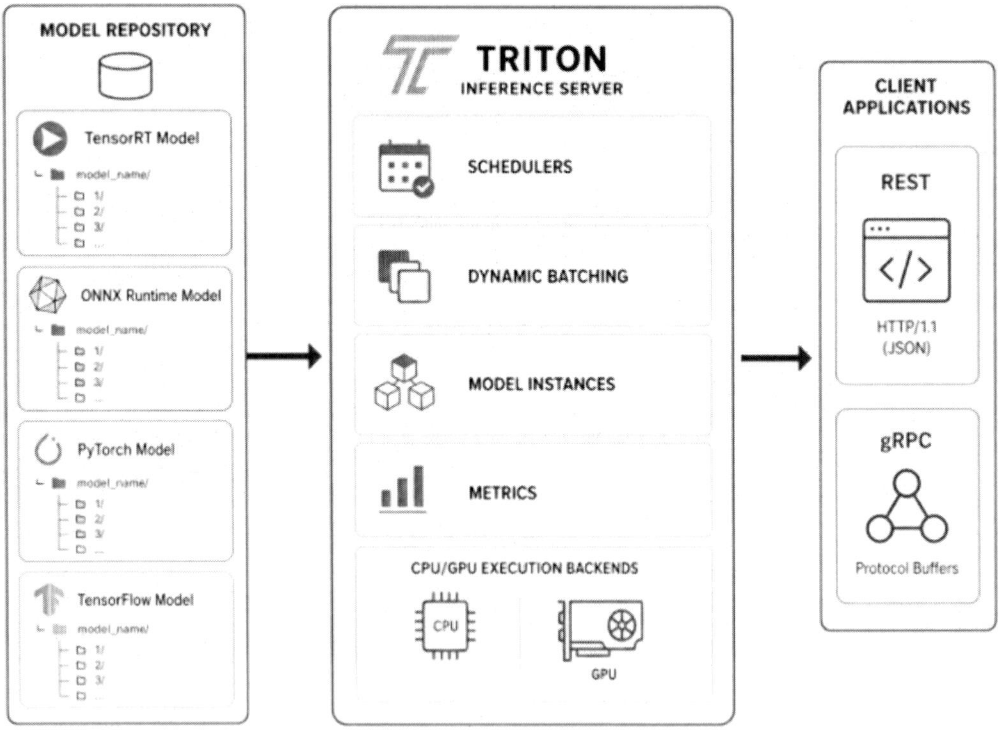

Figure 7.7: Triton between versioned model repositories and inference clients

Figure 7.7 shows Triton accepting models from a repository that can contain several supported formats and exposing them to applications through REST or gRPC. Inside the server, per-model scheduling, dynamic batching, model instances, metrics, and CPU or GPU execution backends handle the operational work required to turn incoming requests into inference results. Triton therefore provides the serving layer around the model rather than replacing the framework or runtime that executes the model itself.

Triton can run on a local system, a GPU server, a Kubernetes cluster, or an edge platform. Several servers can be placed behind a load balancer to improve capacity and availability. This flexibility makes Triton a production component rather than a model-development framework.

The server becomes especially valuable when several requests or models must share the same hardware. Its scheduling features convert incoming traffic into more efficient GPU work.

Dynamic batching, concurrency, and model ensembles

Dynamic batching allows Triton to combine compatible requests into a larger batch before execution. A GPU can often process a batch more efficiently than a sequence of small independent requests because fixed launch and scheduling overhead is spread across more work. The objective is to improve throughput while remaining inside the service latency target.

Concurrent model execution allows multiple models or model versions to run on the same server. This is useful when a shared platform serves several teams or when a deployment must compare a new version with the current one. Resource planning remains important because concurrency can improve utilization but can also create contention if memory or compute capacity is overcommitted.

Model ensembles connect several models or processing steps into one inference pipeline. A request might be preprocessed, classified, and postprocessed without requiring the client to coordinate each stage separately. The ensemble presents one service boundary while Triton manages the internal sequence.

These capabilities answer different performance problems. Dynamic batching improves the execution of incoming requests, concurrency allows multiple model workloads to coexist, and ensembles compose a multi-step inference path. Triton also needs a controlled way to discover and version the artifacts it serves.

The model repository, versioning, and observability

Triton reads models from a model repository. The repository organizes the model name, one or more versions, and configuration information that describes inputs, outputs, batching, and runtime behavior. This structure gives operations teams a predictable deployment artifact rather than an unstructured collection of files.

Triton serves models from one or more configured model repositories, but the way it responds to repository changes depends on its model control mode. In the default `NONE` mode, Triton loads the selected models at startup and ignores subsequent repository changes. `EXPLICIT` mode allows models to be loaded and unloaded through model-management APIs, while `POLL` mode can detect repository changes periodically. Model versions and controlled loading therefore provide the serving layer with a structured way to manage which artifacts are available for inference.

Built-in metrics and integration with Prometheus and DCGM provide observability. Operators can track request latency, throughput, errors, and GPU utilization. The combination matters because high latency may come from the serving scheduler, model execution, preprocessing, or an underutilized GPU waiting for input. The metrics narrow the investigation.

Triton can serve a model in its original supported format, but production targets may require a more portable or optimized representation. ONNX provides the first step in that conversion path.

ONNX as the portability layer

ONNX, the Open Neural Network Exchange format, provides a standardized representation for models. A model trained in one framework can be exported to ONNX and then consumed by another runtime. This is valuable when the development team and infrastructure team use different tools or when the deployment environment needs a format that is independent of the original training framework.

Portability reduces coupling. The training team can choose PyTorch or TensorFlow, while the operations team can evaluate ONNX Runtime, TensorRT, or Triton without requiring the model to be rewritten from the beginning. The exported graph becomes a transfer point between development and deployment.

The conversion still requires validation. The exported model must produce acceptable results, and its operations must be supported by the target runtime. The high-level workflow should be given emphasis on rather than framework-specific conversion commands: train the model, export it to ONNX, validate the representation, and pass it to the selected inference runtime.

ONNX improves compatibility, but it does not by itself perform all NVIDIA GPU-specific optimization. TensorRT provides that role.

TensorRT for GPU-optimized inference

TensorRT is NVIDIA's inference optimizer and runtime. It converts a supported trained model, often through ONNX, into an engine tuned for NVIDIA GPUs. The optimization process can reduce latency, increase throughput, and lower memory usage, making it possible to serve more requests or models on the available hardware.

Precision calibration, graph optimization, kernel autotuning, and layer fusion are important mechanisms. FP16 and INT8 reduce the amount of data used for suitable operations, while graph and kernel optimization select more efficient execution paths. Layer fusion combines operations where possible so that intermediate movement and launch overhead are reduced.

Precision is a performance and accuracy trade-off. A lower-precision engine may deliver greater throughput and a smaller memory footprint, but the result must still meet the model's quality requirement. Calibration and benchmarking are therefore part of the optimization process rather than an afterthought.

TensorRT engines integrate with Triton, DeepStream, and NVIDIA edge platforms. The operational pattern is to optimize once for the target environment and then serve the resulting engine through a managed runtime.

The complete path from training to production inference

The end-to-end path brings the chapter together. A model is developed and trained in a chosen framework. Its runs, parameters, metrics, and artifacts are tracked. The selected model is registered and exported to ONNX when portability is required. TensorRT then produces a GPU-optimized engine, and Triton exposes that engine as a versioned service.

The deployment can run in a container and later be scaled with Kubernetes and Helm. Monitoring captures request behavior and GPU telemetry. If latency rises, quality falls, or input data changes, the evidence feeds the MLOps workflow and starts another development or training iteration.

Figure 7.8 brings these components together by tracing a model from its training framework through portable representation and GPU optimization to serving and production observation.

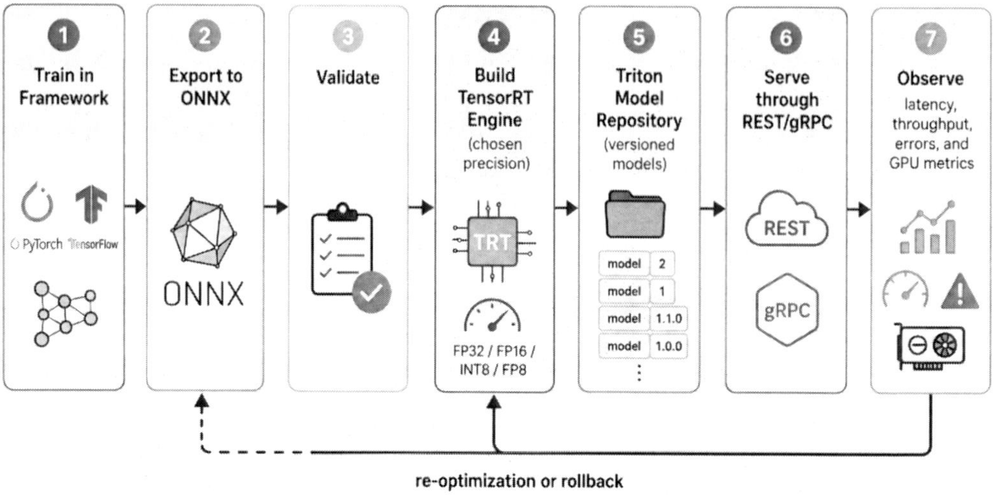

Figure 7.8: End-to-end path from model training to optimized Triton inference

Figure 7.8 summarizes the complete production path. A model is trained in its development framework, exported to ONNX when portability is required, validated, and then optimized for the target NVIDIA GPU with TensorRT. The resulting model version is placed in the Triton model repository and served through REST or gRPC, while latency, throughput, errors, and GPU metrics provide the evidence needed to determine whether the model should remain in production, be re-optimized, or be rolled back.

When choosing among the tools, focus on the problem statement. Use ONNX when the key requirement is framework interoperability. Use TensorRT when the key requirement is NVIDIA GPU inference optimization. Use Triton when the key requirement is a scalable, multi-framework inference service with batching, versioning, and observability.

The chapter has now connected the AI lifecycle, MLOps governance, and inference optimization into one production path. The next chapter widens the view to the NVIDIA delivery ecosystem and the cloud-native platform that operates these services at cluster scale.

Summary

This chapter followed an AI project through development, training, deployment, and monitoring. Development favors fast experimentation and version control. Training introduces larger datasets, GPU scale, containers, orchestration, checkpoints, and experiment evidence. Deployment turns a trained artifact into a real-time or batch service, and monitoring tracks both operational health and changes that may require retraining.

MLOps makes that lifecycle reproducible. Airflow coordinates ordered tasks and scheduled workflows, MLflow preserves experiment lineage and model versions, and Kubeflow executes end-to-end machine learning pipelines on Kubernetes. Used together, the tools replace fragile handoffs with visible, repeatable operating processes.

The chapter objective was to explain how a model becomes a managed production service, and that objective has been achieved. ONNX supplies an interoperable model representation, TensorRT optimizes inference for NVIDIA GPUs, and Triton serves models through a consistent runtime with batching, concurrency, versioning, and metrics. Monitoring then returns production evidence to the next lifecycle iteration.

The next chapter examines how NGC, Kubernetes, NVIDIA cloud-native components, high-speed cluster fabrics, and a disciplined troubleshooting workflow turn this production path into an operable AI platform.

Chapter review questions

Choose the single best answer for each question. The answer key and explanations follow the complete set for this chapter.

1. Why is the AI lifecycle described as iterative rather than strictly linear?
   a. Data never changes after the first release.
   b. Deployment permanently prevents model changes.
   c. Training always occurs after monitoring.
   d. Monitoring and new evidence can send the team back to development or training.
2. What is the typical output of the development stage?
   a. A completed data-center cooling design
   b. A permanently scaled production service
   c. A DPU firmware image for every workload
   d. A working, version-controlled prototype or notebook that defines an initial pipeline
3. Which evidence should accompany a trained model artifact?
   a. No information, because training is complete
   b. Only the model filename
   c. Only the operator's memory of the run
   d. Metrics, logs, checkpoints, parameters, and version information

4. Which tool is the best fit for expressing data preparation, training, evaluation, and notification as a scheduled DAG?

    a. NVLink

    b. Apache Airflow

    c. DCGM

    d. TensorRT

5. Which tool directly addresses experiment tracking and model-registry version promotion?

    a. MLflow

    b. InfiniBand

    c. MIG

    d. BlueField

6. Which platform is built specifically for machine-learning pipelines that run as Kubernetes resources?

    a. vGPU Manager

    b. cuBLAS

    c. Kubeflow

    d. NVIDIA-SMI

7. What is Triton Inference Server's primary role?

    a. Provide a physical GPU interconnect

    b. Serve models from multiple supported frameworks through a unified inference runtime and API

    c. Train every model from raw data

    d. Install GPU drivers on Kubernetes nodes

8. What does Triton dynamic batching do?

    a. Combines compatible incoming requests so the GPU can process them more efficiently

    b. Splits one GPU into hardware-isolated MIG instances

    c. Converts Ethernet to InfiniBand

    d. Creates a virtual machine for every request

9. Why is ONNX useful in a deployment workflow?
    a. It provides a portable model representation between training frameworks and inference runtimes.
    b. It creates a DPU firewall policy.
    c. It monitors GPU temperature.
    d. It schedules Kubernetes pods.
10. What is the correct high-level optimization path for NVIDIA GPU inference?
    a. Install Grafana -> skip model validation -> deploy
    b. Train -> delete metrics -> copy the notebook to every user
    c. Create a MIG profile -> replace the model with a network switch
    d. Train -> export and validate ONNX -> build or select an optimized TensorRT engine -> serve and measure with Triton

Answer key and explanations

Use the explanations to verify both the correct choice and the layer of the stack being tested.

1. D. Production behavior, drift, failures, and new requirements create feedback loops that trigger new experiments and model versions.
2. D. Development emphasizes rapid, controlled experimentation and produces a reproducible starting point for larger training.
3. D. The evidence supports reproducibility, comparison, promotion, rollback, and troubleshooting.
4. B. Airflow orchestrates dependent tasks, schedules runs, monitors status, and retries failures.
5. A. MLflow records runs and artifacts and provides a registry for controlled model lifecycle management.
6. C. Kubeflow provides Kubernetes-native components for preprocessing, training, tuning, and deployment workflows.
7. B. Triton standardizes model serving on GPUs or CPUs and supports features such as batching, concurrency, versioning, and metrics.
8. A. Dynamic batching improves throughput by grouping requests while respecting configured latency constraints.

9. A. ONNX decouples the trained model from a single framework and can serve as input to runtimes such as TensorRT or ONNX Runtime.
10. D. The path preserves portability, applies hardware-specific optimization, and then validates serving behavior with operational metrics.

8

Delivering and Operating NVIDIA AI Platforms

> **Note**
>
> A production AI platform combines trusted software assets, GPU-aware orchestration, high-speed cluster communication, and a troubleshooting process that turns symptoms into evidence.

Operating AI at scale requires more than selecting a GPU or optimizing a model. Teams need a reliable way to obtain compatible software, deploy it consistently, allocate accelerators among workloads, observe the resulting platform, and diagnose failures that cross hardware, drivers, containers, orchestration, and application code. NVIDIA NGC and NVIDIA's cloud-native components provide much of this operating foundation.

This chapter begins with NGC as a delivery platform for containers, models, resources, SDKs, and Helm charts. It then examines GPU-aware Kubernetes through the NVIDIA Container Toolkit, device plugin, GPU Operator, DCGM exporter, and deployment automation. The final section moves to cluster communication with NVLink and NVSwitch and develops a structured troubleshooting workflow using NVIDIA-SMI, DCGM, Nsight tools, container logs, and Kubernetes diagnostics.

By the end of the chapter, you will be able to explain how an NVIDIA-optimized asset moves from the catalog into a managed platform, identify the component that makes a Kubernetes cluster GPU-ready, and approach a performance or deployment failure in a deliberate order. The goal is to operate the full stack as one system rather than troubleshoot each layer in isolation.

- Packaging and deploying AI software with NGC

- Orchestrating GPU infrastructure with Kubernetes and NVIDIA tools
- Scaling and troubleshooting GPU clusters

The operating path begins before a workload starts. It begins with the software artifact and the confidence that its framework, libraries, and dependencies belong together.

Packaging and deploying AI software with NGC

NVIDIA NGC is a curated delivery platform for GPU-optimized AI and high-performance computing software. It reduces the work of assembling compatible frameworks, CUDA libraries, drivers, tools, and deployment definitions. The catalog includes several asset types because an AI project may need more than a container image.

The table below places the major NGC assets in an operational workflow.

NGC asset	What it contains	How an infrastructure team uses it
Containers	A tested user-space software environment with a framework, CUDA-related libraries, and dependencies	Run training, analytics, or inference consistently on supported GPU systems
Pre-trained models	Model artifacts, checkpoints, and related configuration for common AI tasks	Start inference, benchmarking, transfer learning, or fine-tuning without training from zero
Resources and scripts	Notebooks, sample code, configuration files, and training or deployment guidance	Reproduce a reference workflow and understand the expected environment
Helm charts	Reusable Kubernetes templates with configurable values	Deploy multi-component GPU applications repeatedly across clusters
SDKs and toolkits	Domain-focused software, APIs, libraries, and examples	Build specialized applications such as video analytics, data science, or inference pipelines

Table 8.1: NGC asset types and their roles in an AI workflow

The catalog becomes easier to use when it is understood as a complete delivery system rather than as a list of downloads.

NGC as a full-stack delivery platform

The name **NVIDIA GPU Cloud** (**NGC**) can sound like a compute service, but NGC is primarily a repository and delivery platform for GPU-optimized assets. The same artifact can support a local DGX system, a cloud GPU instance, or a Kubernetes deployment. This portability helps teams move between environments without rebuilding the entire user-space stack.

Figure 8.1 maps the main NGC asset categories to the stages of the AI lifecycle in which they can support development, training, deployment, and inference.

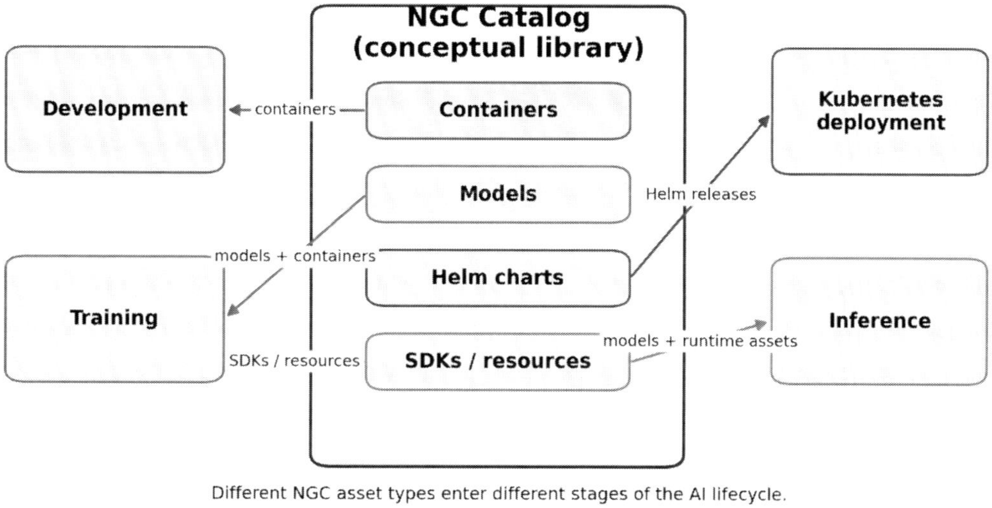

Figure 8.1: NGC asset categories across the AI workflow

Figure 8.1 shows NGC as a common source of assets rather than as one stage of the lifecycle. Containers provide packaged software environments, models supply reusable trained artifacts, Helm charts support repeatable Kubernetes deployment, and SDKs and resources provide development guidance and supporting software. Different assets can therefore enter the workflow at different points according to what the team is trying to build or operate.

Curated assets reduce dependency conflict. A framework container can include CUDA, cuDNN, Python libraries, and the framework versions that were tested together. The infrastructure team still has to provide a compatible host driver and container runtime, but it does not have to assemble every library by hand.

NGC also connects the stages described in Chapter 7. A development team can begin with a notebook or model resource, train inside a framework container, optimize the result, and deploy it through a Triton container or Helm chart. The catalog supplies consistent building blocks across the lifecycle.

The most visible building block is the container, so the next subsection examines what makes an NGC container operationally valuable.

Containers as tested software environments

An NGC container is more than a minimal operating-system image. It packages a user-space environment for a particular workload, including the relevant framework and GPU-accelerated libraries. Containers are available for tools and platforms such as PyTorch, TensorFlow, Triton, TensorRT, RAPIDS, and DeepStream.

Figure 8.2 breaks this packaged environment into layers, showing what the container supplies and where it still depends on the NVIDIA driver and GPU provided by the host.

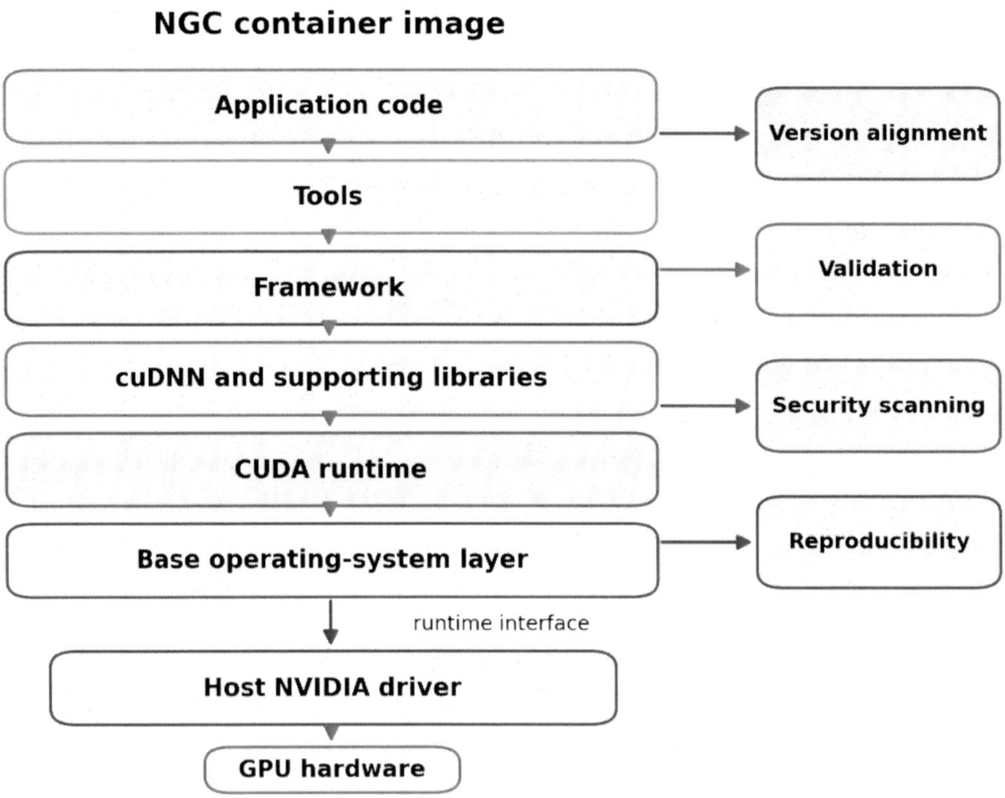

Figure 8.2: What an NGC container packages

Figure 8.2 shows the container's user-space software stack, from the base operating-system layer and CUDA runtime through supporting libraries, frameworks, tools, and application code. Packaging these components together improves version alignment, validation, security control, and reproducibility, but the container still relies on a compatible NVIDIA driver on the host to access the physical GPU. This is why a valid container image can still fail when the host-side GPU software is incompatible.

This packaging improves consistency across development, test, and production. A team can identify the container and tag that produced a result, then reuse the same artifact in a later environment. Pinning a validated tag also prevents an unplanned monthly update from changing the runtime during a critical deployment.

The host and container still form one compatibility chain. The host supplies the NVIDIA driver, while the container supplies the user-space libraries and application. If the host driver cannot support the CUDA requirements of the container, the workload may fail even though the image itself is valid. NGC simplifies the user-space side; it does not remove the need to validate the full stack.

Containers provide the runtime, while pre-trained models and supporting resources reduce the amount of model work required before that runtime can be used.

Models, scripts, and resources for faster iteration

NGC provides pre-trained models for workload families such as image classification, object detection, natural language processing, speech, and recommendation. A pre-trained model can be used for inference, benchmarked on the available hardware, or adapted through transfer learning with organization-specific data.

The related scripts, configuration files, checkpoints, and notebooks are important because a model artifact alone may not explain how it should be loaded or evaluated. Supporting resources establish the expected preprocessing, framework, and deployment path. They also give infrastructure teams a reference workload for validating a new GPU platform.

Using a pre-trained model does not eliminate governance. The team must still understand the model's intended use, test its behavior, and control the version that reaches production. NGC shortens the path to a working environment; the lifecycle controls from Chapter 7 still determine whether the result is acceptable.

Once an asset has been selected, Helm charts provide a repeatable way to move it into Kubernetes.

Helm charts for repeatable Kubernetes deployment

A Helm chart packages Kubernetes definitions into reusable templates. Instead of maintaining a separate collection of manifests for every environment, an operator can use a chart and supply environment-specific values. The chart can define deployments, services, volumes, environment variables, resource requests, and other objects required by a multi-component application.

NGC Helm charts are designed for NVIDIA AI workloads such as Triton, TensorRT pipelines, RAPIDS, or machine learning platforms. A values file can set replica counts, GPU requests, volume mounts, and service configuration. This makes the same deployment pattern repeatable across development, test, and production while preserving controlled differences.

Helm does not replace Kubernetes. Kubernetes remains the orchestration platform, and Helm supplies packaging and release management for the Kubernetes objects. In exam scenarios, a request for a reusable, configurable Kubernetes deployment template points to Helm rather than to a container image alone.

Repeatability is only part of enterprise operations. Teams also need control over access, scanning, updates, and internal distribution.

Enterprise controls and private delivery workflows

Security scanning, updates, and enterprise validation are advantages of NGC. Curated assets can reduce the operational risk of assembling dependencies from unrelated sources. Teams should still pin versions, review release information, test updates, and follow their own vulnerability and change-management processes.

NGC can also support private registries for organization-specific images and controlled internal distribution. A private workflow allows a team to begin with a trusted base, add its own application or model, scan the result, and promote the approved artifact through environments. Access policies determine who can pull or publish content.

This process turns the catalog into the beginning of a software supply chain. The chosen asset is identified, versioned, tested, and delivered to the orchestrator. The next section examines the NVIDIA components that allow Kubernetes to recognize and operate GPU resources.

Figure 8.3 turns this enterprise workflow into a controlled promotion path from a selected NGC asset to production.

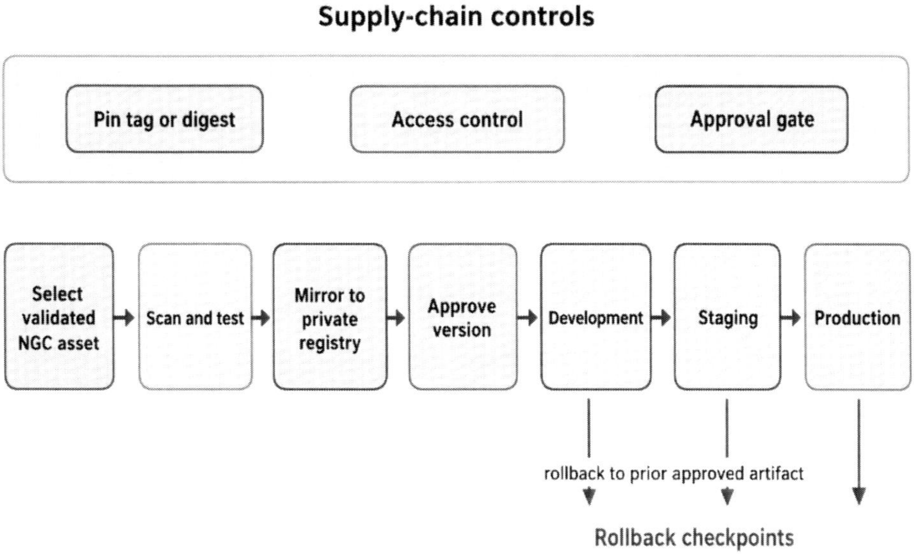

Figure 8.3: Controlled promotion from NGC asset to production

Figure 8.3 shows that an asset should move through validation rather than directly from the public catalog into production. The selected asset is scanned and tested, copied into a controlled registry, approved, and then promoted through development and staging before production. Version or digest pinning, access control, approval gates, and rollback checkpoints preserve the identity of the validated artifact and provide a recovery path if a later release fails.

The chapter has now established how containers, models, resources, and Helm charts form a trusted delivery path. The focus now shifts from the artifact to the cluster that schedules and observes it.

Orchestrating GPU infrastructure with Kubernetes and NVIDIA tools

Kubernetes manages containers across a cluster, but a basic cluster does not automatically understand the full NVIDIA GPU software stack. NVIDIA components expose GPUs to containers, register them with the scheduler, automate node configuration, and export telemetry. Together, they turn general-purpose Kubernetes into a GPU-aware platform.

The following table separates the major components by responsibility.

Component	Primary responsibility	Operational result
NVIDIA Container Toolkit	Connect a container runtime to the host NVIDIA driver and GPU devices	GPU-enabled containers can use CUDA without placing a complete driver inside the image
NVIDIA device plugin	Advertise GPU resources to Kubernetes and support their allocation to pods	Pods can request GPUs as schedulable resources
NVIDIA GPU Operator	Automate installation and management of GPU software components on cluster nodes	Drivers, runtime integration, plugins, labeling, and monitoring components remain consistent
DCGM exporter	Expose DCGM GPU metrics in a Prometheus-compatible format	Cluster dashboards and alerts can include GPU health and utilization
NGC Helm charts	Package GPU applications and services for repeatable Kubernetes deployment	Operators can deploy and update complete AI workloads through controlled values

Table 8.2: NVIDIA components and their responsibilities in a GPU-enabled Kubernetes platform

These components operate at different layers, beginning with access from a container to the GPU.

The cloud-native GPU operating model

Cloud-native GPU orchestration means describing workloads declaratively and allowing Kubernetes to place, restart, and scale them. A team defines containers, resource requests, storage, networking, and policies in manifests or Helm values. The platform then reconciles the running state with that desired state.

Figure 8.4 places these responsibilities into a layered architecture, from application and Kubernetes control at the top to the NVIDIA software components and GPU hardware underneath.

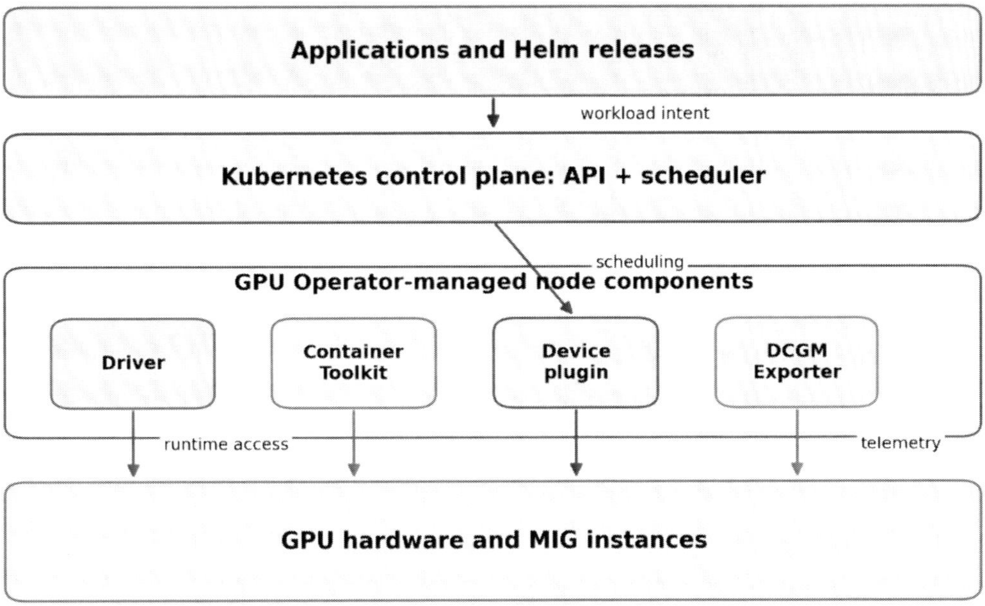

Figure 8.4: NVIDIA Kubernetes GPU stack

Figure 8.4 shows how a Kubernetes workload reaches the GPU through several distinct layers. Applications and Helm releases describe the workload, while the Kubernetes API and scheduler determine its placement. In a GPU Operator-managed environment, components such as the NVIDIA driver, Container Toolkit, device plugin, and DCGM Exporter provide GPU access, resource advertisement, and telemetry above the underlying GPUs and MIG resources. The layers work together, but each solves a different part of the operating problem.

This model is portable across on-premises data centers, cloud services, and edge environments because the application is packaged as a container and the deployment is described through Kubernetes objects. The underlying GPU type and node configuration still matter, but the operating pattern remains consistent.

Kubernetes can run long-lived inference services, batch training jobs, notebooks, and pipeline components. It can also integrate with CI/CD systems so that a validated model or image moves through a repeatable release process. GPU awareness begins with the container runtime and the device plugin.

Container Toolkit and device plugin

The NVIDIA Container Toolkit connects the container runtime to the NVIDIA driver and devices on the host. It allows a container to use the GPU through the host driver while preserving the isolation and portability of the container image. A Docker command or Kubernetes runtime configuration must explicitly make the GPU available; otherwise the application may start without seeing an accelerator.

The NVIDIA device plugin registers GPU resources with Kubernetes. Once registered, a pod can request a GPU in its resource definition, and the Kubernetes scheduler can place the pod on a node with available capacity. The plugin bridges the generic Kubernetes device framework and the NVIDIA hardware present on the node.

The distinction is important. The Container Toolkit enables runtime access from the container to the GPU. The device plugin makes GPUs visible as schedulable Kubernetes resources. A cluster can have one component misconfigured while the other appears healthy, so troubleshooting should verify both layers.

Installing and maintaining these components manually across many nodes can create version drift. The GPU Operator addresses that operational problem.

GPU Operator and DCGM exporter

The NVIDIA GPU Operator automates the deployment and maintenance of the NVIDIA GPU software stack across Kubernetes nodes. Depending on the cluster configuration, it can manage components such as the NVIDIA driver, Container Toolkit, device plugin, DCGM Exporter, MIG Manager, and related node-discovery and validation services. Automation reduces the chance that one node has a different driver or plugin version from the rest of the cluster.

The operator is especially valuable when nodes are added, replaced, or autoscaled. Rather than relying on a manual configuration checklist, the cluster policy describes the desired GPU software state. The operator reconciles nodes with that state and provides a consistent foundation for workloads.

The DCGM exporter adds observability by exposing GPU metrics to Prometheus. Grafana dashboards can then display utilization, memory, temperature, power, and health signals alongside Kubernetes and application metrics. This full-stack view helps operators distinguish a pod scheduling problem from a GPU performance problem.

Figure 8.5 illustrates the operator pattern by showing how GPU node readiness can be established and then restored when nodes are replaced, scaled, or drift from the desired configuration.

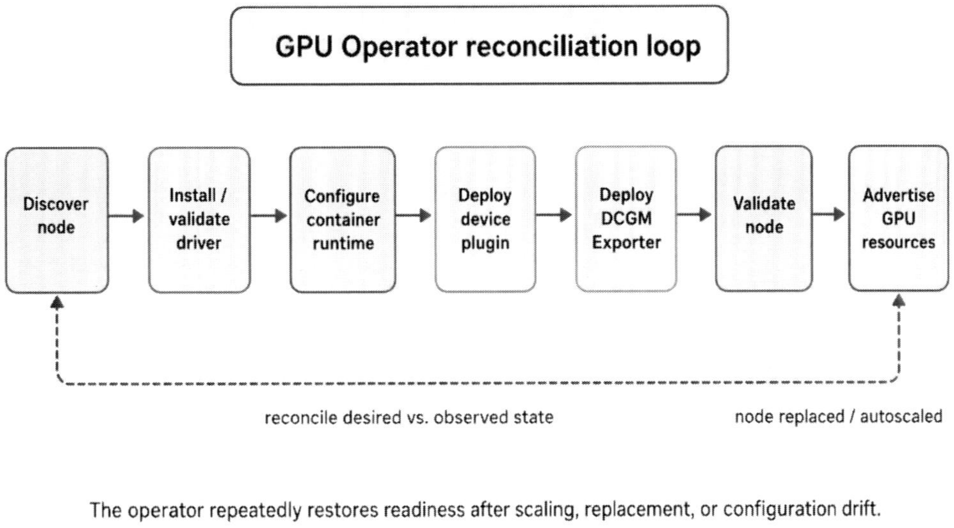

Figure 8.5: GPU Operator node-readiness lifecycle

Figure 8.5 represents node preparation as a reconciliation process rather than a one-time installation checklist. The GPU software stack is established and validated so that accelerator resources can be made available to Kubernetes, and the operator continues comparing the observed node state with the desired configuration. When a node is replaced or the cluster scales, the same reconciliation process helps return the new or changed node to a usable state.

Once the cluster can recognize and observe GPUs, policies determine how those resources are shared among teams and workloads.

GPU-aware scheduling and multi-tenant isolation

Kubernetes can assign a full GPU to a pod or, on supported configurations, expose MIG instances as schedulable resources. MIG allows several isolated workloads to use separate hardware partitions of one physical GPU. This can improve utilization for small inference services while preserving predictable resource boundaries.

Namespaces, quotas, and resource limits provide organizational boundaries. A namespace can represent a team or environment, while quotas restrict how much GPU capacity it can consume. Labels, taints, tolerations, and placement rules can direct workloads to nodes with the required GPU model, topology, or operational role.

Scheduling also includes priority and fault tolerance. Critical inference services may receive higher priority than exploratory jobs. Replica placement can spread services across nodes or zones so that one failure does not remove all capacity. The scheduler must therefore account for both available GPUs and the reliability objective of the workload.

Resource allocation becomes more useful when it is connected to automated release practices and controlled scaling.

Helm, CI/CD, autoscaling, and safe rollouts

Helm provides the deployable package, while CI/CD provides the release path. A pipeline can build a container, run tests, publish it to a registry, update the Helm values, and deploy the new release. The same process can validate a Triton model repository, confirm that the service loads, and measure inference behavior before production promotion.

When scaling uses application-specific or GPU-related signals rather than standard Kubernetes resource metrics, the metric must be exposed through an appropriate custom or external metrics integration so that the autoscaler can consume it. Exporting a metric to Prometheus alone does not automatically make it an autoscaling signal. Scaling should consider the time required to schedule a GPU pod and load the model, because capacity that starts too slowly may not protect a strict latency target.

Blue-green and canary deployments reduce update risk. A blue-green release maintains the old and new environments separately and changes traffic after validation. A canary release sends a small fraction of traffic to the new model or service before expanding the rollout. Both patterns preserve a rollback path if monitoring shows a problem.

Figure 8.6 brings these release practices together in a controlled deployment path that validates a new AI service before allowing it to receive full production traffic.

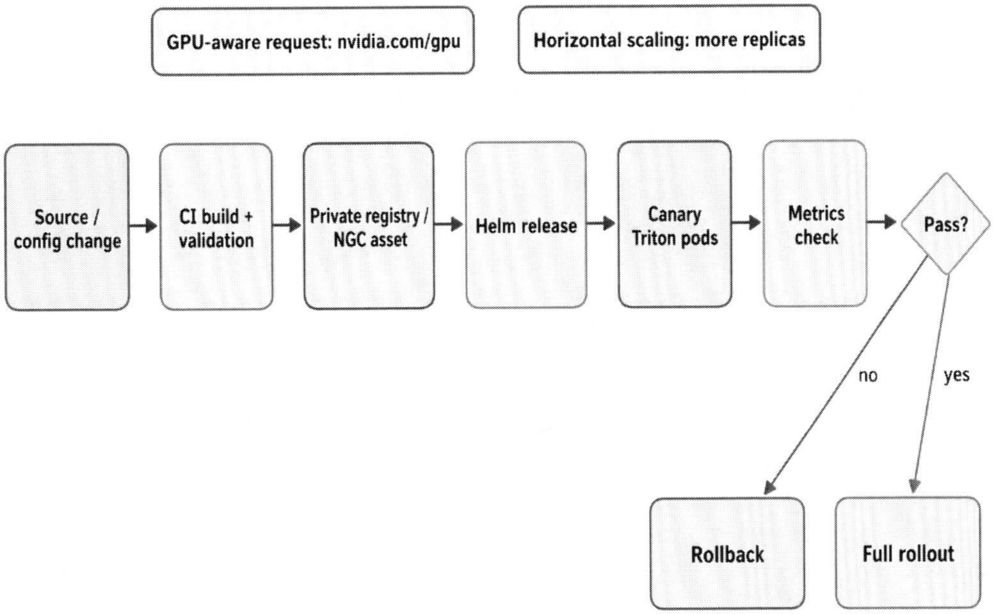

Figure 8.6: Repeatable production rollout for an AI service

Figure 8.6 follows a change from source and configuration through CI validation, artifact storage, Helm deployment, and a limited canary release. Production metrics then provide the decision point: acceptable behavior allows the rollout to expand, while failed validation sends the deployment back through the rollback path. GPU resource requests and horizontal scaling remain part of the deployment configuration so that release safety and capacity management are handled together.

The cloud-native platform is connected to BlueField DPUs and DOCA. That connection is most useful when infrastructure services must run close to the network and storage path.

BlueField and DOCA in a cloud-native platform

Chapter 6 introduced BlueField as a programmable DPU that offloads networking, storage, security, and telemetry from the host CPU. In a cloud-native AI platform, that offload can support traffic inspection, zero-trust enforcement, storage acceleration, and infrastructure observability without consuming the same CPU cycles needed by application services.

DOCA supplies APIs, libraries, and runtime support for applications that execute on or use the DPU. DOCA is connected with monitoring, firewalling, telemetry, DDoS protection, and storage virtualization. These functions complement Kubernetes policy because the DPU can enforce or observe traffic at the infrastructure boundary around the node.

The important distinction is that Kubernetes orchestrates workloads, while the DPU accelerates and secures the data plane beneath them. A production platform may use both: Kubernetes controls where an inference service runs, and BlueField controls how its network and storage traffic is processed.

The chapter has now assembled the delivery and orchestration layers. The final section examines what happens when the platform grows into a tightly connected GPU cluster and when one of its layers fails.

Scaling and troubleshooting GPU clusters

Large AI workloads depend on communication as much as computation. NVLink connects GPUs at high speed, NVSwitch creates a scalable fabric among several NVLink-connected GPUs, and InfiniBand can connect servers into a larger cluster. The resulting platform must be scheduled with topology in mind and operated with a troubleshooting process that follows evidence across layers.

The troubleshooting table below provides an initial map from common symptoms to useful evidence sources.

Observed symptom	Likely area to investigate first	Useful tool or evidence
GPU remains mostly idle during an active job	Data input, preprocessing, runtime configuration, or CPU-GPU synchronization	NVIDIA-SMI, DCGM utilization, Nsight Systems timeline, application logs
CUDA out-of-memory error	Model size, batch size, competing processes, or incorrect GPU allocation	NVIDIA-SMI process and memory view, framework error, scheduler allocation
Container starts but cannot see a GPU	Container runtime access or missing GPU request	Docker run flags, Container Toolkit configuration, pod resource specification
Pod remains Pending	Unavailable GPU capacity, labels, taints, quota, or resource request mismatch	kubectl describe pod, node allocatable resources, namespace quota

Observed symptom	Likely area to investigate first	Useful tool or evidence
Triton cannot load a model	Repository path, volume mount, configuration, or model-runtime compatibility	Triton logs, mounted files, model configuration, container logs
Inference latency spikes	Batching, preprocessing, model optimization, contention, or network path	Triton metrics, DCGM, Nsight, request and load-balancer metrics
Kernel or initialization failure after an image change	Host driver and container CUDA compatibility	NVIDIA-SMI driver information, image tag, runtime error log

Table 8.3: Common GPU-platform symptoms and the evidence sources used to investigate them

A good investigation begins with the architecture because the topology determines where communication and scheduling bottlenecks can occur.

NVLink and NVSwitch as the local GPU fabric

NVLink provides a high-speed connection between GPUs and reduces dependence on a CPU-mediated PCIe path for GPU-to-GPU communication. It is valuable when a model or training job spans several GPUs and must exchange large tensors frequently. The benefit appears only when the workload is placed on GPUs that actually share the required connectivity.

NVSwitch expands that idea by connecting multiple NVLink GPUs through a switching fabric. Instead of relying only on point-to-point links, the system can provide high-bandwidth communication among a larger group of GPUs. This supports data parallelism and model parallelism in tightly coupled systems.

From an operations perspective, the interconnect is a schedulable characteristic. A multi-GPU job placed across poorly connected devices may run but fail to scale. Monitoring must therefore include communication behavior and memory pressure, not only the percentage of compute activity on each GPU.

Figure 8.7 places these communication technologies into a hierarchy, moving from GPU-to-GPU connectivity within a server to the network fabric that connects multiple GPU systems.

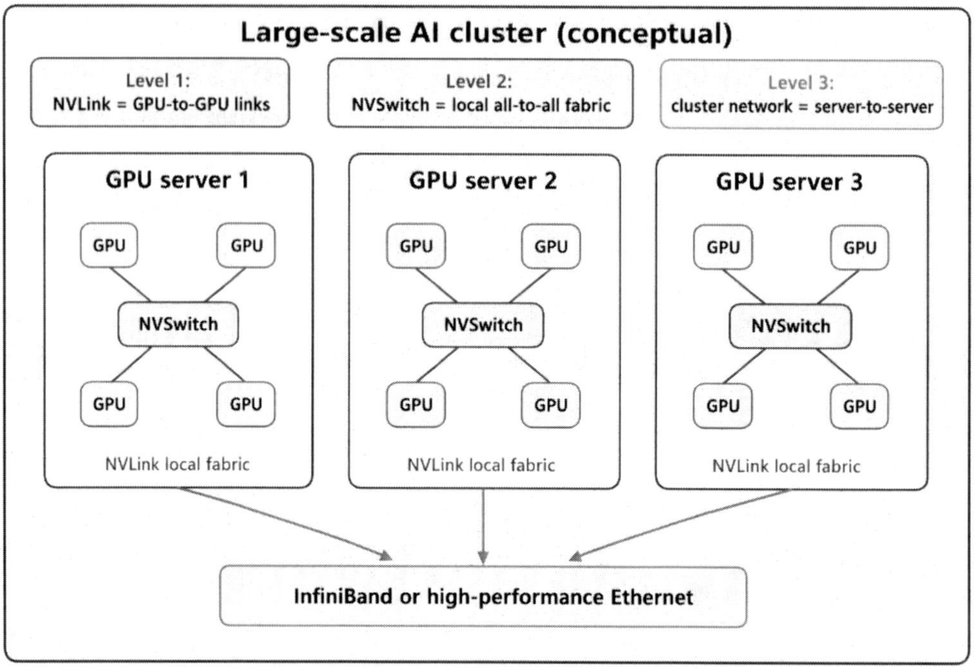

Figure 8.7: From NVLink to the multi-node cluster fabric

Figure 8.7 separates local scale-up communication from communication across the wider cluster. NVLink provides high-speed GPU connectivity within supported systems, while NVSwitch can create a broader local NVLink fabric among several GPUs. Communication between servers then depends on a high-performance cluster network such as InfiniBand or suitably designed Ethernet. The exact topology varies by platform, but the operational principle remains the same: tightly coupled workloads perform best when their placement matches the available communication paths.

Beyond one server, network and cluster-management layers extend the fabric to many systems.

From a GPU server to a managed cluster

We progress from a multi-GPU DGX server to a SuperPOD that connects many systems through high-speed networking, and then to very large GPU deployments. At each level, the management problem grows: jobs must be queued, placed, monitored, isolated, and recovered across more hardware.

Slurm is common for batch and research scheduling, while Kubernetes is common for containerized services and cloud-native workflows. NVIDIA Fleet Command provides centralized deployment and management of containerized AI applications across distributed edge systems. The correct tool depends on the operating model rather than on the number of GPUs alone.

Cluster operation also includes the physical environment. Power, cooling, and thermal design are constraints when GPU density grows. Adding accelerators without adequate facility capacity can lead to throttling, instability, or an inability to deploy the planned number of systems.

These constraints make topology-aware placement and baseline measurement essential parts of capacity planning.

Topology-aware scheduling and performance baselines

A topology-aware scheduler attempts to place a distributed job on resources with the most appropriate communication path. GPUs connected by NVLink or the same NVSwitch fabric are preferable for tightly coupled work. If a job must cross servers, the high-speed network and its RDMA behavior become part of the performance path.

Baseline measurements define what healthy performance looks like for a known workload. GPU utilization, memory use, interconnect traffic, request latency, and data throughput should be recorded before a problem occurs. Without a baseline, an operator may see a number but not know whether it represents normal behavior for that model and batch size.

MIG and resource quotas can protect fairness in shared environments, while placement rules keep large jobs on appropriate nodes. These controls prevent a small service from consuming an entire accelerator and prevent a distributed job from being fragmented across an inefficient topology.

When a workload still fails or underperforms, the investigation should begin with the observed symptom rather than with a favorite tool.

Recognizing common failure patterns

GPU underutilization is a symptom, not a diagnosis. The GPU may be waiting for data, blocked by preprocessing, receiving batches that are too small, or unavailable to the container. Looking only at utilization can lead to unnecessary hardware changes when the actual bottleneck is storage, networking, CPU work, or configuration.

Out-of-memory errors commonly indicate that the model, batch, or concurrent workload exceeds the available allocation. A memory leak can produce a similar symptom over time. The investigation should compare the expected allocation with active processes, model size, batch size, and any other service sharing the GPU or MIG instance.

Driver and runtime mismatch often appears after an image or node update. The container may require a CUDA capability that the host driver does not support. The correct response is to examine the compatibility chain rather than repeatedly restart the application.

Inference latency spikes can arise from poor batching, expensive preprocessing, model contention, network congestion, or an unoptimized model. Because several layers can produce the same symptom, operators need a toolchain that narrows the location of the delay.

The diagnostic toolchain

NVIDIA-SMI provides a quick view of GPU utilization, memory consumption, temperature, power, and active processes. It is a useful first check because it confirms whether the driver sees the GPU and whether another process is consuming resources. It does not, however, replace deeper fleet telemetry or profiling.

DCGM supplies ongoing health and performance data, including utilization, power, temperature, and error information. Exporting DCGM metrics to Prometheus and Grafana supports trend analysis and alerts. A value that looks acceptable at one moment may reveal a recurring thermal or utilization pattern when viewed over time.

Nsight Systems shows the wider CPU-GPU timeline and is useful for finding gaps between data preparation, kernel execution, and communication. Nsight Compute goes deeper into individual kernels, including occupancy, instruction behavior, memory usage, and stalls. Use Systems to locate where time is being lost, then use Compute when kernel-level detail is needed.

The tool choice should follow the depth of the question. Use NVIDIA-SMI for a quick state check, DCGM for fleet health and trends, Nsight Systems for end-to-end timing, and Nsight Compute for kernel-level performance.

Figure 8.8 turns these tools into a troubleshooting sequence that begins with broad configuration and device checks before moving toward increasingly detailed performance analysis.

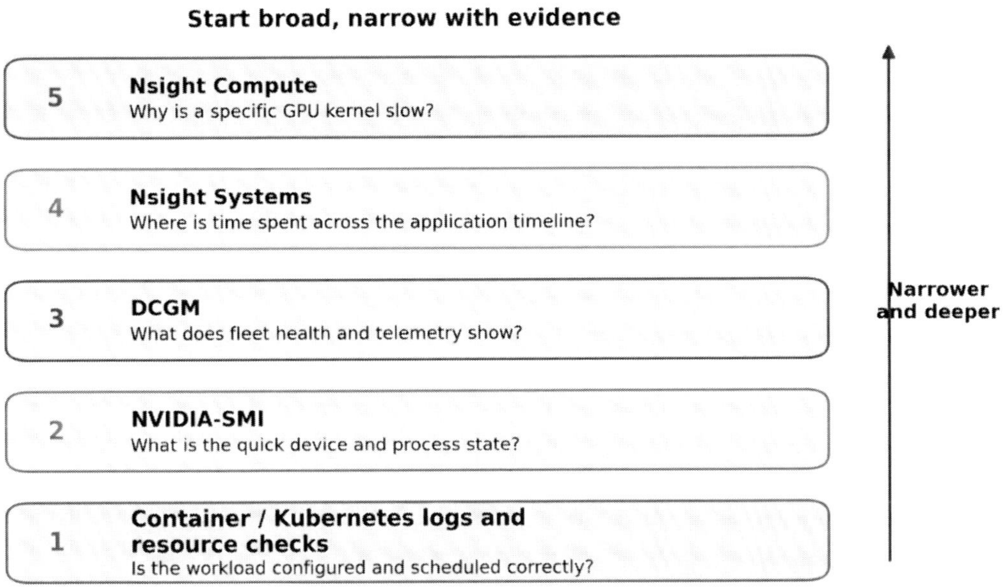

Figure 8.8: Diagnostic ladder for GPU troubleshooting

Figure 8.8 shows why troubleshooting should narrow according to the evidence. Container and Kubernetes checks establish whether the workload is configured and scheduled correctly, while NVIDIA-SMI provides a quick view of device and process state. DCGM adds fleet health and telemetry, Nsight Systems exposes timing across the wider application, and Nsight Compute provides detailed analysis of an individual kernel. Not every incident requires every tool; the correct depth depends on what the earlier evidence reveals.

Container and Kubernetes failure paths

In a container environment, the investigation must include the boundary between the host and the container. A container may have the correct application and still fail because GPU access was not requested, the NVIDIA runtime is missing, or the host driver is incompatible. Checking the launch command or pod resource request is often faster than debugging the model code.

Docker logs and container exit information reveal startup errors. In Kubernetes, kubectl describe pod shows scheduling events, failed mounts, image-pull errors, and resource conflicts. Pod logs show application and Triton errors, while node information shows whether the requested GPU resource exists and is allocatable.

Volume mounts deserve special attention for inference. Triton may start but fail to load a model if the repository path is missing or mounted incorrectly. Similarly, a pod may remain

Pending when its GPU request, label selector, taint tolerance, or namespace quota cannot be satisfied.

A layer-by-layer check prevents the team from treating every container failure as a CUDA failure. Once the immediate problem is fixed, preventive controls reduce the chance of recurrence.

Preventive operations and release validation

The best troubleshooting process begins before an incident. The GPU Operator can reduce configuration drift by keeping cluster components under a consistent policy. Pinning validated container versions prevents an unreviewed update from changing framework or CUDA requirements. Pre-deployment validation confirms that the driver, runtime, GPU, and model repository work together.

Regular DCGM monitoring and Nsight profiling establish baselines. Alerts should focus on actionable conditions such as sustained temperature, repeated errors, memory exhaustion, or abnormal latency rather than on every short-lived fluctuation. Runbooks should connect each alert to the next evidence source and the responsible team.

GPU workloads should also be tested in the release pipeline. A deployment can verify GPU visibility, load the model, send a known inference request, measure response time, and confirm that metrics appear. These checks turn common production surprises into controlled test failures.

The chapter has now followed NVIDIA assets from NGC into a GPU-aware Kubernetes platform and through the cluster and troubleshooting layers needed for reliable operation. The final chapter turns that understanding into an exam-preparation and certification strategy.

Summary

This chapter presented NGC as a full-stack delivery platform rather than only a container registry. NGC containers package tested user-space environments, pre-trained models and resources shorten development, SDKs support specialized workloads, and Helm charts make Kubernetes deployments repeatable. Version pinning, testing, scanning, and private distribution turn these assets into a controlled software supply chain.

The chapter then assembled the GPU-aware Kubernetes stack. The NVIDIA Container Toolkit enables GPU access from containers, the device plugin advertises GPUs to the scheduler, the GPU Operator automates node software, and the DCGM exporter connects GPU telemetry to Prometheus. Namespaces, quotas, MIG, placement policies, Helm, CI/CD, autoscaling, and safe rollout patterns allow several teams and services to share the platform responsibly.

The chapter objective was to operate the full stack as one system, and that objective has been achieved. NVLink and NVSwitch support tightly coupled GPU communication, while Slurm or Kubernetes coordinate work at cluster scale. NVIDIA-SMI, DCGM, Nsight Systems, Nsight Compute, container logs, and Kubernetes events provide progressively deeper evidence when a workload fails or underperforms. Preventive validation and baselines make that evidence easier to interpret.

The next chapter converts the technical material into an exam-ready reasoning process, showing how to recognize scenario signals, avoid common traps, manage the available time, and complete the certification journey with confidence.

Chapter review questions

Choose the single best answer for each question. The answer key and explanations follow the complete set for this chapter.

1. What is NGC primarily used for?
    a. Providing only virtual desktop licenses
    b. Replacing the physical network fabric
    c. Distributing curated GPU-optimized containers, models, Helm charts, SDKs, and related resources
    d. Creating exam appointments
2. What commonly exists inside an NGC framework container?
    a. A tested combination of CUDA libraries, framework dependencies, tools, and runtime components
    b. Only an empty operating-system layer
    c. A Kubernetes control plane with no application software
    d. A physical GPU and NVSwitch
3. What problem does a Helm chart solve?
    a. It templates and packages repeatable Kubernetes application deployment
    b. It replaces the device plugin
    c. It partitions an A100 into MIG instances by itself
    d. It performs kernel-level GPU profiling
4. What is the NVIDIA Container Toolkit responsible for?
    a. Tracking model experiments

   b. Allowing supported container runtimes to expose NVIDIA GPU devices and libraries to containers
   c. Providing an NVLink switch fabric
   d. Creating Airflow DAGs
5. What is the NVIDIA device plugin's role in Kubernetes?
   a. Advertise GPU resources to Kubernetes and support their allocation to pods
   b. Run a hypervisor license server
   c. Store Prometheus metrics
   d. Optimize an ONNX model
6. Why is the GPU Operator valuable?
   a. It replaces all CI/CD tools.
   b. It creates InfiniBand cables.
   c. It serves models through REST and gRPC.
   d. It automates installation, configuration, validation, and lifecycle management of GPU software components across cluster nodes.
7. What does DCGM Exporter provide in a Kubernetes monitoring stack?
   a. A model-conversion format
   b. A virtual-machine disk image
   c. GPU metrics in a format that Prometheus can scrape
   d. A new GPU precision type
8. How do NVLink and NVSwitch differ?
   a. They are both Kubernetes schedulers.
   b. NVLink is a high-speed point-to-point GPU interconnect; NVSwitch creates a switched fabric among multiple NVLink-connected GPUs.
   c. NVLink is for storage only; NVSwitch is for DNS.
   d. NVLink is a model registry; NVSwitch is a container runtime.
9. Which tool should be used to inspect kernel-level stalls and occupancy?
   a. Airflow
   b. Helm

   c. Nsight Compute
   d. NVIDIA-SMI only
10. A container starts successfully but cannot detect the host GPU. What should be checked first?
    a. Whether an Airflow DAG has a retry policy
    b. Whether the cluster uses NVSwitch
    c. Whether GPU access was granted through the NVIDIA container runtime/toolkit and the run configuration
    d. Whether MLflow has an approved model version

Answer key and explanations

Use the explanations to verify both the correct choice and the layer of the stack being tested.

1. C. NGC is a software-delivery catalog for NVIDIA-optimized AI and HPC assets.
2. A. The container packages a compatible user-space software environment while relying on a suitable host driver and GPU.
3. A. Helm charts express Kubernetes resources and configurable values as a reusable release package.
4. B. The toolkit connects container execution with host GPU devices and driver capabilities.
5. A. The device plugin integrates GPU inventory with the Kubernetes resource model.
6. D. The operator reconciles the node GPU software stack and reduces drift across changing or autoscaled clusters.
7. C. DCGM Exporter exposes health and utilization telemetry for collection and visualization.
8. B. NVSwitch expands NVLink connectivity into a more uniform local multi-GPU fabric.
9. C. Nsight Compute provides detailed per-kernel performance metrics. Higher-level tools should normally be used first to narrow the problem.
10. C. GPU visibility is a container-runtime boundary issue before it is a model-serving or experiment-tracking issue.

9

Preparing for the NCA-AIIO Exam and the Next Step

> **Note**
>
> Certification success depends on recognizing the operational problem inside each scenario, selecting the most precise technology, and managing attention as carefully as time.

The NCA-AIIO exam asks candidates to connect foundational AI concepts with infrastructure and operations decisions. Memorizing definitions helps, but practical scenarios demand a second skill: identifying the specific constraint. A container cannot see a GPU, a shared service needs isolation, an inference endpoint has poor throughput, or a cluster requires consistent GPU software. The correct answer is usually the technology that directly addresses that constraint.

This chapter first explains how to read exam questions for keywords, context, and layer boundaries. It then uses recurring operational scenarios to build a repeatable elimination process and shows how flashcards, spaced review, and teach-back strengthen recall. The final section presents a three-pass pacing method, mental-focus practices, test-day preparation, and a plan for turning the certification into further technical development.

By the end of the chapter, you will have a practical method for moving from question stem to evidence, from evidence to a short list of plausible answers, and from that list to the best operational choice. The objective is not to predict every question. It is to make your reasoning reliable under exam conditions.

- Reading exam questions with operational context

- Practicing recall and scenario reasoning
- Managing exam time and completing the certification journey

The first step is to treat every question as a compressed infrastructure problem and identify exactly what the question is asking you to solve.

Reading exam questions with operational context

The NCA-AIIO exam uses a 50-question multiple-choice assessment that mixes definitions with applied scenarios, diagrams, workflows, and operational output. Exam delivery details can change, so readers should verify the current official duration, registration process, policies, and price before scheduling. The reasoning method in this chapter remains useful regardless of those administrative changes.

The following table summarizes common question patterns and the evidence each pattern expects you to recognize.

Question pattern	What it is testing	Useful first question
Definition	Whether you can distinguish closely related technologies	What problem does each option solve?
Scenario	Whether you can select a tool from symptoms and constraints	Which layer is failing or constrained?
Diagram or topology	Whether you understand component relationships and data paths	What is connected, isolated, or bypassed?
Command or output analysis	Whether you can interpret logs, events, metrics, or launch options	Which line proves the condition described?
Best-practice selection	Whether you can choose the most complete and supportable operating approach	Which answer addresses the requirement with the fewest assumptions?

Table 9.1: Common NCA-AIIO question patterns and the evidence they test

Recognizing the pattern helps, but the wording inside the stem determines whether an otherwise correct statement answers the actual question.

Critical words that change the answer

Words such as not, least, best, first, most likely, and completely change the task. A candidate may know the technology and still select the wrong option by reading past one qualifier. Slow down when a question uses a negative or asks for an order of operations.

Best and first deserve special attention. The best long-term fix may not be the first diagnostic step. Replacing a node might eventually resolve a hardware fault, but the first step is usually to gather evidence. Likewise, several options may improve performance, but only one may directly address the stated bottleneck.

Absolute terms such as always and never are often too broad for infrastructure scenarios. Technology choices depend on workload, scale, cost, topology, and operating model. An option that ignores those conditions should be treated carefully even when it contains a familiar product name.

After identifying the qualifier, the next task is to locate the contextual signal that points to the relevant technology layer.

Context signals and technology boundaries

Context tells you which part of the stack matters. Kubernetes suggests scheduling, resource requests, the device plugin, GPU Operator, Helm, namespaces, quotas, or pod diagnostics. A container that cannot see a GPU suggests the runtime boundary and GPU-access configuration. A model portability requirement suggests ONNX, while a GPU inference optimization requirement suggests TensorRT.

Multi-tenant isolation can point to different answers depending on the boundary. MIG creates hardware-isolated GPU instances on supported GPUs. vGPU presents virtual GPU resources to virtual machines through a hypervisor. BlueField and DOCA can enforce network, storage, and security controls around tenants. The stem must indicate which layer requires isolation.

Monitoring language also requires precision. NVIDIA-SMI provides a quick local snapshot. DCGM provides fleet health, telemetry, policy, and diagnostics. Prometheus stores and queries time-series metrics, while Grafana presents dashboards. Nsight Systems exposes the CPU-GPU timeline, and Nsight Compute provides kernel-level analysis.

Once the layer is identified, compare the answer choices according to the problem they solve rather than according to how familiar they look.

Familiar is not the same as correct

A familiar tool can attract attention even when the question asks for a different depth of analysis. NVIDIA-SMI is widely used, but it is not the best answer for kernel instruction stalls. Kubernetes schedules pods, but it does not replace Triton as an inference server. Triton serves models, but it does not make a container see a GPU when the runtime access was never configured.

A useful elimination method is to state each option's primary purpose in one sentence. If the purpose does not match the constraint, remove the option. This is more reliable than asking whether the technology is generally related to AI infrastructure, because most distractors will be related at a broad level.

The correct answer often requires fewer assumptions. If the stem explicitly says a pod is Pending because it requests an unavailable GPU resource, investigate scheduling and capacity before changing the model. If the stem says the host driver supports an older CUDA level than the container requires, compatibility is the direct cause.

The same discipline helps with questions that mix host, container, and orchestrator responsibilities.

Separating host, container, and orchestrator responsibilities

The host supplies the physical GPU and NVIDIA driver. The container supplies the application and user-space libraries. The NVIDIA Container Toolkit connects the runtime to the host GPU. In Kubernetes, the device plugin advertises GPU resources, and the scheduler assigns a pod only when the request can be satisfied.

A failure can therefore occur at several boundaries. NVIDIA-SMI failing on the host points to a driver or hardware problem. NVIDIA-SMI working on the host but not inside a container points to runtime access or compatibility. A valid container that never starts because the pod remains Pending points to scheduling, quota, labels, taints, or unavailable capacity.

Bare metal, virtual machines, and containers also create different sharing choices. MIG is a hardware partitioning feature. vGPU is integrated with the hypervisor and guest driver. Kubernetes can schedule full GPUs or exposed MIG resources, but it is not itself a hypervisor-based vGPU implementation.

Distinguishing these responsibilities turns many complex scenarios into a short sequence of checks. The next subsection applies that discipline to common exam question types.

Definition, scenario, diagram, and output questions

Definition questions reward clear contrasts. AI is the broad category, machine learning learns patterns from data, and deep learning uses multilayer neural networks. NVLink connects GPUs directly, while NVSwitch connects several NVLink GPUs through a switching fabric. Airflow orchestrates tasks, MLflow tracks experiments and models, and Kubeflow runs ML workflows on Kubernetes.

Scenario questions require the same definitions in context. A requirement for many small isolated inference services on one supported GPU points to MIG. A requirement to serve several frameworks with dynamic batching points to Triton. A requirement to move data directly between storage and GPU memory points to GPUDirect Storage.

Diagram questions test the path among components. Look for where the CPU is bypassed, where a hypervisor sits, which GPUs share an interconnect, or which component exports metrics. Output questions test evidence: a driver version, pod event, DCGM error, Triton load message, or missing GPU flag can provide the decisive clue.

The section has established a disciplined reading method: identify the qualifier, locate the layer, define each option, and select the answer that addresses the stated constraint. The next section strengthens that method through repeated practice and recall.

Practicing recall and scenario reasoning

Practice is most useful when it reproduces the reasoning step, not only the final answer. The following walkthrough uses recurring operational patterns: missing GPU access in a container, choosing MIG for isolated small workloads, recognizing driver and CUDA mismatch, enabling Triton dynamic batching, and using the GPU Operator to manage cluster GPU software.

The following table turns those patterns into a compact diagnostic checklist.

Scenario signal	Best-fit concept	Why it fits
A valid GPU container starts, but no GPU is visible	Explicit GPU runtime access, such as the appropriate container GPU option	The image alone does not grant access to host GPU devices
Several small tenant inference services need predictable isolation on one supported GPU	MIG	MIG creates hardware-isolated instances with dedicated resources
A newer CUDA container fails on a host with an insufficient driver	Driver-container compatibility	The host driver must support the CUDA requirements of the user-space stack

Scenario signal	Best-fit concept	Why it fits
Many small Triton requests produce poor GPU efficiency	Dynamic batching	Compatible requests can be combined into more efficient GPU execution
A Kubernetes cluster needs consistent drivers and GPU runtime components across nodes	NVIDIA GPU Operator	The operator automates deployment and maintenance of the GPU software stack

Table 9.2: Common NCA-AIIO scenario signals and their best-fit concepts

These patterns should become starting points, not memorized shortcuts that override the wording of a new question.

Container GPU access as a boundary problem

A container image can include CUDA libraries and an AI framework but still have no access to the physical GPU. Access must be exposed by the runtime. In a Docker scenario, the missing GPU option is therefore more relevant than whether Triton is installed or whether the image tag looks familiar.

The reasoning sequence is simple. Confirm that the host sees the GPU. Confirm that the NVIDIA container runtime integration is present. Confirm that the launch configuration requests the GPU. Only then move deeper into application or framework debugging.

This sequence also prevents a common exam mistake: choosing a sophisticated tool for a basic boundary failure. An inference server cannot correct a container launch that did not expose the device.

The next recurring pattern asks how to share a physical accelerator without allowing one small workload to consume it all.

MIG as an isolation and utilization answer

MIG is appropriate when the workload needs a hardware-isolated slice of a supported GPU. Each instance receives dedicated compute and memory resources, allowing several small services or users to run independently. The key signals are isolation, predictable resource allocation, and improved utilization for workloads that do not require a whole GPU.

MIG is not the best answer when one job needs the maximum memory and compute of the full accelerator. It is also not interchangeable with vGPU. A virtual-machine requirement involving a hypervisor and guest driver points to vGPU, while a container-oriented partition on supported hardware points to MIG.

When the options include several plausible sharing technologies, identify the tenancy boundary first. That one step eliminates most distractors.

Resource sharing is only useful when the software stack can initialize correctly, which leads to the compatibility pattern.

Driver and CUDA compatibility

The host driver and container user-space stack must be compatible. A container that requires a CUDA capability beyond what the host driver supports can fail during initialization, sometimes with an error that appears unrelated to the simple mismatch. The direct evidence is the driver information on the host and the requirements of the selected image.

Do not confuse the CUDA toolkit installed on the host with the driver requirement of a containerized application. Containers normally bring their user-space libraries, while the driver remains on the host. The exam may test whether you understand that division.

The safest operational practice is to use validated image tags, maintain a compatibility matrix, and test an update before broad deployment. In a scenario question, however, select the action that directly confirms or corrects the stated mismatch.

Once the runtime is healthy, performance questions often move to the way inference requests are scheduled.

Dynamic batching and inference efficiency

Triton dynamic batching groups compatible requests so that the GPU can process them more efficiently. The feature is appropriate when a stream of small independent requests creates overhead and low utilization. It improves throughput by increasing the amount of useful work in each execution.

Dynamic batching is not the same as adding more model replicas. Replicas increase service capacity and availability, while batching changes how requests are combined inside the server. The best choice depends on whether the bottleneck is per-request execution efficiency or total service capacity.

Latency targets still matter. A batching policy that waits too long can improve throughput while harming response time. The scenario should indicate which metric is constrained and whether the current request pattern is suitable for batching.

Cluster-wide consistency introduces a different answer: the GPU Operator.

GPU Operator as a cluster-management answer

The NVIDIA GPU Operator automates the GPU software stack across Kubernetes nodes. It is the appropriate answer when the problem is consistent installation or maintenance of drivers, runtime integration, the device plugin, node labeling, or monitoring components.

The operator does not replace the scheduler, edit every application manifest, or interpret model accuracy. Kubernetes still schedules pods, workload definitions still request resources, and model monitoring remains a separate concern. The operator manages the infrastructure prerequisites that allow those workloads to use GPUs.

Stating what the operator does not do is a useful exam technique because distractors often assign a real product a responsibility that belongs to another layer.

The technical scenarios build applied recognition. Flashcards and spaced review build the rapid recall needed to reach those concepts under time pressure.

Flashcards, spaced review, and teach-back

Flashcards are most effective when they test one distinction or decision at a time. A card might ask for the difference between MIG and vGPU, the role of the device plugin, or the data path changed by GPUDirect Storage. The answer should be short enough to recall, followed by a brief explanation that reconnects the term to its operational problem.

I recommend short, spaced sessions rather than one large cram session. Reviewing 10 to 15 cards, shuffling the order, and separating known from uncertain cards forces repeated retrieval. Returning to difficult cards after a delay strengthens long-term memory more effectively than rereading the same page.

Saying an answer aloud, writing it from memory, or teaching the concept to another person exposes gaps that silent recognition can hide. If you can explain why ONNX is not TensorRT, why DCGM is not Grafana, or why a Pending pod is not necessarily a CUDA failure, you are more likely to handle a new scenario correctly.

Combine recall practice with a readiness checklist. Mark each chapter area as explainable, scenario-ready, or still uncertain. Use missed questions to choose the next review topic rather than repeating material that is already secure.

The chapter has now converted operational scenarios into a repeatable diagnostic method and a recall routine. The final section focuses on pacing, attention, test-day execution, and the steps that follow certification.

Managing exam time and completing the certification journey

Time management is not simply answering faster. It is allocating attention so that one difficult question does not consume the opportunity to answer several easier ones. This book recommends a three-pass method that banks confident answers first, returns to questions that need analysis, and reserves the most difficult items for a final pass.

Before the exam, confirm the current official number of questions and time limit, then calculate an average pace and reserve a review window. Use the average as a warning signal rather than as a strict limit for every question. Some definition questions take seconds, while a scenario or output question deserves more time.

The final preparation table organizes the practical tasks that support this method.

Preparation area	Action	Evidence that you are ready
Knowledge coverage	Review each chapter objective and the official topic areas	You can explain the concepts without reading the definition
Scenario practice	Complete the chapter review questions under timed conditions and revisit the scenarios you answer incorrectly; take mock exams	You can identify the layer, eliminate distractors, and justify the best answer
Time plan	Set pass targets and a final review window using the current exam duration	You know when to flag and move on
Technical setup	Check identification, computer, webcam, network, browser, and proctoring requirements	The official system check completes successfully
Mental readiness	Use sleep, breaks, breathing, and a calm review routine	You can maintain a steady pace without rushing

Preparation area	Action	Evidence that you are ready
Post-exam plan	Identify how the credential will support a role, project, or next certification	You have a concrete next action after the result

Table 9.3: Final exam-readiness checklist and indicators of preparation

With preparation organized, the three-pass method provides a practical way to execute the plan inside the exam.

The three-pass method

Pass 1 collects the questions you can answer with high confidence. Read carefully, select the answer, and move on. This builds a reserve of completed questions and reduces anxiety. Do not turn an easy question into a difficult one by inventing facts that are not in the stem.

Pass 2 returns to questions that need comparison or elimination. Identify the layer, cross out options with the wrong primary purpose, and choose the answer that matches the stated constraint. Use the evidence in the stem rather than a memory of a similar but different scenario.

Pass 3 handles the most confusing or time-consuming items and reviews flagged answers. At this stage, make the best supported choice and avoid leaving an answer blank when the exam permits a response. A difficult item should not consume the time reserved for checking clear mistakes elsewhere.

The pass structure manages the order of work. A pace checkpoint manages whether that work is using time as planned.

Pacing, review, and first instincts

Divide the current official time by the number of questions to understand the average available per item, then reserve time at the end for review. Check your progress at planned points, such as one quarter and one half of the exam. If the pace is slipping, shorten the time spent on flagged questions rather than rushing every remaining item.

First instincts are often useful when they come from a clear concept match, but they are not infallible. Change an answer when the review reveals a specific keyword, evidence line, or responsibility boundary that you missed. Do not change an answer only because another option sounds more technical.

Review negative wording and qualifiers first. Then check questions where two options remained plausible. A targeted review protects accuracy better than rereading every completed question without a purpose.

Pacing succeeds only when attention remains stable, so the next subsection addresses mental resets during the exam.

Maintaining focus under pressure

This book recommends brief mental resets: breathe, blink, relax the shoulders, and refocus on the next question. These actions take little time but interrupt the tendency to carry frustration from one difficult item into the next.

Read each stem deliberately. A second focused read can reveal a word such as not, best, or first that changes the task. At the same time, avoid repeatedly rereading a question after the relevant evidence is already clear. The goal is controlled attention, not hesitation.

Confidence should come from the reasoning process. You have identified the layer, defined the options, and matched the technology to the constraint throughout the book. Use the same process under pressure rather than searching for a hidden trick in every question.

A calm exam session also depends on completing the administrative and technical preparation before the appointment begins.

Registration and test-day readiness

Exam providers, prices, delivery methods, and policies can change, so use the current official NVIDIA certification page when registering. Complete any required account setup and system check before the scheduled date. Read the examination policy rather than assuming that a previous online exam used the same rules.

Prepare accepted identification and a quiet, private testing space if the exam is remotely proctored. Confirm that the webcam, microphone, browser, and network meet the current requirements. Restart the system, close unnecessary applications, disable notifications, and remove anything that could interrupt or violate the proctoring rules.

Join the session early enough to complete check-in without rushing. The purpose of this preparation is not only compliance. It protects the mental focus developed during study by removing preventable technical uncertainty.

Certification is a milestone, not the end of the learning path. The final subsection turns the result into a practical next step.

Using the certification as a launch point

The credential validates foundational knowledge of AI infrastructure and operations, but its value increases when that knowledge is applied in real environments. Look for opportunities to work with GPU access, monitoring, resource planning, inference serving, containerized workloads, and NVIDIA software in your own projects or professional environment. When you do, document not only what you configured but also the operational decisions you made and the evidence you used to validate the result.

The subject can lead toward roles in GPU systems administration, data center operations, cloud and DevOps engineering, MLOps, platform engineering, and AI infrastructure support. It can also provide a base for more advanced professional-level training in infrastructure, operations, or networking.

Continue reviewing the technologies as they evolve. Container tags, GPU generations, Kubernetes components, and certification policies change. The durable skill is understanding the problem each component solves and verifying the current implementation details before deployment.

The chapter has now established a complete exam execution plan: read for qualifiers, reason by layer, practice recurring scenarios, retrieve concepts through spaced review, manage the exam in passes, and prepare the testing environment before the appointment.

Summary

This chapter treated the NCA-AIIO exam as an operational reasoning exercise. Definition questions require clear distinctions, scenario questions require layer identification, diagrams require an understanding of data and control paths, and output questions require evidence. Critical words such as not, best, and first determine the exact task, while host, container, hypervisor, and orchestrator boundaries prevent familiar tools from being assigned the wrong responsibility.

The practice section revisited five operational patterns: explicit GPU access for containers, MIG for hardware-isolated sharing, host-driver and container compatibility, Triton dynamic batching, and GPU Operator automation. Flashcards, spaced retrieval, writing, and teach-back turn those patterns into rapid recall without replacing the need to read each new stem carefully.

The chapter objective was to make exam reasoning reliable under pressure, and that objective has been achieved. The three-pass method protects easy points, pace checks preserve a review window, mental resets maintain attention, and advance technical preparation reduces test-day disruption. Certification then becomes a starting point for applying this knowledge to real AI infrastructure and continuing into deeper areas of study.

You have reached the end of this book with a working view of AI infrastructure as a connected system. You have moved from AI workloads and GPU architecture through CUDA, resource sharing, monitoring, storage and networking, virtualization and DPU offload, MLOps, inference, Kubernetes, and production operations. More importantly, you have learned to identify the layer at which a requirement or failure occurs and connect it with the technology designed to address it.

As you prepare for the NCA-AIIO exam, return to the chapter review questions and revisit any concept that you cannot yet explain clearly without referring to the text. Product capabilities, software versions, and certification policies will continue to evolve, so verify current implementation and exam details against NVIDIA's official documentation when necessary. The principles developed throughout this book remain the more durable skill: understand the workload, identify the constraint, follow the evidence, and choose the technology that solves the problem at the correct layer.

Whether your next step is the certification exam, a role working with accelerated infrastructure, or deeper study of NVIDIA technologies, you now have the foundation on which to build.

10

Unlock Your Exclusive Benefits

Your copy of this book includes the following exclusive benefits:

Follow the guide below to unlock them. The process takes only a few minutes and needs to be completed once.

Unlock this Book's Free Benefits in 3 Easy Steps

Step 1

Keep your purchase invoice ready for *Step 3*. If you have a physical copy, scan it using your phone and save it as a PDF, JPG, or PNG.

For more help on finding your invoice, visit `https://www.packtpub.com/en-us/unlock?step=1`.

> Note
>
> **Note**: If you bought this book directly from Packt, no invoice is required. After *Step 2*, you can access your exclusive content right away.

Step 2

Scan the QR code or go to `packtpub.com/unlock`.

On the page that opens (similar to *Figure 10.1* on desktop), search for this book by name and select the correct edition.

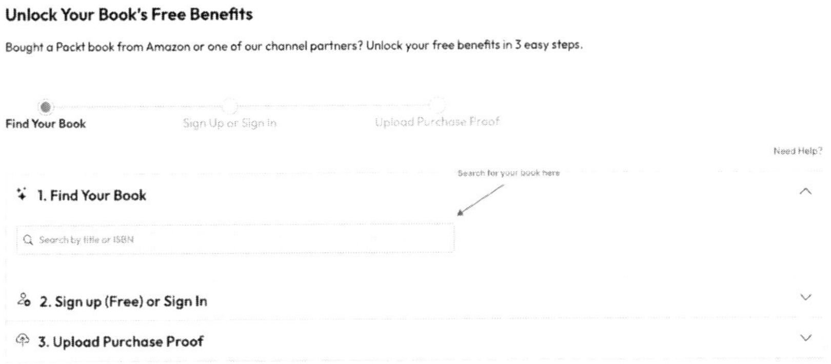

Figure 10.1: Packt unlock landing page on desktop

Step 3

After selecting your book, sign in to your Packt account or create one for free. Then upload your invoice (PDF, PNG, or JPG, up to 10 MB). Follow the on-screen instructions to finish the process.

Need Help

If you get stuck and need help, visit `https://www.packtpub.com/unlock-benefits/help` for a detailed FAQ on how to find your invoices and more. This QR code will take you to the help page.

> Note
>
> **Note**: If you are still facing issues, reach out to `customercare@packt.com`.

Other Books You May Enjoy

If you enjoyed this book, you may be interested in these other books by Packt:

Kubernetes for Generative AI Solutions

Ashok Srirama, Sukirti Gupta

ISBN: 978-1-83620-993-5

- Explore GenAI deployment stack, agents, RAG, and model fine-tuning
- Implement HPA, VPA, and Karpenter for efficient autoscaling
- Optimize GPU usage with fractional allocation, MIG, and MPS setups
- Reduce cloud costs and monitor spending with Kubecost tools
- Secure GenAI workloads with RBAC, encryption, and service meshes
- Monitor system health and performance using Prometheus and Grafana
- Ensure high availability and disaster recovery for GenAI systems
- Automate GenAI pipelines for continuous integration and delivery

Solutions Architect's Handbook

Saurabh Shrivastava, Neelanjali Srivastav

ISBN: 978-1-83508-423-6

- Explore various roles of a solutions architect in the enterprise
- Apply design principles for high-performance, cost-effective solutions
- Choose the best strategies to secure your architectures and boost availability
- Develop a DevOps and CloudOps mindset for collaboration, operational efficiency, and streamlined production
- Apply machine learning, data engineering, LLMs, and generative AI for improved security and performance
- Modernize legacy systems into cloud-native architectures with proven real-world strategies
- Master key solutions architect soft skills

Packt is searching for authors like you

If you're interested in becoming an author for Packt, please visit `authors.packt.com` and apply today. We have worked with thousands of developers and tech professionals, just like you, to help them share their insight with the global tech community. You can make a general application, apply for a specific hot topic that we are recruiting an author for, or submit your own idea.

Share your thoughts

Now you've finished *NVIDIA-Certified Associate AI Infrastructure and Operations (NCA-AIIO) Certification Guide*, we'd love to hear your thoughts! Scan the QR code below to go straight to the Amazon review page for this book and share your feedback or leave a review on the site that you purchased it from.

`https://packt.link/r/1808087496`

Your review is important to us and the tech community and will help us make sure we're delivering excellent quality content.

Index

E

G

V

W

Made in United States
North Haven, CT
04 November 2026

21728187R00130